Seeing Like the Buddha

Seeing Like the Buddha

Enlightenment through Film

Francisca Cho

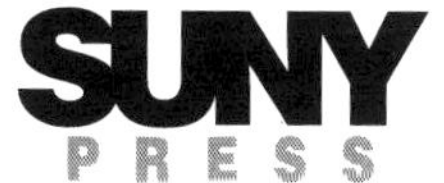

Published by State University of New York Press, Albany

For information, contact State University of New York Press, Albany, NY
www.sunypress.edu

Production, Ryan Morris
Marketing, Kate R. Seburyamo

Library of Congress Cataloging-in-Publication Data

Names: Cho, Francisca, author.
Title: Seeing like the Buddha : enlightenment through film / Francisca Cho.
Description: Albany : State University of New York Press, [2017] | Includes
  bibliographical references and index.
Identifiers: LCCN 2016031461 (print) | LCCN 2017001011 (ebook) | ISBN
  9781438464398 (hardcover : alk. paper) | ISBN 9781438464381 (pbk : alk.
  paper) | ISBN 9781438464404 (e-book)
Subjects: LCSH: Buddhism in motion pictures.
Classification: LCC PN1995.9.B795 C46 2017 (print) | LCC PN1995.9.B795
  (ebook) | DDC 791.43/682943—dc23
LC record available at https://lccn.loc.gov/2016031461

Contents

Illustrations

Acknowledgment

For the students of my Buddhism and Film course offered in the Spring semesters of 2010, 2012, and 2014: It has been a privilege to share my ideas with you and you have inspired me with your amazing insights in turn.

Abbreviations

<table>
<tr><td>A</td><td>Anguttara Nikāya. Translated by Bhikkhu Bodhi as The Numerical Discourses of the Buddha. Boston: Wisdom Publications, 2012.</td></tr>
<tr><td>AdS</td><td>Amitāyurdhyāna Sūtra. Translated by Hisao Inagaki in collaboration with Harold Stewart as The Sutra on Contemplation of Amitāyus. In The Three Pure Land Sutras. Revised Second Edition. Numata Center for Buddhist Translation, 2003.</td></tr>
<tr><td>D</td><td>Digha Nikāya. Translated by Maurice Walshe as The Long Discourses of the Buddha. Boston: Wisdom Publications, 1995.</td></tr>
<tr><td>M</td><td>Majjhima Nikāya. Translated by Bhikkhu Ñāṇamoli and Bhikkhu Bodhi as The Middle Length Discourses of the Buddha. Boston: Wisdom Publications, 1995.</td></tr>
<tr><td>PraS</td><td>Pratyutpanna-Buddha-Saṃmukhāvasthita-Samādhi-Sūtra. Translated by Paul Harrison. Tokyo: The International Institute for Buddhist Studies, 1990.</td></tr>
<tr><td>S</td><td>Samyutta Nikāya. Translated by Bhikkhu Bodhi as The Connected Discourses of the Buddha. Boston: Wisdom Publications, 2000.</td></tr>
<tr><td>SN</td><td>Sutta Nipāta. Translated by H. Saddhatissa. London: Curzon, 1985.</td></tr>
<tr><td>Vm</td><td>Visuddhimagga. Translated by Bhikkhu Ñyāṇamoli as The Path of Purification. Boulder and London: Shambhala, 1976.</td></tr>
</table>

CHAPTER I

Seeing Like the Buddha

Erasing the Buddha

The objective of this book is to demonstrate that films can take on the role that has been played by traditional Buddhist icons and images. Film can articulate Buddhist teachings and, more significantly, put them into practice. This means taking film seriously as a medium for cultivating certain ways of being in the world that have previously been attained through ritual and contemplative practices. Both traditional and filmic practices can be put under the rubric of "seeing like the Buddha," which is intimately tied to the desire of Buddhists to see the Buddha himself. As a founded religion, Buddhists express devotion and piety toward the historical Siddhārtha Gautama of the Śakya clan (Śākyamuni). This means keeping him alive through images and narratives about his life, similar to the way Jesus is kept in mind by Christians. And parallel to Christology, theoretical understandings about the nature of the Buddha as both a historical and transcendent being have allowed Buddhists to "see" him in multiple ways, as well as in multiple things. But throughout Buddhist history, the project of seeing the Buddha has entailed a mandate to see *like* the Buddha, which, paradoxically, erases the individual form of Siddhārtha. The emphasis shifts from *what* is seen to *how* one sees, which in turn renders art and aesthetic experiences into equivalents of the Buddha himself.

This drift toward erasing the Buddha in favor of seeing like the Buddha is the central aesthetic and soteriological theme of this book, and the organizational principle behind the films that have been selected for discussion. The progression of films increasingly loses references to and images of all things Buddhist until "the Buddhist film" is instantiated in ostensibly secular works. This pattern is modeled after a particular dynamic in Buddhist history. This is not to deny that the Buddha's image is revered, preserved, and perpetuated by Buddhists even now, some twenty-five centuries after his death. Depictions of the Buddha are governed by iconographical conventions such as hand postures (*mudras*) that signify certain activities or moments in the Buddha's life, and the thirty-two marks (*lakṣaṇa*) of the great man such as the fleshly protuberance on the top of the Buddha's head (*uṣṇīṣa*) and the imprint of wheels on the soles of his feet.[1] There are other kinds of Buddhist icons such as representations of bodhisattvas (Buddhas-to-be) and *maṇḍala* Buddhas that are endowed with fixed symbolic attributes. But there are also "open form" images that exhibit the layering and substitution of motifs (Shimizu 1992, 207). In such images, the Buddha is "present" primarily as a reference point that deliberately raises the question of what and whom else can be seen as the Buddha.

Itō Jakuchū's (1716–1800) painting entitled *Yasai Nehan* ("vegetable nirvana"), for example, takes the traditional image of the reclining Śākyamuni passing into his parinirvana and replaces him with a daikon radish surrounded by other vegetables that stand in for the various elements of this iconic scene. Eight corn stalks take the place of the Śāla trees under which the Buddha died, and the daikon radish is surrounded by an array of turnips, gourds, mushrooms, melons, chestnuts, and other vegetables to form the assembly of mourners who witness the Buddha's passing. Jakuchū's well-attested Buddhist piety eliminates the possibility that the painting is a mere parody, and the image must be understood in the context of Japanese Buddhist and culinary history. Relevant factors include the tradition of monastic vegetarianism, the association of the daikon with the pure and rustic life, and quite importantly, the Tendai Buddhist creed that even plants and trees attain Buddhahood due to the inherent Buddha-nature in all things. It is this notion that "allowed the interchangeability between the original subject (Śākyamuni) and other subjects, be they poets or mendicant monks"—or even vegetables (Shimizu 1992, 211).

The doctrine of Buddha-nature was not espoused by all Japanese Buddhists, let alone the entire Buddhist world, but it is dominant in the Mahāyāna-leaning regions of East Asia and Tibet.[2] The concept of Buddha-nature originates in the bivalent Indian Buddhist idea of

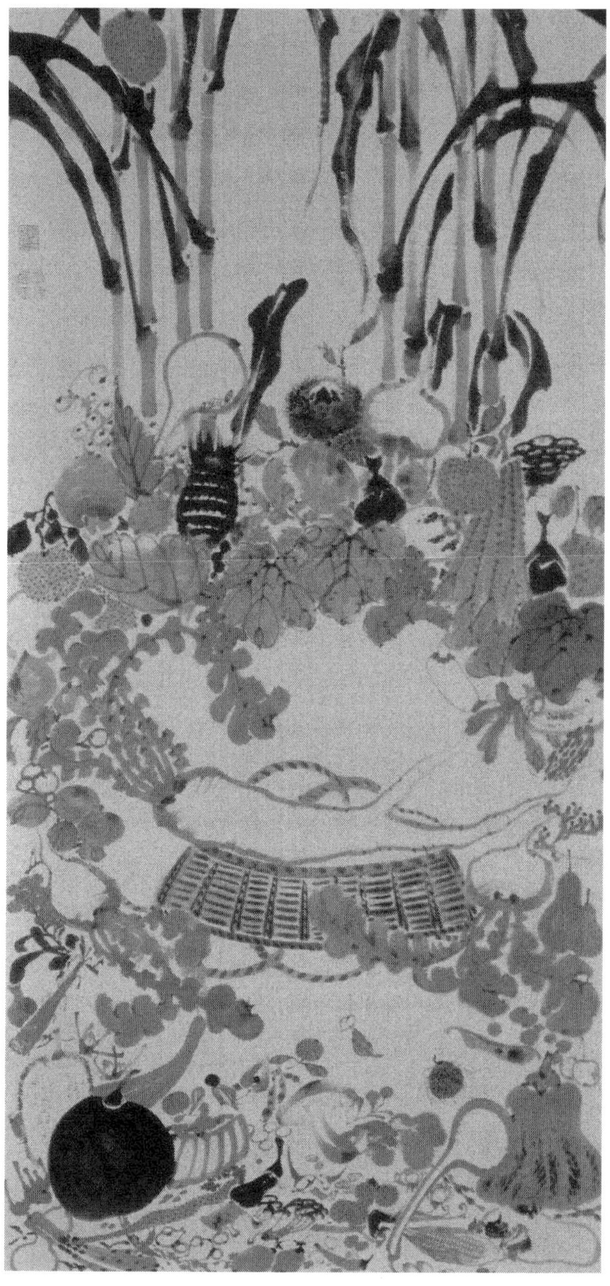

FIGURE 1.1. Itō Jakuchū (1716–1800), *Yasai Nehan* ("vegetable nirvana"), ca. 1792. (Courtesy of Kyoto National Museum)

tathāgatagarbha, which translates both as the "embryo of enlightenment," in the sense of the incipient and potential Buddhahood *within* all beings, and also as the "womb of enlightenment," in the alternative sense of a space that *contains* all beings. Both readings affirm that everyone is a Buddha, either in the future or as a present reality due to the fact that all beings are already contained within the womb of Buddhahood.[3] According to the *Śrīmālādevīsiṃhanāda Sūtra* ("The Lion's Roar of Queen Śrīmālā"), when the tathāgatagarbha is covered by defilements then it is in an embryo state, and when it is not covered by defilements then Buddhahood is a present and actualized reality (Wayman and Wayman 1974, 45). The critical idea here is that even when it is covered with defilements, the tathāgatagarbha is nevertheless present. "Buddha-nature" is actually a translation of the term *buddhadhatu* ("Buddha element"), which is one of many synonyms for tathāgatagarbha, and which emphasizes this idea that it is a quality possessed by and present in all things.

Tathāgatagarbha thought is closely linked to the doctrine of emptiness (*śunyatā*), which deems that the dependently arising nature of all phenomena makes everything empty of inherent essence and identity. To be empty of an inherent essence may sound negative, but it is understood as the quality that enables beings to transform into a Buddha—Buddhahood is possible precisely because suffering and delusion are not inherent to human being and existence. This openness to becoming and change in a felicitous direction may be understood as the quality of the Buddha himself—the tathāgatagarbha. Understanding the truth of emptiness is "a necessary precondition of the realization of tathāgatagarbha" and the idea of tathāgatagarbha in turn corrects "a one-sidedly negative perspective" on the teaching of emptiness (King 1991, 16). Functioning as positive and negative formulations of the same insight, respectively, Buddha-nature and emptiness both erase the separation between the enlightened realm of nirvana and the tainted world of samsara, at least in their earlier interpretation as incalculably distant spatial and temporal domains. This also eliminates the distinction between the Buddha and other beings, and sanctions the idea that even "secular" aesthetic works can function as serious religious practice. This history is notable because it refrains from some characteristic anxieties regarding religious images in our more immediate monotheistic traditions.

Strictures against representing the divine in Judaism, Christianity, and Islam are quite familiar to us, of course, but this is not to suggest a simplistic contrast between an image-affirming Buddhism versus image-fearing monotheisms. The Buddhist world has also had its episodes of aniconism and iconoclasm but this similarity needs to be qualified with the particular reasons why Chan/Zen monks, for example, counseled against the use of religious images.[4] Zen iconoclasts embrace a semiotic worldview different from theists, as I have discussed elsewhere (Cho 2009), and although they express the familiar warning not to mistake the image for what it signifies, the same semiotics is used by other Buddhists to *affirm* the identity between artistic representations and the original reality. This ability to pivot seamlessly between iconoclasm and iconolatry is, paradoxically, the manifestation of a single logic. Some Buddhists reject images on the grounds that they are empty of any inherent qualities and suitability, and other Buddhists—sometimes the same person on a different occasion—embrace and sanction images *because* of their inherent emptiness.[5] We can begin to parse the reversibility of the two positions by remembering that the purpose of the Zen attack on religious icons is to point out the sacred in the *profane,* such as the world of vegetables. The objective, in essence, is to get past the nirvana-samsara distinction and its apparent opposition. This is diametrically opposed to theistic iconoclasm, which zealously guards the separation between the worldly and the divine.

Such differences lead to an interesting contrast when it comes to images of the Buddha and images of Jesus Christ. Depictions of Christ and the controversies they engender help make this contrast clear, and they might be summed up as an underlying anxiety about historical fidelity—given that Christ is understood as the flesh-and-blood embodiment of the divine who walked the earth at a particular place and time. This historical nature is a critical stipulation about who Christ was and central to the logic of his redemptive power. Śākyamuni was also a historical being but the early Buddhist tradition—as evident in the Pāli texts of the Theravāda school—prioritizes the Buddha's teachings over his personhood. In contrast, his historical form-body (*rūpakāya*) is relegated to the realm of the ephemeral and the illusory, to which Buddhist thought consigns all of phenomenal reality. When the Buddha's follower Vikkali complains that he has not seen the Buddha in some time, the Buddha famously responds: "One who sees the Dhamma sees me; one who sees me sees the Dhamma" (S III.120). This passage asserts the importance of the Dharma (Pāli: Dhamma)—that is, the Buddha's teachings—over the person of the Buddha himself. This leads to a distinction between the historical Buddha, who cannot remain in the world, and the Dharma-body (*dharmakāya*) that does. This is a common explanation for early Buddhist aniconism: the recognition of Śākyamuni's impermanence dissuaded his followers from producing images and fixating on him in favor of looking instead to the body of his teachings. We will return to the permutations and implications of this Buddhology below.

A more succinct and illuminating exercise for the moment might be to compare Jakuchū's *Yasai Nehan* to the 1999 photographic installation created by the Jamaican-born artist Renée Cox called *Yo Mama's Last Supper*. Like Jakuchū's depiction of the Buddha's parinirvana, Cox takes on a significant hagiographical moment—this time in the life of Jesus Christ—that is overtly modeled on Leonardo da Vinci's iconic painting of the Last Supper. The composition is actually made from five photographic plates, with Cox herself, who is black and female—and nude—portrayed in the center image as Christ. In each of the two photographic plates on either side of the center piece, a triad of males aggregate into the twelve

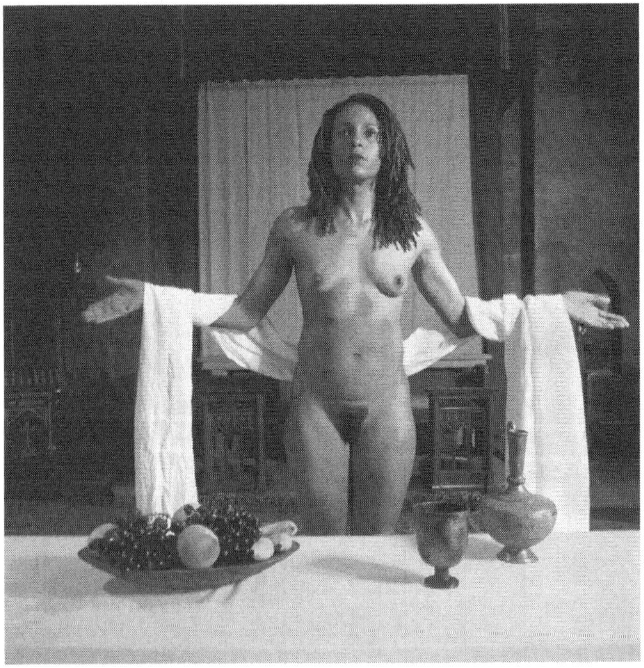

FIGURE 1.2. The artist Renée Cox substitutes for Christ in *Yo Mama's Last Supper*, 1999. (Courtesy of Renée Cox Studio)

disciples—following da Vinci's own compositional structure—except that eleven of them are black and a lone white male sits in the position of Judas. The exhibition of *Yo Mama's Last Supper* at the Brooklyn Museum in 2001 led then-mayor Rudolph Giuliani to call for a decency commission to regulate publicly funded museums. There were also expressions of outrage from religious voices such as the Catholic League for Religious and Civil Rights (*New York Times*, "Affronted by Nude 'Last Supper,' Giuliani Calls for Decency Panel," Feb. 16, 2001).

The expressions of shock and accusations of anti-Catholicism are interesting for their inevitability, on the one hand, and the way they distract from the substantive social and theological issues the photograph provokes, on the other. Cox made this explicit in her response to critics by invoking her Catholic school education and its teaching that all humans are made in the image of God. This prompted the rebuttal that it was simply the offence of her nudity—"There would be no problem if

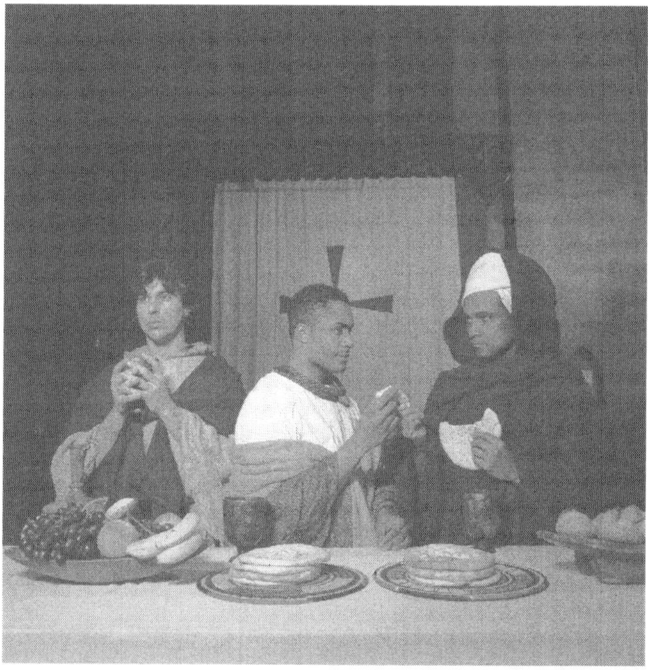

FIGURE 1.3. The plate just right of the Cox/Christ image depicts a white Judas in the triad of disciples. (Courtesy of Renée Cox Studio)

you had kept your clothes on," stated William Donohue, President of the Catholic League (*New York Times*, " 'Yo Mama' Artist Takes on Catholic Critic," Feb. 21, 2001). But this reply conveniently deflects the historical contradictions (and political tensions) in the alternatively accepted norm of the blond-haired and blue-eyed Christ. As a historical being Christ had a certain face and complexion, but social power determines what he looks like and creates difficulties for the purported catholicity of Christian salvation. Cox's work pointedly raises these problems and the expressions of outrage in response to it underscore them even more.

Tensions centering on historical fidelity in the representation of Christ continue in the realm of film. As soon as film became a mass industry in the United States, people began imagining its educational and religious possibilities. A 1910 essay by the Reverend Herbert Jump, "The Religious Possibilities of the Motion Picture," counseled Christians not to be put off by the novelty of the medium or the secularism of the industry, pointing out the potential of movies to function as lively sermons. Jump pays particular attention to the engaging qualities of film: "[T]he picture that is literally moving, that portrays dramatic sequence and life-like action, possesses tenfold more vividness and becomes therefore a more convincing medium of education" (2002, 218).[6] As this essay portended, the power of film for religious ends has not been lost on Christians. One recent and famous realization of this is Mel Gibson's *The Passion of the Christ* (2004), which was treated by Christians as a sermon and a religious meditation in much the same way that paintings, sculptures, and Passion narratives have been experienced since the medieval period.[7]

The Passion was engulfed in controversy, however, because of the way it inflames anti-Semitism. In this, the movie continues a long-standing legacy of both theological readings and artistic depictions that blame Jews for Christ's crucifixion. Hence, much of the pushback on the film consisted of challenges to its historical accuracy on multiple counts—not only the actions of Jews, but the languages spoken, the nature of the torture and crucifixion, and the personality of Pontius Pilate. These rebukes were induced by Gibson's own claim to tell the story of Christ as it "really" was, which reinforces the sense of realism that film dramatizations already possess. New Testament scholar Paula Fredriksen writes, "For better and (probably) for worse, Christianity in America is mediated as much through popular media as through the traditions and institutions of our various churches. Convictions both about the Bible and about Christianity can be as heart-felt as they are uninformed."[8] In Fredriksen's estimation, Gibson problematically purveys the standard Hollywood blockbuster commodity, with its gratuitous violence and simplistic "good versus evil" action, in the guise of religious history.

Accuracy becomes a big question because historical claims are intimately tied to spiritual and moral ones in the Christian conception of Jesus. His story is linked to that of others, and when it comes to the Passion, Adele Reinhartz observes, "filmmakers do have a responsibility to think through the potential negative consequences of their films" because Jews are indelibly written into that history (2004, 28). Furthermore, the Christian understanding of Jesus is itself fraught, particularly in its attempt to balance his human and divine natures. The Jesus film often steps into this fray by making Christ either too superhuman or too human (Deacy 2001). For that reason, the Jesus film is doubly vulnerable to controversy, from the perspective of theological orthodoxy as well as historical accuracy. The protests over Martin Scorsese's *The Last Temptation of Christ* (1988) for making the savior too recognizably mundane in his longings are a case in point. Gibson's own Christ, on the other hand, survives such an excess of physical brutality that he is rendered into an action superhero, compromising the theological view that it is Christ's very humanness that enabled the redemptive power of his suffering.

The sociopolitical and religious stakes in how one sees Christ, then, impose qualifications on Reverend Jump's enthusiasm for the motion picture, which he sanctions on the grounds that Jesus himself preached by means of exciting and accessible stories. He singles out Jesus's parable of the Good Samaritan because it was taken "from contemporary experience. It was the sort of thing that might have happened any day and to any one in the audience" (2002, 217). But this very approachability also creates the justification for iconoclasm. As David Freedberg observes, the power of images to attract and hold the attention is a double-edged sword, for, "What if the lingering is occasioned by color, line, and pleasure in anatomy, and not by reflections of sacred history and dogma?" (1989, 187). The moving action that film provides only adds to this litany of aesthetic pleasures. In the course of Christian history, the mesmerizing powers of art have required interventions in order to "draw the mind away from the attractive sign to the meaningful signified . . . [to] prevent our dwelling on quality and form" (Freedberg 1989, 188).

The Buddha was also a historical figure, but his human existence is contrasted to—and subsumed under—the ever-present Dharma-body of his teachings, which appropriately includes the idea that all beings are ultimately insubstantial, impermanent, and not to be clung to. As theorizing about the nature of the Buddha progressed, the Buddha was understood in terms of the ever-present dharmakāya, understood both as a transcendent realm such as the *dharmadhātu* ("dharma dimension," "dharma sphere," dharma element") and as a personified being such as Vairocana, the Universal Buddha.[9] The impulses that initially minimized the historical Buddha through aniconism eventually gave rise to the view that Śākyamuni is only one historical manifestation of the ever-present dharmakāya.[10] Ironically, this provided a justification for reversing aniconism on the grounds that even images of the Buddha—as yet another historical manifestation—can also lead sentient beings to liberation. This logic is demonstrated in the well-known story of the first image of Śākyamuni and its implication that there is no functional difference between the image and the original person. This image was reputedly commissioned by King Udayana of Kauśāmbī when the Buddha was absent for three months preaching to his mother in the Trāyastriṃśa heaven ("heaven of the thirty-three").[11] Stricken by the absence of the Buddha, the king had an artist transported to the heaven to create a likeness in sandalwood. Quite interestingly, it is said that when the Buddha returned to the palace, the sandalwood image rose and greeted the Buddha, who in turn responded to the image and said: "The work expected from you is to toil in diligence to convert the unbelieving and to lead in the way of religion the future ages" (Beal 1980, 255).[12]

This mythical tale encapsulates Buddhist historical practice, in which the longing to see the absent Buddha has led countless followers to recreate him in likenesses that are animated into "living images" that are thought to be equal in every way to the original Buddha. The Jowo Śākyamuni housed in the Jokhang temple in Lhasa, which is often described as the most important image in Tibet, is another that was supposedly constructed during the Buddha's lifetime. It was purportedly brought to Tibet by Wencheng Gongzhu (628–680) from the Chinese Tang court as a part of her dowry when she was wed to the first Tibetan emperor, Songtsen Gampo (d. 649). Its status as a living image means "devotees do not view him as simply a statue but rather as a manifestation of the Buddha himself" (Warner 2011, 3). The Śākyamuni image in Seiryōji temple in Kyoto is another statue that is invested with the same status. It is supposedly a copy of King Udayana's sandalwood image that was brought from China to Japan by the monk Chōnen in the tenth century (Henderson and Hurvitz 1956).[13] Both the Jowo and Seiryōji

Buddhas are venerated as "first Buddha images" that were carved from life while the Buddha lived, and we can see a concern with historical continuity here in that the veracity of the images is vouchsafed by the claim that they were modeled on the actual Buddha.

But this conceit seems undermined by the fact that the Seiryōji Buddha, for example, is acknowledged to be a *copy* of King Udayana's sandalwood image, which means that it cannot be a "first Buddha image" that was modeled on the living Buddha. This apparent inconsistency actually holds the key to understanding how the power of Buddha images is rendered. A comparison to Buddhist relic worship provides helpful illumination. The centrality and power of relics in Buddhist ritual practice is tied to the fact that relics are either remains of the Buddha himself or were in direct physical contact with him, such as his begging bowl. Relics therefore make the absent Buddha present through the power of synecdoche and contact. Buddha images are also recognized as a kind of relic, but one that acts on a different kind of power:

> Images . . . gain their authority by their capacity to re-present the Buddha visually. . . . Images, unlike relics, can be reproduced endlessly, and they are accepted as worthy of veneration because they embody basic iconographic conventions. Images are also, in many cases, ritually consecrated. . . . In general, however, the ease of reproducing images allows for their proliferation outside monastic control to an extent that distinguishes them from relics, which are usually confined within the ritually defined boundaries of monastic complexes. (Trainor 1997, 30–31)

The power of images arises from the fact that they are ritually consecrated in monastic ceremonies that bring them to life as living Buddhas (Bentor 1996; Swearer 2004). Some images such as the Jowo and Seiryōji Buddhas are given distinction by virtue of a lineage that is traced back to the historical Śākyamuni. This logic works for the Seiryōji Buddha because it is connected to Udayana's sandalwood Buddha, which in turn is connected to the original Buddha. This idea of an unbroken physical lineage partakes in the logic of relics, which are also authenticated by chronicles of successive transmission from the Buddha down to the present day. But this proximity to the actual Buddha, which seems to guarantee the "likeness" of these images, has less to do with physical similarity than with ritual efficacy. The consecrated images are "like" the Buddha in that their presence has the same potency in allowing devotees to generate merit.[14] And unlike relics, each of which must be an actual physical remnant of the Buddha, images can proliferate to the point where the criterion of physical proximity becomes far less relevant. This trend is reinforced by developments in theories about Buddhahood that see the potential of multiple historical entities to function as manifestations of the dharmakāya.

We can see this development in Buddhist locations that adhere closely to Mahāyāna tradition. Yael Bentor's study of Tibetan Buddhist ritual texts reveals that consecrated images and *stūpas* (Buddhist reliquary monuments) are "regarded as parallel to the emanation of a Buddha in the *saṃsāric* world" (1996, 5) because the act of consecration "establishes" (Sanskrit: *pratiṣṭhā*; Tibetan: *rab-gnas*) the dharmakāya in the physical object.[15] In Mahāyāna theory, the Buddha's form-body (rūpakāya) is only one of many "manifestations" or "emanations" (*nirmāṇakāyas*) that can appear in the world.[16] This signals an important shift in the conception of Śākyamuni, who is demoted into merely one agent in a universe of entities that function for the sake of liberating sentient beings. In the Tibetan consecration texts:

> [w]riters distinguish three types of emanation bodies. The supreme emanation bodies are the Buddhas; the born emanation bodies are various incarnations of Buddhas and bodhisattvas born in the world, such as the Dalai Lamas and other incarnate lamas; finally, the made emanation bodies are emanations made by artists and consecrated by lamas, such as *stūpas* and images, and even bridges. (Bentor 1996, 5–6)[17]

The nature of the dharmakāya that is established in these objects needs some parsing here. The Dharma-body may simply be the physical texts that preserve the Buddha's words even though he himself is gone. In the Pāli *Nikāyas*, the dharmakāya simply means the teachings of the Buddha (Xing 2005, 22). But the Dharma-body came to be understood in a second sense as the qualities (*dharmas*) of the Buddha's knowledge and enlightenment.[18] This enlarges the idea of the Buddha into something more than a historical person or even a body of teachings, focusing instead on the Buddha's knowledge (*adhigama*) as an abiding possibility that is ever-present in the world: "By implication, it is also a place where the student or the worshipper can follow the Buddha's example and realize the Perfection of Wisdom for himself or herself" (Eckel 1992, 99). To say that the Dharma-body remains in the world, then, is to say that the virtuous qualities that the Buddha attained are an ever-present possibility for all beings. As a result, the importance of the historical Śākyamuni is diminished, as he is turned into one temporary manifestation of this larger principle of an abiding Buddhahood. The early tradition's aniconic sign—such as the footprint of the Buddha—emphasizes the Buddha's absence as a reminder that his "importance lies precisely and only in the *effects* he has upon those others to whom he appears to be present" (emphasis added; Griffiths 1994, 94). The point of seeing the Buddha is not so much to see *him* but rather to see what he sees.

In Mahāyāna Buddhism, the desire to see what the Buddha saw deemphasizes Śākyamuni Buddha by creating a bewildering proliferation of Buddhas. This trend actually begins in Theravāda texts, where Śākyamuni recounts a lineage of six previous Buddhas who lived parallel lives in prior cosmic ages.[19] The Mahāsāṃghika, another early school, originated the idea of numerous Buddhas living in other worlds. Mahāyāna cosmology develops this idea to reveal countless simultaneously existing Buddhas and bodhisattvas in multiple world systems and Buddha-fields (*buddhakṣetra*), or Pure Lands. Working around the early teaching that only one Buddha can arise in a world system, the Mahāyāna emphasis on innumerable bodhisattvas who strive for complete liberation fueled the logic that there must be many Buddha lands for them to occupy (Xing 2005, 166).

The preeminence of bodhisattvas in Mahāyāna Buddhism may have created the need to provide realms for them to occupy, but the idea that the universe is teeming with Buddhas and bodhisattvas in every direction also exhibits a soteriological principle: if the eternal Dharma-body can manifest as one specific being in a particular time and place, then there is no limit to the number and forms it can take. According to the *Daśabhūmika Sūtra* ("Ten Stages"), when beings reach the eighth stage of the bodhisattva path they are able to pervade "an unspeakable number of universes and undertake manifestations in the forms of the beings there according to their various inclinations, by means of knowledge of how to appear as a reflection" (Cleary 1993, 768).[20] In the twenty-fifth chapter of the *Lotus Sutra*, which focuses on Avalokiteśvara, it is stated that this bodhisattva can manifest in the form of a Buddha if needed, but also as numerous other beings ranging from gods, kings, laymen and women, boys and girls, and even demons. This ability to take on many forms in order to respond to the needs of different beings is elaborated by the fifth-century commentator Vasubandhu through substance metaphors for the dharmadhātu ("dharma element") such as water or gold, which can take many forms while still remaining itself (Eckel 1992, 102–105).[21]

The Pāli texts describe another version of Buddha-proliferation with the idea of "mind-made bodies" produced by meditative concentration for the purpose of performing Buddha works. Just as a sword can be drawn from its scabbard, or a snake from its old skin, the monk "draws that body out of this body, having form, mind-made, complete with all its limbs and faculties" (D I.77). As a fruit of the homeless life—that is, the Buddhist path—this capacity to produce mind-made bodies is shared by Buddhas and bodhisattvas, who out of compassion for all beings produce many efficacious Buddha-bodies. The idea of mind-made bodies develops into an explicit theory of magically emanated bodies that appear in human or heavenly Buddha realms for the purpose of liberating all beings.[22] In this manner, the Buddha "seems to be present to different living beings in different ways, to different extents" (Griffiths 1994, 109).

In sum, all Buddha-bodies are expedient illusions, or works of art. This idea also proposes that there is no need to privilege one form over another if they produce the same effects. This point is explicitly affirmed in the Mahāyāna text *On the Merit of Bathing the Buddha*. The sūtra begins with the Buddha at Rājagṛiha amid an immense assembly of monks and bodhisattvas. There the Pure Wisdom Bodhisattva wonders how it will be possible to see the Buddha once the latter has passed out of this world. The Buddha responds by offering substitutions for his own body. In the early tradition, the Buddha's bone relics were placed in stūpas as a way of extending the physical presence of the Buddha (Strong 2007). In this text, the Buddha sanctions the use of a Dharma "relic" in the form of a four-line verse, replacing the physical Buddha with his teachings. Archeological evidence from India confirms that canonical texts eventually replaced physical relics in stūpas. The rise of Dharma "relics" and image worship eclipsed relic veneration in those parts of India under strong brahmanical influence, with its abhorrence of corpses as ritually polluting (Bronkhorst 2011a, 193–206). This led to the substitution of images and verses for bodily remains.[23] The rise of Mahāyāna Buddhism also promoted the worship of texts as a way of bypassing the stūpa cults under the control of more orthodox schools (Schopen 1975). This "cult of the book" actively substituted texts for the relics of the Buddha, on the principle that the Buddha and the Dharma are equivalent.[24] *On the Merit of Bathing the Buddha* provides a spiritual rationale for the efficacy of relic, text, and image veneration alike:

> If men, women, or the five groups of mendicants would build an image of the Buddha . . . it would be like doing homage by offering up a rare jewel. If in accordance with one's own strength and ability one can be truly sincere and respectful, it [the image or stūpa] would be *like my present body, equal without difference.* (Boucher 1995, 65; emphasis added)

The sūtra affirms that all three forms of Buddha homage can promote the ability to be truly sincere and respectful. Paying obeisance to a relic, text, or image is uniformly equivalent to worshipping the Buddha himself because they all enable Buddha qualities, such as attention, compassion, and insight. This eighth-century Chinese text, which is purportedly based on an Indian Sanskrit sūtra,[25] seems to reconcile what were once competing practices by emphasizing a unified soteriological aim—that is, the *experiences* enabled by ritual veneration, which is ultimately more important than the physical vehicles employed. In this act of reconciliation, the text reaffirms the original principle that seeing the Buddha is more a matter of the virtuous qualities attained, rather than the actual bodies seen.

The Necessity of Form

The other side of this picture, however, is that the history of Buddhism displays a need for concrete bodies that engage the senses and the imagination. The Buddhist tradition has availed itself of every means of seeing the Buddha—through stories, poetry, paintings, carvings, statuary, and dramas.[26] The necessity of concrete manifestations of Buddhahood, in contrast to philosophical abstractions such as nonduality, no-self (*anātman*), and emptiness, has been felt by monastics and laypeople alike. Rather than being a concession to human weakness, the use of forms agrees with the Buddhist view that sensory perception is prior to the conceptuality of words. This is particularly evident in the way the sense of sight is emphasized. The vision metaphors that characterize the Buddha's enlightenment as "seeing" and "insight" are not just poetic images but also describe the content of the Buddha's wisdom as a "direct perception" (*pratyakṣa*) of reality. To see the Buddha, in other words, is not a matter of ideas and concepts but rather an actual *seeing* that is unencumbered by conceptual labels.

In the Buddhist phenomenology of the person articulated in the Pāli texts, sensory perceptions emerge from the body, and thoughts arise afterward as a form of distortion. Hence, "perception [is] primary in the sense that it reveals the world prior to the imposition of conceptual elaboration" (McMahan 2002, 48). The sensations (*saṃjñā*) that arise in the wake of contact between the body and external objects are observed to immediately trigger a naming process that imposes categories upon the world. This "cognitive process is based on not seeing things as they really are: and this misperception is what constitutes the ignorance which generates continued *saṃsāric* existence" (Hamilton 1999, 56). This phenomenon is later identified with the "proliferation" (*prapañca*) of concepts set into motion by the process of naming, and which needs to stop in order for liberation to take place. This results in Buddhism's enduring ambivalence toward words, doctrine, and scriptures even while it makes ample use of them. But in the end, the point is clear: "Words may be essential to convey certain types of meaning, but they are no substitute for direct perception. To see something is to know it more directly than to hear about it through words" (Eckel 1992, 149).

But a paradox arises here, in that the specificity and materiality of the Buddhas seen are supposed to help one in apprehending an ultimately formless and empty reality. The physicality of the Buddha disperses first into a set of teachings and finally to a purely mental state of understanding.[27] This understanding is described as nondual knowledge, which arises from the insight that the insubstantial nature of all things (their "empty" quality) means there is no fundamental difference between things. Thus, the Tibetan consecration texts, for example, acknowledge that the act of consecrating an image as a receptacle of the dharmakāya is only a conceit because the dharmakāya is "as vast as space" and therefore non-localizable in any single object. This also means that the quality of emptiness is already in the image/stūpa without ever having to be established there. This nondual knowledge undermines the necessity of any particular receptacle and discerns the Buddha-nature in all things. To really see the Buddha, then, means letting the Buddha go—at least as envisioned as a particular form.

But even the practice of "direct seeing" means that one must look at *something*. As Bentor observes, "It is not an easy matter to perceive the omnipresent nature of the [dharmakāya], nor to regard the entire universe as sacred. One prefers to confine the ultimate powers in certain identifiable places" (1996, 18). The difficulty of visualizing the nondual and the formless is not lost on those who construct sensory imaginings of the Buddha. Consider the following poem by the Chinese poet Qiu Wei (694–789):

> On the precipitous peak, a bracken hut,
> A climb straight up of thirty *li*.
> I knock at the gate—no servant boy;
> I peak in the room—only a table and bench.
> If he's not abroad in his covered cart,
> He must be fishing in the autumn waters.
> This way and that, we do not meet
> After all that effort, in vain I gaze, awed.
> The color of grass in the new rain,
> The sound of pines in an evening window.
> Arriving here at the summit of solitude,
> Perfect contentment washes over my heart.
> While there's been no understanding of guest and host,
> There is something of the sense of limpid purity.
> When my desire abated, then did I descend the mountain,
> What need is there to see the master?[28]

This poem rehearses the well-known poetic theme of looking for the Zen master and not finding him in. The popularity of this trope testifies to how much the Buddhist challenge to see an unseeable "emptiness" spurred on the aesthetic imagination. In this poem, the absence of the recluse is the main event and echoes the absence of Śākyamuni himself. The success of the poet's encounter with this absence pivots on a series of substitutions that are both tacitly and explicitly invoked. The master sought out for instruction is himself a substitute for the historical Buddha, who in turn is merely an apparitional body of the formless dharmakāya. In the absence of the master, the speaker finds "perfect contentment" in the landscape, which now substitutes for the master. But lest this gets misunderstood, it is clearly the speaker's "awe," "solitude," and "sense of limpid purity" that embodies his attainment. What is crucial is the attentiveness of the poet in traversing the physical landscape rather than the environment, per se.

This meditative attention is normally understood as the primary *means* to enlightenment, but as the poem suggests, this practice is also the *substance* of enlightenment itself. The dualism of subject and object is dissolved because what the poet does is not separate from the stated goal of his activity: meditative attention is both the means and end. Furthermore, the poem's focus on nature, as the broadest reiteration of the Buddha, signifies how readily we can find the means of liberation at our disposal. This tacit exhortation to let go of particular forms and utilize what is immediately at hand neutralizes dualistic distinctions between "religious" and "nonreligious" objects. To see the Buddha everywhere is a strategy for "seeing" the formless in all forms. The process of seeing the Buddha is also the process that allows one to see *like* the Buddha by exerting an attentive gaze that goes beyond conventional labels and comes alive to the nature of things—to the point of seeing a universe of Buddhas and bodhisattvas in the ordinary and even the abject. This principle is a tremendous boon to aesthetic practice.

Visions of the Buddha

The medium of film—particularly its visual and temporal nature—stands out for how it can attend to the sensory and phenomenal world. Film can direct our gaze and form connections between things, which is a way of telling a story, and it can also lead us to look at objects and events that contribute nothing to the development of plot and that even undermine the intelligibility of the narrative. The films examined in this book do both, but they are ordered from the first kind to the second in order to replicate how Buddhist traditions have patterned levels of Buddhist insight. The first film, Kim Kiduk's *Spring, Summer, Fall, Winter . . . and Spring* (2004), is the most overtly Buddhist in content and the film weaves its episodes together according to the narrative logic of the doctrine of karma, which can be summarized as a postulated connection between actions and consequences. According to the East Asian and Tibetan Buddhist schemas of doctrinal classification, karma doctrine and its focus on reward and punishment is a preliminary teaching that is ultimately superseded by the realization of emptiness and Buddha-nature.

For that reason, the final chapter examines the films of the American director Terrence Malick, particularly *The Thin Red Line* (1998), *The Tree of Life* (2011), and *To the Wonder* (2013), which lack any mention of Buddhism. I construct this progression of works that increasingly erase references to the Buddha and to Buddhism to make the point that film itself can stand in for the Buddha and the kind of seeing he is understood to have attained.

My analysis of Malick's cinema appears to participate in what might be called "Buddhist film criticism," in which contemporary Western films such as *Groundhog Day* (1993), *American Beauty* (1999), and *Donnie Darko* (2001) are analyzed through the lenses of Buddhist teachings and values.[29] John Whalen-Bridge refers to such films as "draftees" that have become Buddhist by virtue of being discussed in Buddhist terms (2014, 46), and he suggests part of the reason for this phenomenon (particularly in the context of the Buddhist Film Festival) is to appeal to mainstream Western audiences. Hollywood feature films avoid the potential turn-off of films that are too devotional or hagiographical, such as Martin Scorcese's *Kundun* (1997)—a biopic about the current Dalai Lama's early life—and provide an accessible way of introducing Buddhist teachings. My choice of Malick is a departure from this general feature of the "draftee" Buddhist film because Malick's cinema is hardly accessible or representative of Hollywood filmmaking. Watching a Malick film can require a fair amount of effort for the average viewer and it frustrates the usual filmic norms of narrative sensibility. I choose these films as examples of the highest and most difficult form of Buddhist vision precisely because they defy thematic handling and put the emphasis on how the viewer experiences the sensory filmic event itself.

Through the five chapters of film analysis in this book, I construct three progressive ways of seeing the Buddha loosely based on an artistic precedent from the ancient Buddhist world—the temple known as Borobudur on the island of Java in Indonesia. Constructed during the late eighth and early ninth centuries, this stone temple is a rising structure that peaks with a central stūpa. The bottom levels consist of four nested galleries that progressively ascend toward the center. These square-shaped galleries are relatively enclosed spaces formed by high walls on the sides that face the center, on the one hand, and by balustrades on the sides that look out and away from the temple, on the other. All four galleries feature highly elaborate relief carvings that are viewed by circumambulating each level before moving up to the next gallery level.

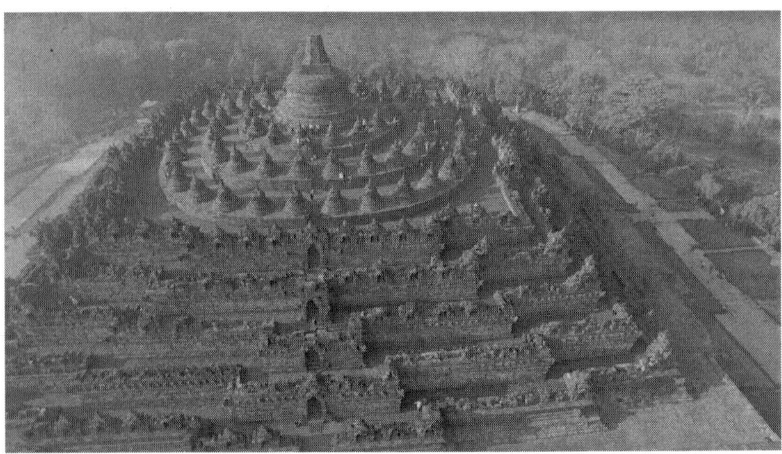

Figure 1.4. Borobudur Temple, ninth century. Central Java, Indonesia.

After the fourth gallery, the pilgrim emerges onto three nested and circular open-air terraces. There are no view-obstructing walls here but an open space that offers panoramic vistas of the countryside. In addition, a total of seventy-two small stūpas sit atop the three terraces, each with a sitting Buddha that can be seen through the latticed openings of the stūpa covers. At the very top of the temple sits the main stūpa, made of solid and visually impenetrable stone.

A notable feature of Borobudur is the way the depictions on the relief carvings closely follow Buddhist scriptures, particularly the *Gaṇḍavyūha*, a Mahāyāna text that became part of the *Avataṃsaka Sūtra* in Buddhabhadra's Chinese translation of 420 CE. But as Julie Gifford points out in her study of the monument, it is a mistake to simply "read" Borobudur as a visual illustration of Buddhist texts. This discounts how Borobudur is meant to be experienced: "The visual program of Borobudur as a whole was not designed precisely to be 'viewed,' but rather to be contemplated in the context of ritual, devotional, and possibly meditative practice" (Gifford 2011, 4). Taken in as a whole, the "visual program" of Borobudur stages a progression of visions of the Buddha from the particular to the ultimate. The experience of Borobudur moves the pilgrim from discrete narratives about the Buddha to a final wisdom in which the Buddha, as represented by the central stūpa, is completely obscured and replaced by an open and panoramic view of the world. The visual and experiential program of Borobudur provides a blueprint for how films can also be Buddhist.

Legend has it that when the Buddha attained enlightenment, he gained the "divine eye" that allowed him to see the past and future of all living beings, including his own past lives. This is the knowledge of karma, or of the connection between events. The practice of seeing connections between the past, present, and future encourages greater awareness of how one's dispositions in the present derive from the past and in turn lead to future conditions. This karmic lesson has been conveyed for centuries in both stories and visual representations of cause and effect, particularly in the accounts of the Buddha's past lives known as *jātaka* ("birth story") tales. Borobudur commences with such narratives at its base by depicting scenes from the *Karmavibhanga*, which features general tales of moral cause and effect.[30] From there, the first two galleries of Borobudur depict the former and present lives of the Buddha himself, based on the *Jātakamālā* and *Lalitavistara,* respectively. In the Mahāyāna worldview that Borobudur embodies, the teaching of karma is one of the most elementary, in the sense of a beginner's meditation: "The Buddha manifests in this way for the benefit of practitioners who are capable of understanding morality only in terms of punishment and reward" (Gifford 2011, 172). The visual logic of these sections is narrative and linear and in that respect resembles a movie. In fact, the detailed temporal sequencing of the panels can be likened to a primitive film in which "the eye elides the frames and runs the images together so that the illusion of motion is achieved" (Gifford, 55). The first film to be considered, *Spring, Summer, Fall, Winter . . . and then, Spring,* is likewise a vision of karma that offers a clear message about actions and their consequences in the mode of a cautionary tale.

Spring is considerably more nuanced than this, however, and its invocation of circularity (which is apparent in the title) ends up posing a challenge to the distinction between (and transition from) the "not-enlightened" to "enlightened" that linear tales narrate. This parallels the way linearity is also discarded in Borobudur's third and fourth galleries, where the images shift to scenes from the *Gaṇḍavyūha*. The *Gaṇḍavyūha* concerns the story of the pilgrim Sudhana who visits the Bodhisattva Maitreya (the future successor to Śākyamuni) at the climax of his journey. The revelations at Maitreya's palace—which Borobudur features in 221 relief panels—consist of the visions Maitreya creates of innumerable

Buddhas in their Buddha-fields across the universe, and the totality of Maitreya's own past, present, and future in his career as a bodhisattva. These visions are Maitreya's own sermon in visionary rather than narrative form, in which the distances of both space and time are collapsed to suggest that the cosmos is always and everywhere pervaded by the body of the Buddha—the dharmakāya. At this point, Borobudur abandons narrative images in favor of picturing one setting repeatedly—such as the interior of Maitreya's palace—by featuring different elements of the same scene in successive panels. The point of the images clearly shifts from telling stories to aiding the practice of focused seeing, tying such contemplation to one's ability to see the dharmakāya in one's own world.

The second and third films to be analyzed likewise offer "visions of emptiness" by provoking viewers to be mindful of what they see and offering the insight that human conceptions of reality are ultimately illusory. The Buddhas and bodhisattvas that Maitreya conjures in his palace are illusions, emphasized by the fact that they appear and disappear with a mere snap of Maitreya's fingers. When Sudhana asks where they come from, Maitreya replies that "those supernal manifestations are not internal or external, yet it is not that they are not seen, by the magical power of the enlightening being, and because of your own capacity" (Cleary 1993, 1499). In other words, what we see attests to our own abilities, inclinations, and foibles. Therefore, the question of what we see becomes a question of what we choose to see, and its consequences. *Nang Nak* (1999), by Nonzee Nimibutr, is a Thai film based on a popular folk tale about the ghost of a devoted wife. Described as a "tale of horror," this commercially successful movie focuses on the taming of the intractable and murderous wife-ghost. Despite the "horror" billing, what the film offers is two competing visions of Nang Nak: that of an unnatural and murderous demon, on the one hand, and that of a piteous and very human woman, on the other. The former vision, which is articulated by the villagers, results in their own violent deaths. The latter vision, which is depicted through the meditative insight of a Buddhist abbot, successfully lays the ghost to rest. As the film demonstrates, the way we see the world is its own karma and its own form of punishment or reward.

Akira Kurosawa's classic *Rashomon* (1950) established a landmark in filmmaking with its consecutive and utterly conflicting versions of the rape of a woman told from multiple viewpoints. The film's refusal to reveal the "true story" of what happened has been read as a condemnation of human mendacity. The Buddhist roots of the film's literary sources, however, suggest an alternative emphasis on the inevitable relativity of all perspectives and the need to refrain from dogmatic renditions of "the truth." As *Rashomon* demonstrates, films have the capacity to propagate this vision by refusing the "God's-eye" point of view. Film can hold conflicting views in productive tension and encourage one to see the humanity in each. This kind of relativism cultivates a more penetrating and compassion-inducing vision, and both the visions of emptiness displayed in *Nang Nak* and *Rashomon* trump the question of what is really real with inquiries about the compassion (or absence thereof) in our own ways of seeing things.

The open terraces on the top of Borobudur are ringed with stone Buddhas that create a physical Buddha-field. The central stūpa forming the apex of the temple is made of solid stone, embodying an invisible

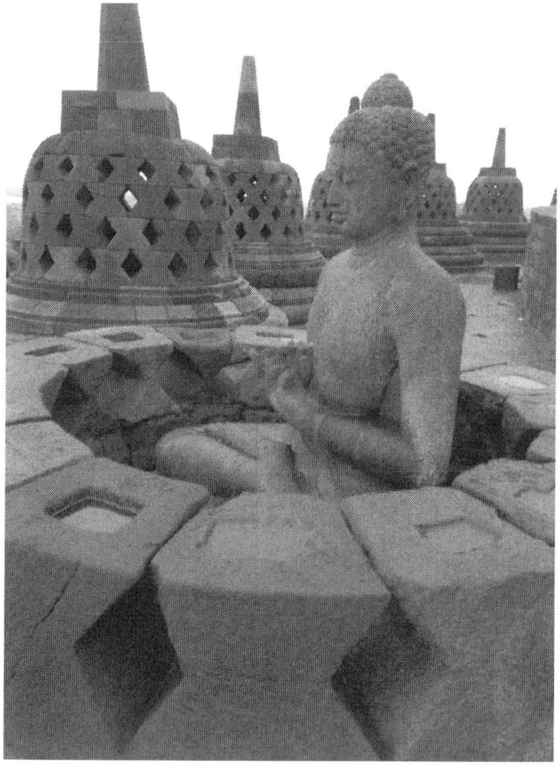

FIGURE 1.5. An exposed stūpa Buddha on the circular terrace of Borobudur. (Photograph by Robert DeCaroli)

Buddha that is analogous to the invisible dharmakāya that cannot be seen through ordinary vision. The pinnacle of Borobudur presumes that the pilgrim has undergone a meditative journey by means of the temple itself, and now the seeing *of* the Buddha can be replaced with seeing *like* the Buddha that discerns him in all phenomena without requiring his explicit form. The vista onto the surrounding landscape beyond the temple points to the anywhere and everywhere that the Buddha can be found. This is the final perspective that I call the "aesthetic vision." In Mahāyāna Buddhism, the inherently empty and open-ended nature of all phenomena has been expressed through poetic and artistic visions of the intrinsic "Buddha-nature" in all things. In this practice, art and religion become indistinguishable because both draw attention to the infinite openness of the ordinary world, which becomes a Buddha-field when it is seen properly. In East Asia, for example, composing poetry and brushing paintings were ways of contemplating one's immediate surroundings that look past their conventional meanings. In examining poetry and land-scape painting during the Muromachi era in Japan (1336–1573), Joseph Parker notes that these arts were taken to be Buddhist spiritual practices sanctified by the Zen view that "there can be little distinction between the sacred realm of the natural world and that of human civilization" (1999, 158). Aesthetic practice, in short, is a way of liberating oneself from limited and conventional ways of experiencing things.

The medium of film can actualize this kind of aesthetic practice quite virtuously because as an experience that centers chiefly on the suc-cession of images, it has the ability to control how we look at something, as well as what we look at. Many movies entertain us with rapid and action-centered images, but some capitalize on the camera's ability to fix our attention on what seems incidental or unrelated to the movement of the plot. In so doing, the images tell their own story and become the main characters. *Maborosi* (1995) by the Japanese director Hirokazu Kore'eda, is about a young woman whose husband commits suicide for no apparent reason. Although her life moves on, the young wife's struggle with this senseless death comes to a peak at the end of the movie. Rather than resolving the mystery, the film is largely taken up with offering images, particularly arresting tableaus of shadow and light that do not advance the story in any discernible way. The title of the film, which may be translated as "a trick of light" invokes the stock Buddhist metaphor that life is nothing but a magical creation, a shadow, a mirage, and a dream. The title also refers to the illusion of cinema, which is ultimately nothing more than an arresting play of light and shadow that has the power to entrance. The way *Maborosi* insists on shifting away from discursive explanations to sustained contemplation and appreciation of what is ultimately illusory forms a version of the Buddha's vision.

Finally, the films of Terrence Malick demonstrate how this aesthetic vision is a possibility of film itself regardless of its geographical or cultural origins. The central feature to note is how Malick's filmmaking favors images over attempts at a discursive moral and philosophical clarity. Utilizing film's capacity for movement, Malick juxtaposes images in a way that goes beyond the limiting "either/or" distinctions of both common perceptions and intellectual formulations. Malick's work instantiates both a wholeness and ambiguity that transcend the necessary dualisms of language and puts the emphasis on the question of what each character—and viewer—chooses to see. In this manner, Malick's cinema is particularly virtuous in demonstrating the ability of film to convey the world beyond the restrictions imposed by normal habits of mind. In doing so, it offers the potential to train the viewer to see the world in the same way.

Conclusion

This book illustrates the ways in which film instantiates traditional ways of seeing the Buddha, and thereby becomes the latest artistic technology within a long tradition of cultural practices that have seen art as religion. This demonstration is modeled on the visual and meditative program of Borobudur, which resembles a maṇḍala, or the stylized diagram of the universe employed in Buddhist (particularly Tantric) ritual.[31] A maṇḍala is an "imaginative vision" that "harnesses the creative power of mind to produce a new divine vision of reality" (Newman 2000, 588). In maṇḍala meditation practice, the deities depicted are recognized as aspects of the self as seen in purified form. These deities are in turn treated as manifestations of emptiness, which comprises the ultimate vision. Although there are many different maṇḍalas in Buddhist traditions (not to mention the rest of the Tantric world), they display a basic structure in which the supreme transcendent/immanent principle (the dharmakāya) sits in the center and radiates outward into differentiated forms. The discrete forms in the outer limits "participate in the outward flow of the godhead, and are in some way emanations or hypostases of the deity himself" (White

2000, 9). In Buddhist language, the immanent and unseeable Buddha at the center flows outward as innumerable enlightening beings of many discrete and expedient appearances.[32]

It should be noted that my visualization of Buddhist films on the model of Borobudur is an artistic creation of my own. This creation is not meant to encapsulate all of Buddhist history or ways of defining the Buddhist film. But all art—as well as life—must be experienced through temporal moments and spatial locations that form a sequence. I have arranged the films in this book to do just that in order to exhibit one specific way in which films can replicate—and perhaps even improve upon—how Buddhists have imagined the possibilities for seeing the Buddha, and seeing like the Buddha. I take encouragement in how readily it is possible to identify works that fit into the schema that I construct, and fancy that this book can offer a template for one way of identifying and talking about Buddhist cinema. It is possible to add more works to each of the three categories I identify, or to refine the categories further. I hope to offer a skeleton that can be further fleshed in by others, particularly when it comes to films with no explicit Buddhist references. The template I create allows us to visualize the Buddhist muscles of filmic art because the logic of Buddhist "manifestation bodies" affirms the possibility of there being countless enlightening beings who are "equal without difference" to those who are "truly sincere." Hence, the celluloid bodies of cinema validate the claim of the *Gaṇḍhavyūha* that "birth in all states of being is phantomlike" but that at the same time these phantoms "are tireless in guiding and perfecting all beings, because they are aware all is selfless" (Cleary 1993, 1500).

CHAPTER 2

The Karmic Narrative of
Spring, Summer, Fall, Winter . . . and Spring

Kim Kiduk's *Spring, Summer, Fall, Winter . . . and Spring* (2004) is a product of Korean cinema, which boasts a steady stream of Buddhist-themed films. Among these, the works of Im Kwon-taek such as *Mandala* (1981) and *Come, Come, Come Upwards* (1989) have been oft-noted, as is Bae Yongkyun's *Why Has Bodhidharma Left for the East?* (1989). Im's movies feature Buddhist monastic figures (both monks and nuns) who negotiate the tension between world renunciation and social engagement. Both *Mandala* and *Come, Come, Come Upwards* ponder the same question: "What is socially at stake in the choice between a pure ascetic life in the mountains and a life of active participation in the world's affairs?" (James 2002, 61). The righteousness of religious seclusion is questioned in the face of social injustice and suffering, displaying a contemporary vision of the bodhisattva ideal of acting in the world. Bae's *Why Has Bodhidharma Left for the East?* also plays on the tension between the worlds inside and outside of the Buddhist hermitage, suggesting that one can never really leave one for the other, on the one hand, but presenting this as a conflicted experience for the main monastic character. Social consciousness is at the heart of these films, mirroring the national consciousness and political turmoil of Korean society during the 1980s.

Kim Kiduk's film is the product of a different era, however. In *Spring*, the Buddhist hermitage is not an escape from the world of samsara and its competing moral obligations, but rather a setting that provides the space to truly see the world "outside." Various characters come in from and go back out to the world beyond, bringing their troubles with them. The hermitage is not a place to escape worldly dilemmas but rather a stage on which they are mirrored, magnified, and sometimes even resolved. The unusual structure of the hermitage, which comprises a small hut fronted by a proscenium-like platform that floats unanchored on the middle of a lake, enhances the suggestion that the hermitage is a stage where one can watch worldly dramas unfold. The cast of characters that enters this space all come to ends that are within the purview of traditional Buddhist thought while surrounded by the scaffolding of overtly Buddhist rituals and symbols. Furthermore, *Spring* translates canonical Buddhist metaphors and long-standing ritual techniques into cinematic art. To the degree that *Spring* reflects its present cultural context—as all art must—it conveys a transnational and contemporary Buddhist consciousness marked by the modern Western interest in doctrine, on the one hand, and by traditional Asian symbols and tropes, on the other. Front and center to both is the use of karmic cause and effect as a narrative device that both structures the story and conveys Buddhist religious lessons.

Observing the Buddhist Drama

Spring is set in a tiny Buddhist hermitage that floats in the middle of a lake surrounded by mountains. The final shot of the movie offers a perspective from the peak of those mountains, which reveals the distant lake dwarfed and nestled within the folds of a vast landscape. The lake is miniscule in comparison, and the people who occupy the floating temple are likewise integrated into the vaster world of trees, rocks, and water. The human characters—initially a young boy novice and elder master—are appropriately unnamed, for the film evokes timeless patterns rather than telling the stories of individuals. The scarcity of personalizing dialogue reinforces this quality, and most of the spoken words observe perennial realities. As the film (and seasons) progress, the little boy becomes a young man in the flush of sexual awakening, then an older man in the wake of violent disillusionment, and then finally returns to take the place of the mature master, thus completing the cycle.

Kim Kiduk is a self-taught filmmaker and was a painter before that, which perhaps accounts for the cinematography of *Spring* and the way it evokes the panoramic scale of classical Chinese landscape paintings. Humans never dominate the canvas in such works, which include the much larger environment within which human existence is embedded. The Buddhist perspective on this existence is conveyed through a statue of the Bodhisattva Guanyin who gazes upon the distant lake from the mountaintop at the end of the film. Guanyin, the bodhisattva of compassion, is the Chinese version of the Indian Avalokiteśvara, and the full three characters of the bodhisattva's name—*guan* 觀 ("observe, see"), *shi* 世 ("world"), *yin* 音 ("sound, cries")—faithfully renders the meaning of the Sanskrit version: "the one who looks down upon the cries of the world." This is precisely what Guanyin does in the film's final shot, signifying that everything below is encompassed within the bodhisattva's vision. The lake-top hermitage is far from the bustle of life in the mundane realm of human strivings, but for that very reason it is a quiet microcosm where human life is carefully observed rather than escaped.

The essence of what *Spring* observes, as a work of film, is the law of karma. In this manner, the film replicates the vision of the Bodhisattva Guanyin, who replays what the Buddha saw when he attained his divine eye: the law of dependent arising. Canonically, this is expressed as a simple observation of causality: "When this exists, that comes to be; with the arising of this, that arises. When this does not exist, that does not come to be; with the cessation of this, that ceases" (S II.28). According to accounts of the Buddha's enlightenment, he first attained knowledge

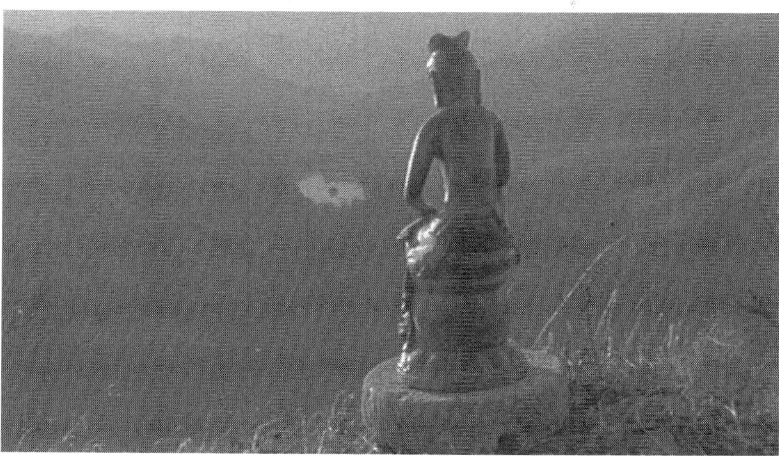

FIGURE 2.1. The Bodhisattva Guanyin looks down upon the world and hears its cries.

of his former lives, and then he saw the births and deaths of all other beings in the following manner: "These living beings who perform evil deeds end up in miserable states; But these others who perform virtuous deeds, rise up to the triple heaven" (Olivelle 2008, 405). These two visions then culminate in the Buddha's knowledge of dependent arising and the Buddhist law of cause and effect as the true nature of the world.

Reflecting this account of the Buddha's own awakening, the Buddhist teaching of causality is frequently glossed as the law of karma in which the moral nature of one's deeds is recompensed in kind through successive lives. The teaching of cause and effect naturally lends itself to storytelling, and the many prior lives of the Buddha in the form of various animals, kings, deities, and other figures form an important class of literature known as the *jātaka*.[1] Another form of Buddhist literature called the *apadāna*, which, expanded into the later genre called *avadāna*, tells the story of persons other than the Buddha by recounting their past deeds in order to explain their present circumstances.[2] The importance and ubiquity of such narratives in the lives of ordinary Buddhists have not always been appreciated by outside observers, who might consider them inferior to doctrinal texts.[3] Their fable-like quality is self-evidently accessible to mainstream audiences but the lessons they convey seem to be predictable and unvarying: good actions lead to good consequences, and evil actions to sorrowful ones.[4] The karmic drama appears to assure us that everyone gets his just deserts in the end through the mechanism of rebirth.

It is tempting to read karmic narratives as a Buddhist theodicy that explains why bad things happen to apparently good people, but this in fact misses their more profound meaning. What the Buddha sees with his divine eye may assure us that justice ultimately prevails, but the law of karma assumes a cosmic scale much grander than the concerns of individual beings. *Spring* helps us to see this by scaling down its temporal view: the cycle of rebirth is abbreviated into a single seasonal circuit—from spring to spring. This synecdoche is layered, however, in that the seasons also represent the chapters of the life journey of the young boy, who evolves into the new mature master at the end of the film. The story falls short of depicting rebirth, but the explicit allusion to recycling seasons allied to life stages suggest multiple and interchangeable scales of analysis: a single year also represents a full lifetime (from boy to master), and even multiple lives (in the repetition of the pattern in which boys become masters). This in turn indicates that what is actually at the heart of the karmic drama is the natural mechanism of cause and effect that drives the plot of human existence, rather than the particular individuals who instantiate these recurring dramas.

In this, the karmic narrative differs markedly from the norms of Hollywood storytelling in which the will of the protagonist drives the mechanism of cause and effect. It is always the main characters who drive the story, or perhaps clash in their desire to do so, but the agency of such individuals is a given. Even when the characters are engulfed by natural or historical forces beyond their control, these factors form a mere backdrop that showcases the self-determined actions of the main players. Thus, in classic Hollywood cinema, "history [is] unknowable apart from its effects upon individual characters. . . . A storm may maroon a group of characters, but then psychological causality takes over. A war may separate lovers, but then they must react to that condition" (Bordwell, Staiger, and Thompson 1985, 13). In contrast, the characters in *Spring*, who are not even identified by personal names, serve to illustrate the inexorable processes that condition both human and natural existence. The main character is the impersonal law of causality itself.

This impersonal law functions morally by highlighting what is common to the human condition writ large. The frequent tales of the Buddha as an animal in a former life operate similarly. By clothing the Buddha in the form of multiple animals, he is divested of any social identity and its bias-inducing function, particularly in a society where caste status automatically shaped estimations of a person's worth. These tales convey that there are no inherent properties to or differences between living beings, but rather a single web of cause and effect. This "can help us to perceive the generic nature of persons, such that we are better able to perceive universal obligations and rights in a world characterized by social diversity" (Hallisey and Hansen 1996, 316). The fruit of pondering the karmic drama, then, is the cultivation of compassion for all beings by enhancing one's sense of a shared human predicament. The assurance that everybody gets one's just deserts in the end is a far less significant aspect of the idea of karma.[5]

Spring's vision of the cyclical human drama begins in spring, the season of planting and sowing that will yield later fruits. This is a time of excursions into the mountains to collect herbs, and, for the boy, to play. After one outing, the master teaches the boy to distinguish between nutritious and poisonous plants that appear almost identical—that is, to see properly. But soon thereafter, the child engages in all manner of play, some consisting of innocent idyll such as cavorting with a puppy, and some ultimately cruel, when he ties stones to a fish, frog, and snake. The boy is equally enthralled with his various pastimes because he cannot foresee their outcomes: in weighting down the small animals with unbearable burdens, the fish and snake die as a result. The boy ends the season in tears, already bearing out the master's warning that the stone he uses to harm others will become his own burden. Although the master teaches the law of action and consequence by tying a boulder to the boy's back as punishment, the long-term outcomes of his deeds do not manifest themselves until the seasons progress through their cycle.

When summer opens, the boy is now a young man. New characters are introduced in this season—specifically, a nubile young woman who is brought to the hermitage by her mother to nurse an illness. The appearance of this woman suggests the ripening sexual consciousness of the young man, for whom a female is now a new and powerful presence. After some frustrated misadventures, the young man wins the woman's sexual consent and a whole new world of powerful attachments is awakened. The elder master's response is muted but decisive: he observes that this is merely a matter of nature, but that lust and possessiveness soon lead to violent feelings. He sends the woman home since she has healed. The young man, however, decides to leave the hermitage and follow her into the world.

With the opening of fall, we see a visibly older master to whom the young novice of summer returns, now a bitter and enraged man of thirty years. He has just murdered the woman he pursued at the end of the prior season for betraying him with another man. The disillusioned man—now murderer—is angry and racked with hatred. He has returned to evade the police but also to seek resolution for his pain, which the master treats by imposing punitive austerities and beatings. The final penance the master levies on the man is to carve out the *Heart Sutra* on the wooden platform of the floating hermitage. The carving of each character, he says, will cut away the anger and kill the self, which is much harder to accomplish than taking the life of another. The master persuades the two detectives who arrive at the hermitage to wait until morning so that the man can finish his labor of expiation. When morning arrives, the detectives lead the man back into the world to serve his time. At the conclusion of the season, the master also finishes his time—having arrived at the end of his life—by immolating himself.[6]

With the arrival of frozen winter, the man who was led away at the end of the previous season now returns as a much older and mature person, ready to take the place of his master. He collects the relics from his master's cremation site and deposits them into a Buddha he carves from ice. His accomplished *gongfu* training signifies his maturing practice, but he has not yet completed his karmic cycle. This happens when a veiled and troubled young mother arrives to deposit her infant child at the hermitage. As she flees in the middle of the night, she falls into the water hole the man had carved into the frozen surface of the lake and drowns. Now the man has killed two women, mirroring the deaths of the two animals he burdened in the spring of his life. These deaths have now turned into the burdens he himself bears. Tying a millstone around his waist, he retrieves the Guanyin Bodhisattva image from the cupboard and makes an arduous and hindered climb to the top of the mountain.

The Bodhisattva's Vision

Guanyin is the bodhisattva of compassion who looks down and hears the lamentations of the world. Two of the three characters forming her name refer to sensory perceptions—those of seeing and hearing. At the beginning of the *Heart Sutra*, Guanyin meditates deeply on the Perfection of Wisdom and sees the inherent emptiness of all phenomena. The text goes on to state that the eyes, ears, nose, tongue, body, and mind—that is, all the sense faculties and their objects—do not ultimately exist. The "perfection of wisdom" (Sanskrit: *prajñāpāramitā*) refers to a class of Mahāyāna texts to which the *Heart Sutra* belongs. In this literature, correct perception of the inherent insubstantiality of all phenomena (emptiness) is of utmost importance, but this wisdom is also coupled with the compassion of the bodhisattva for all suffering beings and the promise that all will eventually attain liberation.

Spring alludes to classic Buddhist practices to underscore the theme of heightened perception. The use of the Guanyin image at the end of the film is an explicit reference to what a Buddha sees, and this theme is repeated throughout the film through another icon—the Buddha image that occupies the modest central alter within the hermitage. This location gives the Buddha a vantage point for observing the major events that unfold, because everyone who enters this space offers obeisance to him in seeking resolution for their pains. *Spring* makes effective use of camera techniques to enliven this Buddha: the "shot/reverse shot" sequence is used to link what is seen (as established by the first shot) to a viewer (as revealed by a 180-degree reverse shot), which is the Buddha himself. The shot/reverse shot technique is in direct contrast to an establishing shot, which reveals the subject of the scene from a disembodied god's-eye perspective that is tied to no one. The reverse shot, on the other hand, immediately identifies the one who is looking, and allies the perspective with a particular subjectivity. With this technique, the camera reenacts the Indian ritual practice of *darśan,* or seeing and being seen by the deity. The very opening sequence of the film begins with a frontal shot of the Buddha image, immediately followed by a reverse shot of the bowing master from the vantage point of the image. The master looks at and is seen by the Buddha, and in many sequences to follow, we see the Buddha *looking at* as well as being seen by those who come before him.

The shot/reverse shot is used repeatedly throughout *Spring* to reveal interaction between two characters with little or no use of dialogue. A particularly charming instance of this technique appears very early in the film, soon after the opening shot/reverse shot of the master and Buddha image just described. The master and young boy board the small rowboat that ferries them between the lake and the shore throughout the course of the film. In the first shot we see the master rowing, looking directly into the camera; the reverse shot reveals the boy looking straight back. The two shots in sequence indicate their mutual gaze, their half smiles and open faces signifying an affection that words cannot capture. Much of their relationship is indicated in this scene—to each other and to the film's viewers—in an effective and economic manner.

The shot/reverse shot sequence is most often used, however, to suggest that it is the Buddha who is watching the events unfold in this quiet microcosm. When the young woman arrives to convalesce at the temple in summer, she prays in front of the Buddha and the reverse shot of the statue proposes that the Buddha is looking at her—an impression that is reinforced a second later when the perspective switches to a view of the woman from directly behind the Buddha. When the murderous man of fall sits convulsing with torment before the Buddha, the reverse shot suggests that the Buddha sees his suffering. Later in winter when the veiled mother cries in front of the Buddha, the reverse shot of the statue again implies that the Buddha is watching. Everyone looks at the Buddha and the cries of each person are seen and heard by him in return.

The camera work renders the Buddha image into an active character of the film that interacts with humans as much as they interact with each other. The silence of this Buddha is rarely a hindrance, given the

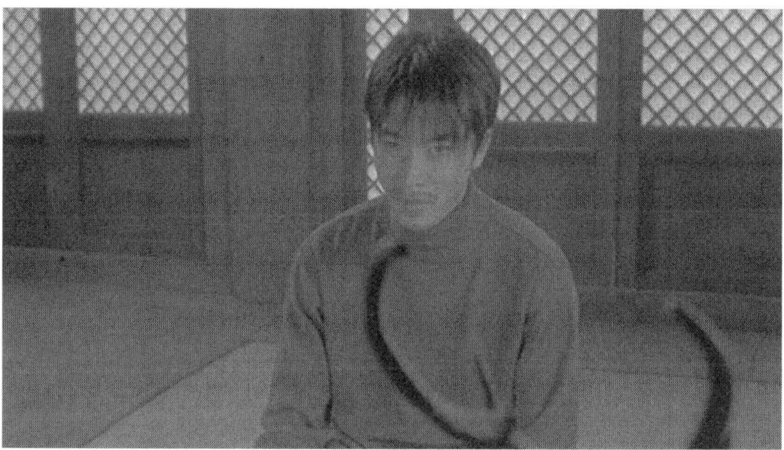

FIGURE 2.2. The man looks at the Buddha and seeks resolution for his pain.

minimal dialogue in which the humans themselves engage. In the world of *Spring*, it is the act of seeing and being seen that matters. This premise actively retrieves the traditional ritual practice of treating Buddha images as no different from the living Buddha himself. The countless legends of Buddha statues that weep and perform miracles testify to a widespread view of images as both efficacious and alive.[7] *Spring* treats the Buddha

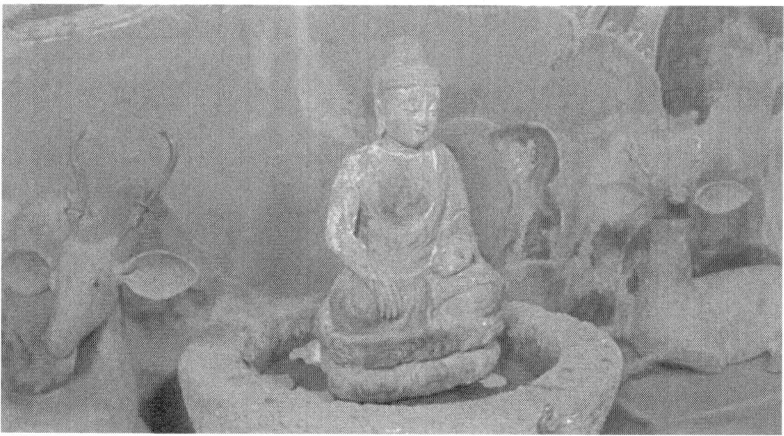

FIGURE 2.3. The Buddha is a live character who looks back at the people who come before him.

image in this traditional manner by skillfully employing the technology of film to maintain a classic religious premise. Melissa Conroy suggests that the way the film employs the shot/reverse shot technique teaches "the audience how to see themselves, and each other, in the way of the Buddha" (2007, 6). The final shot of the Bodhisattva Guanyin gazing upon the hermitage, lake, and surrounding vastness seems to reinforce the idea that seeing the Buddha as alive can help the viewer to see what the Buddha sees.

The audience is assisted in such seeing through the cues given by the human master, which is a second way in which *Spring* takes up the theme of heightened perception. The elder master witnesses the law of causality unfold through the life of his young charge, and in watching the actions of the latter, the film suggests a certain supernatural aspect to the master's powers of perception. When the young boy discovers that the animals he has teased are dead, for example, the master is also there—but in a rather mystifying manner, as the boy previously took the rowboat necessary to cross unto land. It is not clear how the master managed to traverse the water to follow the boy. Similarly, when the boy-turned-man returns in the fall after murdering his wife, the master inexplicably appears to see the man's tormented rampage in the mountains. The master exhibits other supernatural abilities, such as the power to call the rowboat across the water of its own accord and to momentarily halt its departure when the two detectives row the man away to his prison term. These actions suggest the workings of the master's own mind: when he briefly immobilizes the boat to delay the man's departure, the master's momentary regret and attachment are suggested.

This depiction of occult-like powers faithfully reflects the Buddhist idea that mental concentration produces various paranormal abilities. The *Samannaphala Sutta* ("the fruits of the homeless life") of the *Digha Nikāya* describes many such powers, such as the ability to create a "mind-made body" so that "being one, he becomes many" and to "walk on the water without breaking the surface as if on land." He also attains the divine ear with which "he hears sounds both divine and human, whether far or near" and gains knowledge of others' minds, discerning which one is filled with passion, or hatred, or delusion, or concentration (D I.77–80). The cultivation of mental concentration, in other words, enables superior perception, very much like the ones the Buddha attained during the three phases of his enlightenment. The multiplication of the body suggests the ability to be "present" even where one is physically absent, as when the master appears to witness the boy/man's sufferings. It is the master's depth of knowledge that allows him to see and hear what is happening, whether it is near or far, and to know the minds of others.

The particular nature of what the master discerns is worth examining. Although he appears to have supernatural powers, the master does not attempt to circumvent the various events—and their sorrowful consequences—that unfold. He does not stop the young boy from harming helpless animals, and he does not attempt to interrupt the utterly foreseeable sexual dalliance between the young novice and the young woman. The master's admonitory words are never to condemn the actions as such, but rather to foresee their outcomes. He does not try to disrupt the cycle of existence but rather accedes to its inevitability and its drama. It is as if he willingly consents to it and plays his own role within it, even though he already knows what will happen—like a story he has heard many times before. This too is indicated in the way the film title evokes repetition.

This idea of storytelling is explicitly suggested in *Spring* through the visual motif that opens the beginning of each new season: the gates to the hermitage magically open of their own accord, like the opening of a book that leads the viewer into each chapter of the story. The presence of these doors is patently symbolic—the gate is freestanding, with no walls on either side, making its existence and use purely figurative. These self-operating doors clearly invite the viewer to come inside and watch what happens, with the attention that is customarily rendered in reading a book or watching a play. But for the person who is familiar with the story, as is the master, the act of watching entails a balance between being involved and being detached. One is involved because life must be lived, but detachment is simultaneously possible through foreknowledge of life's inexorable patterns. This equilibrium between engagement and detachment can be described through the traditional Buddhist practice known as "guarding the doors of the senses," to which *Spring* overtly alludes.

The *Salayatanavagga* ("book of the six sense bases") of the *Samyutta Nikāya* describes the practice of guarding the sense doors in this manner:

> Here, having seen a form with the eye, a bhikkhu does not grasp its signs and features. Since, if he left the eye faculty unrestrained, evil unwholesome states of covetousness and displeasure might invade him, he practices the way of its restraint, he guards the eye faculty, he undertakes the restraint of the eye faculty. (S IV. 176)

The same instructions are repeated regarding the other sense faculties. Guarding the sense doors does not mean shutting off the senses and inducing insentience. Instead, the bhikkhu (monk) is instructed to actively look, listen, smell, taste, and touch, in order to engage in a deeper practice of sentience. This contemplation entails being aware that all sensory experience leads to positive or negative responses on one's own part, which in turn activates craving or aversion. According to the *Heart Sutra*, all sensory and mental objects are inherently empty and do not possess the quality of being intrinsically pleasant or unpleasant. The understanding of this truth begins with the practice of watching over one's response to sensory stimuli, as exhorted in the *Samyutta Nikāya*, in order to discern the causal mechanisms behind it. Therein lies the beginning of detachment from it as well. The signs of this discipline populate the imagery of *Spring*, particularly through the symbolism of doors.

The gate doors that open each chapter/season of the story invite the viewer to open their senses to what will unfold within. But the opening doors simultaneously evoke caution via the guardian figures painted on their surface. These traditional images of two fierce and warrior-like deities frequently guard the entrance of Buddhist temples in East Asia. The iconography is a derivation of the Indian bodhisattva Vajrapāṇi, who functions in many images as a protector of the Buddha. The gates open to allow entrance but they also demand discipline, which those who enter the hermitage observe by vigilantly going in and out through the doors. To ignore them is to become unmindful of one's experiences, which results in becoming disordered.

This conceit of the wall-less doors that signify mental discipline is repeated inside the hermitage, where the residents not only worship but sleep. The sleeping area is simply demarcated by a door, again with no anchoring walls. The master and boy dutifully use the door to pass from one area and function to the other in the course of their ordered life. The notable exception occurs when the young man of summer ignores the door and breaches the invisible wall in his eagerness to share the bedding of the young woman lying on the other side of the room. The correlation between disrespecting the door and the breach of discipline is overt. The transgressive act, which is outwardly manifested as sexual congress within the hermitage, is not a matter of despoiling a sacred space as much as it is the failure to maintain the clarity of one's inner mental space. The young man is too busy giving in to his desires to mind either the physical or mental doors of awareness.

The most severe version of this discipline comes again through the image of doors. When the young boy becomes the fugitive in fall, the penitential austerities imposed upon him by the master are carried out with the Chinese character for "shut" pasted over his eyes, ears, nose, and mouth. The ideograph for the word "shut" (閉) depicts two doors of a gate that are propped closed with a stick. The master admonishes the man to shut the doors of his senses as recompense for having lost control of them. This "discourse" is again pictured rather than uttered, through what the camera shows rather than what the actors say. This picture/word device is used one more time in the same season after the man is led away to prison, leaving the old master behind. When the master pauses the boat to exchange one last glance with the man, a premonition is suggested in this fleeting act of attachment: the master will never see his disciple again because he will die soon. As the master sits over the cremation pyre he has constructed for himself, he too dons the graph for "shut" over his sense faculties, but this time, it signifies the natural conclusion of life rather than a compensatory rite.

And yet, the symmetry of the man and the master is distinctly evoked and the theme of repetition sounded once more. Their parallel natures are made explicit in the final chapter of *Spring*, when the film returns to the opening season—spring—as if to pointedly assert that the same story will unfold again. This time, the master is the newly matured man we saw in winter, and he has his own young charge—the infant child left behind by the mother who drowns in the lake. As the second spring season opens, the new boy is the same age and played by the same child actor who occupied the role in the previous spring. The invocation of circularity seems to suggest an inescapable drama that renders all individuals into generic repetitions. This cannot help but raise a serious question and doubt about what the bodhisattva sees: the cycle of life seems inexorable and ultimately futile, as wisdom continually reverts back to ignorance. What, then, is the point of these repetitions? The ever-present nature of what the bodhisattva sees requires further investigation in order to see how progress is possible in this universe.

Repetition and Awakening

The Buddhist Wheel of Life diagrams the cycle of death and rebirth within the six realms of existence, which is driven by the twelvefold chain of dependent origination (which is another way of imagining karmic cause and effect). This wheel is firmly held in the grip of Yama, the Indian god of death appropriated in Buddhist cosmology to preside over the realms of hell and determine the destiny of the dead. The Buddha always stands outside of the wheel of samsara, frequently pointing to the moon that symbolizes the possibility of liberation. The moon is also pictured outside of the samsaric circle. This graphic rendition of basic Buddhist teachings demonstrates how readily and easily the liberation of nirvana is imagined in physical distinction and opposition to the seemingly endless repetitions of samsara. Quite simply, samsara is over *here* and nirvana is over *there*—that is to say, somewhere else. In Mahāyāna Buddhism, the length of time it takes to attain complete liberation was fixed at three incalculable aeons.[8]

The difficult and distant nature of liberation seems to be signaled in the theme of repetition that *Spring* persistently evokes. The circularity of the seasons not only undoes the progress of a strictly linear narrative, it seems to indicate something like reversion. This is strongly suggested by the progression of animals that accompany each season, which gradually climbs the evolutionary hierarchy and then abruptly reverts back to the beginning of the scale. In the first spring season, the animals that the young boy harms (fish, frog, snake) are cold-blooded, egg-laying species associated with the water, where the earliest and most primitive forms of life began in evolutionary history. The choice of these chordate varieties parallels the nascent state of wisdom that the young child exhibits. When the film moves into summer, the animal most prominently featured is a rooster that makes its first appearance in the hermitage space. From an evolutionary point of view, this clearly represents a progression of species: fowls are land animals that evolved at a later point in time. But its evolution in terms of Buddhist wisdom is still quite limited. The first shot of the rooster appears when the young woman is rowed to the hermitage platform, and it makes its second appearance immediately after the young man attempts to grope the sleeping and prostrate woman. The juxtapositioning of this scene, in which we see the awakening of the young man's lust, with the figure of the rooster pointedly refers to its symbolic meaning in the Buddhist Wheel of Life: the rooster represents lust and craving and is one of the three poisons that give rise to the cycle of existence and rebirth.[9] The rooster appears prominently in the foreground of various scenes in which the amorous couple cavorts and plays. When the master discovers their nude bodies sleeping in the rowboat after a night of lovemaking, he tosses the tethered rooster into the boat to pull it back to the temple. The animal is a clear emblem of the couple's activities. And quite noticeably, when the young man leaves the temple at the end of the season to follow the woman, he takes the rooster with him, literally carrying the burden of his attachment.

In the fall, yet another animal takes center stage—a white cat that is immediately introduced as the master returns from an excursion to the outside world for provisions. The cat's head pokes out of the top of the rucksack the master bears on his back. This image is a striking parallel to the scene in which the young man of summer leaves the hermitage—with the head of the altar Buddha also sticking out of the top of his sack. The master appears to be replacing the Buddha with the cat. Juxtaposing the cat with the Buddha suggests both an evolutionary and spiritual leap. The cat—or rather the cat's tail—also serves as the master's writing brush when he copies out the *Heart Sutra* on the hermitage platform for his penitential charge to carve. The master dips the cat's tail in ink to trace out the characters, rendering the animal into a direct instrument in the ritual process toward healing.

But at the end of the fall season, when the old master immolates himself, a water snake emerges from the blazing pyre (built on top of the rowboat in the lake) and climbs unto the hermitage platform. In the next season, the snake can be seen coiled on top of the old master's robes. The snake seems to be an incarnation of the master, who reappears rather unexpectedly in lower rather than advanced life form. The snake is also an embodiment of the poison of hatred and aversion in the Buddhist Wheel of Life, making the idea of spiritual reversion quite explicit. It is as if even the master's religious progress was only temporary and that he too must begin all over again from the bottom of the cycle. *Spring* does not seem to allow for the possibility of true progress from samsara to nirvana, trapping all of existence in a repetitive and futile cycle—like the endless labor of Sisyphus who was also burdened with a boulder that had to be hauled up a hill.

What the Bodhisattva sees, then, appears to be forbidding, and perhaps also accounts for why most Buddhists have considered the goal of nirvana to be beyond their present capacity. But it is important to remember that *Spring*, by virtue of its Korean provenance, operates within the Mahāyāna Buddhist universe of compassionate bodhisattvas and assertions of emptiness. A prominent feature of these Mahāyāna institutions is their skepticism regarding the samsara-nirvana polarity, with its linear conception of the Buddhist path in which one makes slow and steady progress toward a distant goal. There is an alternative version of Buddhist practice, then, that is built upon the foundations of Indian Mahāyāna literature that speak of such things as emptiness and Buddha-nature, and which further evolves in East Asian Zen postulations of innate Buddhahood. In this version of things, enlightenment is not a far-off destination but rather the prior and innate condition that makes Buddhist practice and progress possible at all.[10] When framed from this point of view, the apparent futility of the cyclical world of *Spring* can be read in an entirely different way.

If Buddhahood is already innate to sentient beings, as Zen teaches, then the passage of seasons represents neither progress nor reversion on the spiritual path. Rather, it is the stage on which both ignorance and defilement, on the one hand, coexist with the Buddha-nature of all beings, on the other. Carl Bielefeldt describes the Zen attitude in this manner: "Once we are assured of liberation, there is nothing to do but be liberated; once we have put the issue of awakening behind us, there is only the waking life before us" (1992, 499). The movement of the seasons, then, is an ever-present opportunity to surrender the distinction between liberated and not-liberated; between nirvana and samsara. The idea of "guarding the senses" that the film repeatedly invokes appears to distinguish between right and wrong, counseling dispassion over passion. But the old master never rebukes his young charges for their preoccupations; he merely foresees the resulting discriminations—between life and death, between possession and loss—that will bring pain. Guarding the senses means being aware of sensory discriminations and the inevitable pleasure and grief they bring. Neither can be avoided, only accepted. In Zen parlance, this is the state of "no-mind" in which one outgrows the preferential attitude that is normal to human beings and instead accepts both sides of the equation. This then provides the Zen adept with a "moment-to-moment means for taking the world as it comes to him, in all its ambiguity. For no-mind, then, the karmic law of birth and death in samsara holds no fear" (Bielefeldt 1992, 499).

When the murderous man in winter carves out the *Heart Sutra* on the temple platform, something like this nondiscrimination is attained, which allows him to conquer karma even while under its yoke. This scene depicts the rather undramatic turning point of the adept's life, in which his rage and anger give way to acceptance. There is no magical, mystical, or spectacular transformation: only the exhaustion of carving all through the night that wears the pain away. In the oft-invoked Zen image, mental defilements are like clouds that obscure the bright moon. Clouds are wispy and insubstantial, and the moon is always there. Thus, parting clouds are not monumental or rare events, and the gathering and obscuring clouds must also be countenanced. Both are really all of apiece. The carving man uses the knife with which he slew his wife—its history made clear by its conspicuous bloodstains. But in carving the *Heart Sutra*, the instrument of death is now the means of redemption. The knife is not inherently good or evil, and its nonduality also muddies the putative distinction between enlightened and not-enlightened.

A closer look at the cyclical structure of *Spring* reveals this Zen tendency to collapse the distance between nirvana and samsara. In the course of one full seasonal cycle from spring to spring, we see a young boy grow into a mature master, replacing and taking on the role of his prior caretaker for a new young child. In abbreviating a full life into one seasonal rotation, the film compresses the time scale that is traditionally posited for any discernable religious progress to take place. It is as if to live and mark time is to necessarily awaken, as a function of time itself. The pain of samsara is not the negation of some utopic nirvana but the inherently empty condition that is necessary to precipitate enlightenment. The rebirth of the old master as a snake then need not mean the near-impossibility of nirvana. Rather, it extinguishes the illusion of the distance between *here* and *there* to suggest that this apparent opposition always works together. As we plainly see late in the winter season, the development of the young novice into the mature adept does not exempt him from the residue of his prior karma—a second woman dies as a result of his presence, by falling into the hole of the icy lake. In his self-imposed penance, the monk elevates the Guanyin Bodhisattva to the top of the mountain so that she may look down upon the cries of the world. The power of her vision does not transform the condition of sentient beings, because that condition does not require transforming. Instead, her compassionate vision of what is already within all beings encourages others to see the same thing.

The Collapse of Time

In the third and fourth galleries of the temple Borobudur, the exquisitely detailed stone relief carvings noticeably shift from a linear narrative mode to one that collapses time into simultaneous visions of past, present, and future. This transition in vision reflects a development in Buddhist texts on the nature of the Buddha and his appearance in the world. According to narrative accounts such as Aśvaghoṣa's *Buddhacarita* ("life of the Buddha"), Śākyamuni undergoes a transformation from an ordinary being to the enlightened Buddha. This creates certain tensions for Buddhist soteriology. As Mark Woodward states:

> While [Buddhism] makes universal claims and presents itself as the only path leading to salvation, it is grounded in the religious experience of a single individual. This presents a number of problems, among which is that of establishing the truth of the [dharma] as prior to the person of the historical Buddha." (1997, 50)

The historical Buddha Śākyamuni is first an ordinary unenlightened being (although quite handsome and noble) and then becomes a Buddha at the age of thirty-five. What does this mean about the nature of enlightenment and its possibility before and apart from the path taught by Śākyamuni? If the Dharma is universal, how can it be tied solely to the life and teachings of one man? The problem is resolved by "describ[ing] the true nature of Buddhahood (insofar as it *can* be described) in partly metaphysical and completely atemporal terms" (Gifford 2011, 59). The path to this atemporality is paved with stories about past and future Buddhas, and Buddha-fields in which countless Buddhas and bodhisattvas can be seen simultaneously. The resolution is clear: the possibility of liberation cannot be localized to a particular time or place. Even more, the *moments* of liberation are likewise no longer tethered to a chronological and dualistic conception of "before" and "after" states.

Spring collapses the linearity of the karmic drama by abbreviating the vision of countless lives on the gradual path to nirvana to an ever-cycling story in which action and its outcomes are themselves liberating. In the most common view of karma, good actions lead to worldly rewards that are in turn inducements to follow the Buddhist path.[11] This immediate enticement paves a very long road to eventual liberation in which one is supposed to transcend the concern with such mundane benefits. A deeper view of karma, however, suggests that the inherently empty and malleable nature of the self means that "being" a person amounts to nothing more than the qualities of one's actions in the present. One's intrinsic emptiness is what makes progress and liberation possible in the first place, and, in some readings, comprises the Buddha-nature that is already a reality rather than a distant goal. In that case, the karmic lesson of action and its consequences is a continuous and ever-repeated awakening to who one is—of how it feels to be where one is presently and to activate the possibilities of what one might become. *Spring* depicts this endless process, which might be thought of as the action of liberation itself.

This version of karma collapses time and deflects concerns about both the near and distant future, with their fear of punishment or hope of reward. That is because all actions are their own forms of liberation or suffering that do not require a future time: the concept of karma "highlights a structure of personal accountability in which every act contains its own internal, natural rewards or consequences" (Wright 2007, 30). Conversely, the way each act shapes one's character and dispositions means that the past is always present because persons are essentially the accumulation of their actions. But this does not result in the ironclad determinism that some imagine karma to be. Dispositions and intentionality also function in the present so that "there is always room for improvisation with respect to where and how things are heading. . . . Karma is not just the experienced result of prior purposeful actions. Karma is also the inflection of things as-they-are-coming-to-be" (Hershock 2007, 183). Every time one utilizes this knowledge to attain the internal rewards of action, one accesses the Buddha-nature of both self and others to change their present world.

As *Spring* demonstrates, film compresses time and eliminates the great distance that appears to separate the present from the desired end of nirvana. The result is a meditation on the constant malleability and open-endedness of human experiences, and to suggest that it is ultimately the actors themselves who determine the nature and meaning of their actions. The compression of time is a capacity inherent to film, which gives this medium an advantage in exploring the interconnectedness between events and in juxtaposing the possibilities of experience. Therefore, it is not surprising to find other films that have borne out these themes. *Three Times* (2005) by the Taiwanese director Hou Hsiao-Hsien also utilizes the technique of using the same actors cross-temporally to suggest the repetition of cycles: it features two lead actors (Shu Qi and Chang Chen) who portray different couples in three different eras—the years 1911, 1966, and 2005, to be exact, all in different Taiwanese locations. *Three Times* invokes the traditional Chinese idea of the karmic bond between couples that requires multiple lives to play out, which is the framing premise of the eighteenth-century classic novel *Dream of the Red Chamber* by Cao Xueqin. Interestingly enough, each of the three stories in *Three Times* has its own title that features the word *dream* (*meng*), mimicking not only Cao Xueqin's novel but a plethora of classical Buddhist-themed literature.[12] The English subtitles do not reflect this use of the Chinese character for "dream" (夢) however. The 1966 episode is subtitled "A Time for Love" when it is actually "Dream of Love"; the subsequent 1911 episode is titled "A Time for Freedom" rather than the literal "Dream of Freedom"; and the final 2005 episode is titled "A Time for Youth" rather than "Dream of Youth."[13]

The choice to eliminate the dream reference is unfortunate because it erases the symbolic evocation of the Buddhist teaching that life is fleeting and illusory. But the cinema of *Three Times* maintains the theme by depicting three different and equally possible versions of the couple's relationship as modulated by the impact of context and time. The 1966 episode is the most hopeful, suggesting the burgeoning of possibility, whereas the 2005 story is bleak and the ubiquity of modern social media communications only broadcast messages of disconnectedness and despair. Hou's choice to move back and forth chronologically (from 1966, to 1911, to 2005) discourages the notion of a progressive narrative arc, suggesting instead a range of experiential possibilities. The immediate recognizability of the lead actors (despite their varying dress and hair-styles) juxtaposes their different relationships as side-by-side options that are equally conditioned by circumstance and therefore equally possible. There is no true version of their relationship, and in all three episodes the actions and images of transience abound as if to accentuate the instability of all events: characters always seem to be arriving and departing, and there are constant images of movement across bodies of water and bridges. Everything is in a state of flux, which means that happiness is always temporary, but no more or less significant than experiences of alienation. Hou's lingering visuals and limited dialogue seem most interested in how such varied moments emerge and feel, instantiating these possibilities for the viewer as well.

Cloud Atlas (2012), by the Wachowskis and Tom Tykwer, features an ensemble cast that reappears in six different stories that straddle the years 1849 to 2321 in locations all over the globe. Unlike *Three Times*, *Cloud Atlas* runs in chronological order and establishes a connective thread between adjacent stories, whether it is a character, a musical composition, or a political manifesto. In this sense, *Cloud Atlas* resonates with the idea of karma in more mainstream fashion (in the way that *Spring* does as well) by showcasing the links between events across time. The scale of the cast and historical settings creates a plot-driven focus that is more typical of Hollywood filmmaking, and its narrativity is enforced throughout its length of almost three hours. Though overlong by general movie standards, the number of stories folded into *Cloud Atlas* again displays how film can compress time and create a meditation on the interplay of the actions within it. At the same time, we also see a moral progression in the characters played by the same actor—such as Tom Hanks—which juxtaposes the vast range of possibilities that can be occupied by the same person. *Spring* exhibits both the cause-and-effect connections featured so robustly in *Cloud Atlas,* and the possibilities of experiences captured so delicately in *Three Times.* The next two films to be examined in this book focus on the latter theme by depicting how the multiple possibilities in experience means that humans ultimately exercise a choice in what they see.

CHAPTER 3

The Meditative Discernment of *Nang Nak*

Nonzee Nimibutr's *Nang Nak* (1999) is a ghost story based on a folk legend set in the nineteenth century about a young wife (Nak) who dies in childbirth while her husband (Mak) is away at war. Nak materializes as a ghost to resume her life with her husband after his return, and she terrorizes and murders the villagers who attempt to enlighten the unsuspecting Mak about the spectral nature of his wife and baby. The story of Nak is familiar to the Thai people, and has been the subject of radio broadcasts, live opera, comic books, graphic novels and some twenty-three films. Some of these versions cast Nak as a vengeful and bloodthirsty demon. Nonzee's telling, however, is a touching love story. To be sure, Buddhist warnings against domestic attachment are regularly sounded in the film—in the advice of monks and in Mak's ultimate entry into the monastic order. In this manner, the conventional view of women and domesticity as hindrances to Buddhist liberation is expressed. The villagers' view of Nak as a demon also reflects folk religion with its fear of restless female spirits, which arise from the tragic ends to which women were historically prone—particularly death during childbirth. At the same time, Nak and Mak's love for each other is poignantly portrayed, and the suffering it brings is sympathetically rendered. This compassionate vision of the human condition is manifested by the Buddhist abbot Somdet To at the end of the film, which succeeds in banishing the demon that is terrorizing the village. The abbot's meditative vision is yet another way of understanding karma, with its discernment of cause and effect. But it distinguishes better from worse ways of understanding it, and the consequences that each brings.

49

Nonzee's *Nang Nak* was a great artistic and commercial success, becoming the third highest grossing film of Thai cinema. It has been described as a Thai "heritage film," marked by high production values and promoted by a marketing campaign that conveyed it to international audiences (May Adadol 2007). This boost to Thai prestige has led scholars to see the film in terms of nationalist aspirations and anxieties. May Adadol Ingawanij, for example, sees it as a response to cultural anxieties about the loss of native identity due to the infiltration of global forces: "Because films such as *Nang Nak* reanimate the past as an expression of the nostalgic sentiment of Thai filmmakers, they then connect with Thai film viewers who harbour a yearning to relive bygone days" (2007, 187). The film indeed offers a ravishing and romantic vision of the agrarian past, centering around Nak and Mak's traditional home-on-stilts by the Prakanong canal in southern Thailand. Another observer notes, "These images serve the dual function of elegizing the past and broadcasting the film's national origins; they loudly and clearly tell us, 'Made in Thailand' " (Knee 2005, 144).

The film is also seen as reflecting gendered anxieties about modernization, as new social and economic arrangements erode traditional images of women even as it reignites deep-seated cultural fears of female sexual power. The classic literary motif of the lustful female ghost who possesses human males, it is asserted, dramatizes contemporary anxieties about women's autonomy and freedom of movement. Fear of female ghosts, "with their rapacious and uncontrollable appetites, translate these same characteristics of modern womanhood into frightening harbingers of death and destruction" (Mills 1995, 259). The difficulty of exorcising Nak "points to a fear of feminine recalcitrance and willfulness, of female agency as a threat to patriarchal systems of power" (Knee 145). But the complexity of Nak is that she is also a paragon of wifely duty and devotion. Her ghostly incarnation and transgressions are a function of her desire to serve her husband—a feminine quality for which she is still revered by Thai people at shrines in her honor (McDaniel 2011). Arnika Fuhrmann reads Nak, then, as "an icon of updated traditional femininity" and Nonzee's film as "a strong example of Buddhist-nationalist cultural recovery in the domain of sexuality" (2009, 222).

These insights into the national-cultural context of the film are firmly trained on the contemporary era and the ghostly Nak is read as the embodiment of distinctly modern anxieties. But stories about malevolent ghosts and spirits—and their intersection with Buddhist practice—go far back into the past. Although Buddhist teachings about suffering and its resolution do not require belief in the supernatural, Buddhist literature is full of the ghost, spirits, and demons that populate cultures across Asia. From the inception of Buddhism in India, there are tales of monks possessed or killed by menacing spirits as well as of monks who are able to exorcise them. Robert DeCaroli's consideration of early Buddhist literature shows the depth and complexity of the relationship between Buddhism and spirit cults (2004). Spirits and demons function as foils that demonstrate the protective powers of Buddhist discipline against spirit possession and the danger of unbridled desire and emotion, which the malevolent demons are made to embody. Buddhist tales often function to bring these minions of folk belief under the Buddhist yoke, resulting in coexistence rather than the eradication of native spirit cults. In Buddhist tales, demons and spirits sometimes call upon the Buddha or the *sangha* (the monastic community) for aid and protection, which they receive, and malevolent spirits converted to the Buddhist path even turn around to police undisciplined monks. While Buddhists evidently utilized widespread belief in the supernatural to advertise the curative and protective powers of their own rites, it is also clear that Buddhist monks and followers themselves took the existence of this nether world for granted.

Contemporary Thai Buddhism is a perfect example of this situation. The figure of Somdet To (d. 1872), the famed abbot of Wat Rakhang who figures largely in the tale of Nang Nak, is a well-known personality due to his reputation as a powerful magician and healer. He is indelibly linked to Mae Nak ("Miss Nak") as the monk who tamed her, and the two in turn occasion a popular religious cult of sorts. Justin McDaniel describes the centrality of these two figures in contemporary Thailand, and the kind of Buddhist religiosity they exemplify:

> As with many Irish and Mexican Catholics, and Chinese Taoists, among others, magic and ghosts are part of a Thai Buddhist's normal life. Many of the practices of religiosity associated with Somdet To and Mae Nak are so pervasive and popular that they can only be called mainstream expressions (neither aspects nor features) of central Thai Buddhism. (McDaniel 2011, 10)

Biographical accounts of Somdet To differ significantly but his popularity in Thailand draws in large part from his reputation as a magical healer—a power that he reputedly acquired by training with the Lao people along the northern Thai border. One way Somdet To's popularity is channeled is through the cult of protective amulets, for which there is an active market in Thailand. The amulets attributed to Somdet To are particularly valuable, given his reputation for protective powers. To is also known as a fierce nationalist who defended Thai autonomy during an era when most of its neighboring states fell to colonial rule. To's outspoken nationalism articulates the pride felt by contemporary Thai people in having avoided the yoke of colonialism. Fuhrmann (2009) therefore interprets To's appearance in *Nang Nak* as another sign of the film's nationalist and cultural agendas. Somdet To's reputed religious powers are also a significant reason for his presence, however, along with his close association with Mae Nak. In the following analysis of *Nang Nak*, my focus will be on Somdet To as a Buddhist religious figure and the way his persona exemplifies long-standing traditions of ritual technology and meditative practice within Thai Buddhist culture.

The Karma of Ghosts

The centrality of ghosts, demons, and other supernatural beings throughout the Asian Buddhist world is evident in the literary record. Early Buddhist scriptures teem with Indian spirits and deities, and as Buddhism traveled to other parts of Asia, the native spirits of those regions were incorporated as well. What Bryan Cuevas says of premodern Tibet holds true broadly across Asia: "There was widespread consensus that the world of human beings was overrun by a host of malicious spirits and roaming manifestations of the dead" (2007, 318). In East Asia, the didactic Chinese Buddhist tales known as *zhiguai* ("accounts of the strange") and their Japanese adaptations called *setsuwa* ("explanatory tales") are short narratives that purport to account for actual supernatural events.[1] Trips to hell, ghostly retribution, and human interactions with animals and spirits feature prominently in these stories and were popular ways of teaching the Buddhist doctrine of karma. Zhiguai and setsuwa tales became the subject of later performance traditions, such as the Japanese Nō drama and the late medieval storytelling performances that produced the literature called *otogizoshi* ("companion tales").[2] Tales of ghosts and spirits provided exciting and compelling subject matter for Buddhist sermons and medieval dramas. Not surprisingly, they also translate well into the modern medium of film. Kenji Mizoguchi's classic 1953 film *Ugetsu* ("Rain and Moonlight") has particular resonances with *Nang Nak* and is therefore worth a brief consideration.

Mizoguchi's film draws upon Ueda Akinari's (1734–1809) *Ugetsu Monogatari* ("Tales of Rain and Moonlight"), which consists of nine stories adapted from medieval Chinese and Japanese Buddhist sources. Mizoguchi's film features two female ghosts attached to a potter named Genjuro. The first is the ghost of Lady Wakasa, a beautiful noblewoman who died young before getting the chance to enjoy the pleasures of love and marriage. This ghost seduces and possesses the unsuspecting Genjuro when he travels far from home to sell his pottery.[3] The second ghost is that of Genjuro's abandoned wife Miyagi, who is murdered by soldiers while he is away. Miyagi reappears as a ghost to spend one last evening with her husband when he finally returns home, having learned of Lady Wakasa's true nature.[4] Nak is in many ways a composite of these two female ghosts in *Ugetsu*. Like Miyagi, Nak is a devoted wife who is cheated by war of a full life with her husband. Her devotion survives even death so that she reappears to him, in the land of the living. And like Lady Wakasa, Nak dies before she can fully experience the joys of marriage and domesticity, and her unfulfilled desires drive her ghostly manifestation. These female ghosts personify the Buddhist idea that it is the power of desire that drives existence within the cycle of samsara. Simultaneously, these spectral figures materialize the widespread fear of restless spirits throughout Asia, especially of those who die young, tragically, and unfulfilled. Lastly, in both films it is a Buddhist monk who is capable of seeing beyond the surface of things to their underlying nature.

No literary source for the story of Mae Nak has been identified to date, and the tale is likely the product of oral storytelling.[5] But its basic elements suggest a lineage that begins with Indian literature and develops into a native vernacular story driven by Buddhist sensibilities. One clear evidence of this pattern is provided by the Thai collection of stories called the *Nang Tantrai*, which are based on the third-century BCE Indian collection of animal fables known as the *Pancatantra*.[6] The *Pancatantra* derives from the same folklore tradition that produced the Buddhist jātakas and it also features didactic stories with talking animals. The Thai *Nang Tantrai* features a section of "ghost stories" (the *Piśācapakaranam*) about a spirit king who wants to marry a human princess. He is advised against it through a series of embedded tales that illustrate the disasters that result from such unnatural liaisons. The *Nang Tantrai* was thought to teach wisdom and bring merit, and was actively promoted by both Buddhist monks and kings.

But what, exactly, is the nature of the wisdom gained by tales of ghosts and demons and the way they menace the living? The tale of Mae Nak, especially as rendered by Nonzee's film, displays a contest of interpretations and ritual technologies that are typical in the history of Buddhist practice throughout Asia. The first interpretation underscores pervasive cultural fears of the dead, and the dangers thought to arise when the proper ritual and moral boundaries between the living and the dead are not observed. The competing Buddhist interpretation takes the form of a wisdom tale that illustrates the suffering that arises when one is unable to look more deeply into this fear and see an alternative reality therein. The Buddhist perspective accepts but at the same time redefines these cultural anxieties about supernatural menaces. And if belief in ghosts is largely gone from rationalized societies such as ours, the Buddhist translation of such specters makes them relevant still.

The Buddhist Taming

A good part of *Nang Nak* is occupied with Nak's ghostly wrath toward those who infringe upon her domestic happiness with her husband and baby. Fears of ghostly ire are particularly ignited by those who suffer untimely and violent deaths, such as Nak who dies during the agony of childbirth. In northeastern Thailand, mothers and newborns who die in this way are singled out as a class of spirits that remain strongly attached to the life-world (Hayashi 2003, 213). Nak has been deprived of motherhood and her full measure of domestic happiness. The same sort of deprivation attends Prig, the friend with whom Mak goes off to war: Prig dies painfully in the war and subsequently haunts Mak in his dreams. These restless spirits are aggrieved, and their power to cause illness and to trouble the living is enabled by the horror and pity of those who survive them.

Buddhist cosmology has its own category of ghosts that is adapted from general Indian mythology. In this tradition, the dead are known as *pretas* ("the departed") and are believed to haunt their descendants unless the appropriate rites (*śrāddha*) are performed that transform them into proper ancestors. If the living do not perform the rites, or if the preta is guilty of evil deeds during his or her human life, then these departed spirits are believed to be condemned to hell. Buddhist cosmology adopted the preta as one of six possible forms of rebirth. The preta realm is not actually a hell, which Buddhism counts as a separate domain, but it is certainly a very wretched realm of rebirth. The *Petavatthu*, contained in the *Khuddaka Nikāya* of the Pāli canon, contains fifty-one stories of people who acted reprehensibly and became pretas. In later Buddhism, pretas are generally known as "hungry ghosts" because their needle-thin necks condemn them to perpetual hunger and thirst. This suffering mirrors their transgressions during their human lives, when their enormous greed led them to stinginess and lack of charity. The fourteenth-century Thai Buddhist cosmological text known as *Trai Phum Phra Ruang* ("Three Worlds According to King Ruang") provides many graphic descriptions of these "suffering ghosts"—all of whom are racked with hunger as punishment for their uncontrollable appetites.[7] As we will see, this motif of monstrous desire is key to the way Buddhist sources understand the origins of ghosts and demons alike.

In the realm of ritual practice, however, Buddhist monks have fully accommodated the desire to appease the dead in Asian societies. In the Buddhist ritual economy, charity toward the sangha was extolled as a way of making merit that could be transferred to ancestors—particularly to hungry ghosts—to send them on to better destinations (Teiser 1988; Holt 2007). Buddhist ritual, then, taps into this anxiety about the dead that predates Buddhism but which presents an opportunity to extol its own efficacy. The calculus of karma and the ritual potency of monks combined to promote a system in which communal support of the sangha assured that restless and tortured spirits could be laid to rest. The degree to which Buddhist monks have been involved in mortuary rites across the Asian world is therefore not surprising, even though it has entailed accepting classes of spirits that are outside of original Buddhist soteriological concerns. In addition to the Indian and Sri Lankan preta, these native spirits also include the Thai *phi,* the Burmese *nat,* the Chinese *guei,* and the Japanese *kami.* According to both Buddhist reformers and early Western scholars, the widespread funerary services provided by Buddhist clerics are driven by finances and inconsistent with the fundamental Buddhist goal of nirvana. Contemporary scholars, however, are more sympathetic to this admixture of Buddhist and indigenous practices in Asia, seeing "the very tensions between them as itself constitutive of Buddhist approaches to death" (Cuevas and Stone 2007, 8).

Nang Nak exemplifies these tensions in a way that establishes a clear ritual and moral hierarchy regarding the treatment of the troublesome departed. This hierarchy might be articulated using the Buddhist strategy of distinguishing between provisional and ultimate teachings, in which conventional views are initially utilized but then dispensed and replaced by a deeper wisdom. The Buddhist embrace of local spirit cults can be seen as an example of this pedagogy in action, in which anxieties about the dead are engaged because of their powerful hold on the human imagination, but subsequently "rehabilitated" into a distinctly Buddhist vision of the universe. This vision is uncompromisingly orthodox in understanding the presence of ghosts and demons as the embodiments of our own karma. This redefines their genesis as the human fears, guilt, and regrets that empower them.

There are three moments in *Nang Nak* when villagers fall prey to the demon Nak. The first victim is the midwife Urb, who botches Nak's delivery and pilfers Nak's wedding ring after her death. The second is Um, the friend who attempts to persuade Mak that his wife and child are really unnatural apparitions. The third is the inflamed posse of young men who decide to purge the ghost by burning down her house. In these scenes, Nak is envisioned as an evil menace, although she is not actually depicted as such until the scene where the young village men torch her house. Here, Nak emerges to confront her antagonists in a spectral and menacing form, with her home in brilliant flames against the night sky. The young men upbraid Nak for her murderous deeds, but she retorts that it was the victims' own karma that brought about their deaths. Nak's inhuman appearance seems to undermine her protest of innocence, and yet she speaks a Buddhist truth that the film reiterates in the way it depicts each death.

The villagers are possessed by a reckless terror that seems to be the actual cause of their undoing. Hence, the violent storms that seem to indicate Nak's vengeful presence before somebody dies can just as easily indicate the internal turbulence that drive the fearful to their own demise. Urb is scared to death in her own home as violent winds tear open her doors. But is the vengeful ghost (whom we never actually see) a preternatural entity or an externalization of Urb's own guilty conscience? As a lashing storm whips up the village, Um and his wife argue furiously about the ghostly ire his actions may have provoked. Mad with anger and panic, Um defies the spirit of Nak to come and get him and runs out into the wilderness. Shortly thereafter, he is discovered dead, floating in the water. Was Um done in by a ghost or by his own recklessness? Nak appears to the posse determined to banish her by destroying her home, but their wild actions only create avalanches of burning beams that crush and immolate them instead. None of the villagers can heed the village abbot's admonition to "remain calm" and their turbulent states of mind determine their fates. The realms of rebirth within Buddhist cosmology "can be seen as distinctive types or categories of embodied sentience associated with specific qualities of consciousness" (Hershock 2007, 183).[8] This is a way of accounting for Nak's own identity as a ghost and the villagers' fate as victims. The interdependence of these two roles creates an ambiguity about the true nature of the supernatural and how it arises.

The figure of the village abbot who resides locally in Thonburi provides another opportunity to make this point. His strength of perception is emphasized in contrast to the husband Mak, who manifests the classic Buddhist diagnosis of one who lives in a dream by the power of his own desires. When Mak returns from war and believes that he has been reunited with his wife and baby, the camera depicts the world through his eyes: he not only sees his family but a clean and tidy home, frequently bathed by the camera in a romanticizing and glowing light. In contrast, when the village abbot visits, he sees that the seat he is given is covered with dust and dead leaves and that the entire house is desolate and disarranged. Mak's blindness to the truth is further displayed in the food he offers, which is petrified with dust, and the cradle he rocks, which is filled with nothing but cobwebs. The dialogue plays overtly on the contrast between the abbot's perception and Mak's blindness. Mak implores the abbot to "see for himself" the baby in the cradle and to "see with his own eyes" his wife who will soon be home, which only emphasizes his own inability to truly see. The abbot in turn tells Mak that he must concentrate if he wants to "see the truth." He advises Mak to bend over and look between his legs to truly see, and when he eventually does so, Mak finally sees Nak's preternatural form.

But the abbot's perception is itself limited, which accounts for the limited power of his rituals. The abbot believes in the conventional reality of ghosts, which he himself fears and seeks to flee. In this, the abbot exemplifies a lesser understanding in contrast to "accomplished monks [who] fare better against spirit-deities than those who easily give in to fear" (DeCaroli 2004, 134). The Buddha Śākyamuni is the exemplary model, particularly during his enlightenment when he overcomes the visions that Māra generates of both his tempting daughters and his menacing plagues. The one who attains full Buddha knowledge is swayed neither by desire nor fear. The village abbot, in contrast, is unnerved by Nak, and his attempts to council his flock are amusingly peppered with flabbergasted interjections such as "To hell with it!" The abbot is not fully capable of mental mastery and his own fear surrenders the greater power to the spectral Nak. This is evident in the merely deflective powers of his protective rituals. His chanting and the sacred string he uses to surround the huddled novices succeed in fending off Nak's apparition at the monastery where Mak has taken refuge. But the exorcism is only temporary.

If the villagers exhibit ordinary ignorance, and the village abbot only partial mental discipline, the greatest foil to Buddhist vision is provided by the Brahmin priest hired by the villagers in a last ditch attempt to exorcise the ghost. The figure of the Brahmin, who is clearly brought in from outside regions, evokes a social reality going back to ancient India when Buddhism and Brahmanism formed competing ritual systems. Brahmins specialized in the sciences of mathematics and astronomy, which reputedly gave them divinatory abilities. Their use of formulas and incantations based on Vedic mantras also gave Brahmins their reputation for wielding powerful rites of exorcism. Johannes Bronkhorst states, "Buddhists could not compete with Brahmins in this respect, and there are indications to show that they did not wish to" (2011, 108). In the early Buddhist Pāli canon, it is stated that the Buddha refrained from "base arts" such as predicting the future, interpreting signs, and casting spells. But as Brahmins became more politically and socially influential based on these reputed powers, Buddhists eventually offered their own protective rites, particularly with the rise of Tantrism in the seventh century.

This response to Brahmanism, along with performing rites for the dead, demonstrates the Buddhist responsiveness to local demands. The literary sources reveal that when most people approached the Buddhist sangha, it was "more often than naught . . . for two basic reasons: either they [were] seeking merit through donations or they needed help in dealing with a supernatural problem" (DeCaroli 2004, 38). The reputation of Buddhist monks for possessing protective and thaumaturgical powers greatly enhanced the reception of Buddhism in regions outside of India, particularly in the courts of Tibet and East Asia. But as *Nang Nak* demonstrates, this expediency does not necessarily mean capitulating to the moral and symbolic meanings of these external ritual systems. In Thailand and other parts of Southeast Asia where the Brahmin presence remained strong, Brahmanical and Buddhist ritual systems form directly competing ones.[9] *Nang Nak* portrays this reality by depicting the ineffectual nature of the Brahmin's ritual as a penultimate staging ground for the appearance of Somdet To and his ultimate resolution.

The Brahmin priest's technique is to exhume Nak's corpse and crush her skull with a rock. This violence goes beyond fear to ritual aggression and violation, and the consequences are immediate: as the priest pounds the skull with a rock, Nak possesses him and aims the blows at his own head, causing his death. This symmetry between transgression and consequence evokes the standard Buddhist notion of karmic retribution. As the priest violates the corpse, the demonic Nak materializes through the sound of preternatural and maniacal laughter that possesses the Brahmin and turns his blows against himself. His vision of Nak as an evil power is exactly what animates her in that manner—to his own doom. The failure of his exorcising ritual is due to the faulty nature of his own perception, similar to the village abbot and the villagers themselves. The Brahmin is distinguished only by the catastrophic degree of his ignorance. The film accentuates this point by sharply contrasting the priest's violence with the reactionary visions of the husband Mak: every strike the Brahmin makes against the corpse is countered by Mak, whose memory flashes back to the very human and vulnerable wife he has lost. The sequencing evokes pity and questions the Brahmin's proposal that Nak is a fearsome entity that must be destroyed. Mak's competing images hint at the necessity of a much deeper vision of Nak.

The Eye of Wisdom

In contrast to the hysteria of the villagers, Somdet To is the eminently calm and efficacious monk who arrives from Thonburi and succeeds in "banishing" the ghost. This is not the first time Somdet To appears in the film, however. He is introduced earlier as the monk who heals Mak's battle wounds, which allows the latter to return home to his village and begin the saga of his unnatural domestic life. The depiction of Somdet To in the first half of the film neatly bookends his appearance in the second half by displaying his healing powers, again in pointed contrast to a competing ritual technology. In crosscutting scenes, we see the Venerable To attend to Mak's battle wounds, while in a parallel space the midwife Urb administers much less successfully to Nak's birthing pains. Both Mak and Nak are in a fight for their lives, their mirror circumstances signifying the depth of their karmic connection. But Mak is in much better hands: in closely intercutting scenes, we see the monk attending to Mak's wounds, uttering his signature mantra (the *Jinapañjara*) and dressing Mak's body with herbs. Mak is soon fully healed. Urb, on the other hand, attempts to deliver Nak's baby by adhering to folk customs such as opening the window and avoiding bad omens. In the final parallel segment, Somdet To spits on Mak's wound, which aids the healing process; Urb spits on Nak to prepare for a cut but Nak bleeds out and dies instead.

The introduction of Somdet To immediately testifies to his curative powers, which includes the use of herbal remedies. This reflects the Buddhist practice of medicine as a legitimate science—in contrast to its condemnation of spells and incantations as an illegitimate one. It also distinguishes Buddhist practice from Brahmanism, which denigrated medicine as lowly and impure. When Somdet To appears at the end of the film to lay Nak to rest, however, he turns to yet another and perhaps more distinctively Buddhist remedy: he meditates. As Nak is already dead, it is too late for medicine or other physical treatments. The monk's cure consists of doing nothing to Nak except to *see* her. The ultimate Buddhist prescription is the curative power of perception, which, in transforming the perceiver also transforms and tames what is perceived.

The first thing Somdet To does upon approaching Nak's open grave is to call her to arise, reconstituting her in human form, cradling her baby. What comes next is a sequence of highly structured scenes, comprising four cycles of a tryptic. The first part of each cycle is always a black and white flashback to Nak and Mak in earlier and idyllic days;

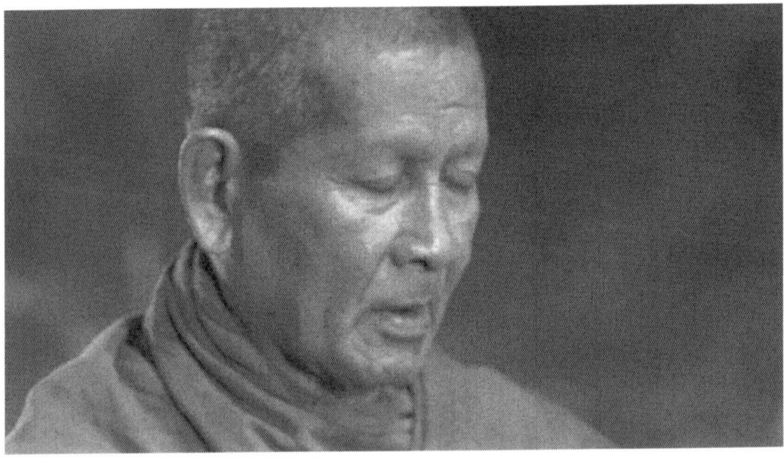

FIGURE 3.1. Somdet To sees Nang Nak through meditation on the cycle of life.

the second part cuts to an image from nature; and the third returns to the present where Somdet To sits chanting and meditating before Nak. These last anchor scenes, set in the present, suggest that the first and second vignettes are the monk's meditative insights. In the first flashback, he sees Nak and Mak in the idyll and pleasure of their courtship; in the second, he sees them cavorting in the river in front of their house; in the third vision, Mak bends his ear to the belly of his pregnant wife; and in the fourth, we see Nak again in her labor pains, just at the point of her expiration. The black and white sequence suggests a cycle of a hopeful but all-too-brief life. The cyclical theme is reinforced by a sequence of nature shots that immediately follow the black and white images of Nak and Mak: the first displays a close-up of a verdant leaf with a dewdrop gliding off its surface; the second is a wider shot of lush green grass, fresh with moisture; the third pans up the trunk of a magnificent and mature tree and visualizes its spreading boughs; the final scene tracks a withered leaf that falls before Somdet To, bringing us back to the present.

The flashbacks and nature scenes closely parallel each other in displaying the cycle of life and death, and their symmetry integrates human and natural existence. The dew on the young leaf evokes a classic Buddhist symbol of evanescence, completed by the brown and shriveled version that is the destiny of all life. The effect is powerfully moving and transforms Nak into a most ordinary yet tragic figure. In Somdet To's

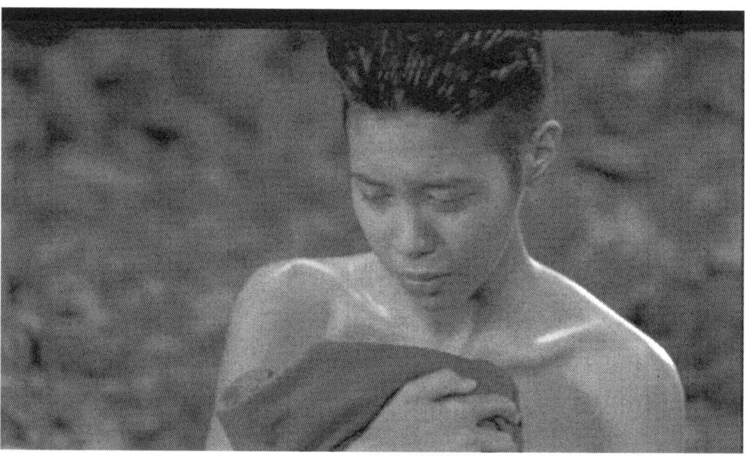

FIGURE 3.2. Nang Nak as seen through the humanizing vision of Somdet To.

perception, she is not a malevolent power. She simply suffers the pain attendant upon everything that lives—accentuated by her short existence and traumatic death. The demise of a young woman in childbirth evokes the universal fragility of life, which, when approached with lesser vision, is rendered into something fearful and even monstrous. It is Somdet To's penetrating insight that overcomes the specter of ghosts to see instead a natural condition that evokes a quiet sense of pity and acceptance. This vision brings peace to both the restless spirits of the dead and the fearful anticipations of the living.

The final scenes of Nonzee's *Nang Nak* are a remarkably virtuous visual translation of a long-standing Buddhist discourse on menacing spirits. The *Maitrībala Jātaka*, for example, is the story of the Buddha in his prior life as King Maitrībala, whose ability to protect his kingdom from demons is said to come from the strength of his moral qualities rather than his sword. One day, five yakṣa demons disguise themselves as humans and demand an offering of human flesh and blood, which is the only food that satisfies them. King Maitrībala sees through their disguise for what they are, and is instantly filled with compassion. He observes:

> By living off this type of food,
> These pitiless, evil-hearted demons incinerate
> Their welfare in this world and the next.
> When will their sufferings end? (Meiland 2009, 175)

The king recognizes that the yakṣas' abnormal appetites are a symptom of their uncontrollable desires, which imprisons them in the cycle of suffering. This reading of the yakṣas is significant: the conventional view of demons as inhuman monsters is translated into the Buddhist idiom of suffering and understood primarily as a mental rather than supernatural affliction. The Thai *Trai Phum* blends the Indian yakṣa with the native Thai spirit known as *phi su'a*, and classifies it as one kind of hungry ghost (Reynolds and Reynolds 1982, 96). This suggests that demons are essentially equivalent to humans whose insatiable appetites condemn them to penance as pretas.

Akinari's *Ugetsu Monogatari* displays strikingly similar themes. In the tale "The Blue Hood" (*Aozukin*), the abbot of a mountain temple falls in love with a young acolyte. The latter's untimely death drives the monk crazy with grief, so that he actually eats the corpse. This triggers a demonic rampage in which the abbot raids the village for fresh corpses to consume, terrorizing the villagers. When the situation is explained to the Zen Master Kaian, he notes, "There are countless examples, from the past down to the present, of those who, led astray by the karmic obstacles of lust and wrong thoughts . . . turn into demons or serpents to take retribution" (Ueda 2007, 193). Again, demonic identity is explained as a function of outsized desires—in this case, the transgressive attachment of the abbot to the acolyte. Master Kaian continues:

> It was probably his single-minded nature that caused him to turn into a demon when, once having entered the maze of lust, he was burned by the karmic flames of unenlighten-ment. *He who fails to control his mind becomes a demon*; he who governs his mind attains to Buddhahood. (ibid., 194; emphasis added)

The equating of monstrosity with the untamed mind is made explicit in the Zen Master's words. In Buddhist cosmology, all forms of birth within the cycle of life are the results of unwholesome mental states, normally condensed into the three "poisons" of greed, anger, and delusion. The *Trai Phum* states, "When any of these . . . kinds of evil mind occur to anyone he will, as a result, be born in an evil place, for example, one of the four realms of loss and woe" (Reynolds and Reynolds 1982, 64). The four realms of loss and woe refer to birth as hungry ghosts, hell beings, animals, and the bellicose demigods known as *asuras*. Although the realms of rebirth are often described as distinct and separate places, the ease with which humans and fiends intermingle in Buddhist narratives suggests that different forms of life are largely a matter of psychic reality.[10]

In these tales, such uncontrollable desires are neutralized by the powers of compassion and generosity. Master Kaian tames the hapless abbot by first offering him his own flesh to feast on. The abbot is awed and humbled by this selflessness and accepts instead the Master's blue hood and a koan, which the abbot is found reciting uninterruptedly even a year later. Master Kaian's manner of taming repeats the strategy of King Maitribala: unable to relinquish his compassion or charity, the king drains his own blood and slices his own flesh to satisfy the yakṣas. The yakṣas are so amazed by this that they become followers of the king. On its face, the purpose of this tale is to demonstrate Śākyamuni's perfection of virtues in his previous life. At another level, however, it also testifies to the way Buddhist tradition encompassed spirit cults by redefining the malevolence of ghosts and demons as the suffering brought about by unbridled desire. In this view, they are to be won over by compassion rather than defeated by force.

A key ingredient in taming and converting demons, then, is the ability to see their true nature by looking beyond their immediate appearances. As the Prince Sutasoma in another jātaka tale, the Buddha confronts the cannibal king Kalmaśapada. As with the yakṣas, the desire to eat human flesh signifies the demonic, which in turn connotes the untamed mind: "He has lost all self-control," Prince Sutasoma observes of the cannibal king (Meiland 2009, 337). This insight into the true nature of "demons" allows the Buddha to transcend the fear that possesses everyone else and respond with generosity: Prince Sutasoma willingly surrenders himself to the cannibal. The prince's insight—and the actions it allows—in turn liberates the demon. Kalmaśapada declares, "Now that I see my hideous conduct reflected in the mirror of virtue, I may feel a strong impulse to yearn for morality" (Meiland 2009, 369). The Buddha's depth of perception is the standard against which the shortcomings of others become clear. These shortcomings are not only exhibited by demons, but by the people who fear and become victimized by them. The Buddha's insight proves to be the superlative technology for taming fiends. In this way, the Buddhist tradition incorporates spirit cults by employing its own distinctive understanding of them.

In the final scenes of *Nang Nak*, we see Mak with the shaved pate and robes of a Buddhist monk, first presiding over Nak's cremation and then collecting alms as a religious adept. The voiceover narrates how Nak's spirit was tamed and transferred into an amulet that Somdet To created from a fragment of her skull. Here the film invokes a major reason for Somdet To's popularity today—the reputed powers of the amulets he manufactured. The film ends by alluding to the monk's magical efficacy, but this power clearly flows from the strength of his meditative perception. The overall framing of *Nang Nak*—a tale of lost love that ends with world renunciation—is a modern rendition of the Buddhist-inspired morality tale. Such tales are related to the Buddhist tradition of confession or revelation in which the events that precipitate such awakening are revealed (Childs 1987). Contrary to the Christian sense of confession, however, it is not specific acts of wrongdoing or the goal of redemption that are at play. Instead, it is *recognition* of the nature of human life and of its inevitably painful ties. Such revelation is a contemplative act rather than a condemnation of sins. Somdet To's religious potency is outwardly manifested in the power of his amulets and filmically depicted in his meditative vision of Nak.

Keeping It Real

Buddhism has coexisted with spirit cults for its entire history in Asia, and has engaged in rituals designed to appease, tame, and exorcise the dead. This ubiquitous practice is often referred to as "folk religion," which gives the false impression that it was limited to rural populations and disparaged by the upper echelons of the sophisticated and educated. But, as DeCaroli notes, "There are numerous literary accounts that represents individuals such as kings, brahmans, and even members of the samgha at times turning to these spirit-deities for help" (2004, 14). Aside from the problematic "folk" designation, the label "religion" is perhaps confusing because it creates the impression that talk of ghosts and spirits form a creed sanctioned by institutional authorities. This creates the apparent problem of two separate traditions—Buddhism and folk religion—being practiced together, thereby mixing and adulterating them.

This is not very helpful, however. Stories about ghosts and spirits do not form a confessional faith but are rather the language that enables people to express certain sensibilities and experiences. These expressions may be anxieties and regrets about the dead, or a keenness to the life that animates the world—including the domain of trees, mountains, rivers, and the like. The assumption that these sentiments are "beliefs" that conflict with the rational tenets of Buddhism entails a very limited view of how language and imagery function, and it limits what can be recognized as important and therefore "real" in human experience. But the long tradition of visionary experiences cultivated by Buddhist practitioners suggests an attempt to move in the opposite direction—to expand the human capacity to inhabit extraordinary states of mind and therefore realities. Both visionary and "commonsense" experiences arise in the same manner, due to causes and conditions that depend on the quality of mind. But Buddhist visionary practice understood that "the everyday perception of the subject is overpowered by the imaginative one" (Shulman 2012, 59). Stories of "supernatural" phenomena help illustrate this aspect of human experience in a vivid and arresting way.

To embrace fantasy is very fitting for Buddhists, given their habit of proclaiming that "reality" itself is an illusion. The baselessness of all phenomena is precisely because of the transience of all things, in which the difference between dream and fantasy, on the one hand, and waking life, on the other, is only a matter of degree. This is perhaps the reason why Buddhists are not so fastidious about distinguishing between the real and the unreal. Given this metaphysically level playing field, "the *imaginaire* of rebirth is employed as a support for seeing *all* beings as part of a 'moral economy' in which their individual and collective 'fortunes'—not only within, but across lives—correspond with patterns of sustained values-intentions-actions" (Hershock 2007, 182). The power of such values, intentions, and actions renders each individual into a magician and conjurer in relation to his or her own life.

If ghost stories do not have the same presence in the modern West as in traditional Asian cultures, there are other fantasy genres such as science fiction that can function in similar ways. The Russian filmmaker Andrei Tarkovsky's *The Stalker* (1979) is a story about the Zone, an area that has the mysterious property of being able to fulfill a person's deepest desires. A writer and a scientist are guided into the Zone by a "stalker" who knows how to approach the dangerous territory. In the course of their journey, they discover that the true treachery of the Zone is that it grants the hidden and unconscious desires of its visitors rather than their overt wishes. Because these deep-seated thoughts and desires are unknown to their possessors, they bring about their ruin. Tarkovsky's *Solaris* (1972) has the same theme. The film depicts the strange occurrences manifested by the sentient ocean of the planet Solaris, which causes the crew of the planetary base to go insane. Tarkovsky again uses a supernatural vehicle as a mirror of the psyches that confront it. The realm of fantasy can be used to demonstrate that all life forms are the reflections of our own fears and desires, and subject to the same law of consequences. This is another version of karmic cause and effect and the idea of the interconnectedness of all things. Stated in terms of traditional Buddhist cosmology, hellish and heavenly existences are heightened visions of human possibilities rendered in the most vivid and didactic of forms.

CHAPTER 4

Rashomon and the Indiscernible Emptiness of Being

Rashomon (1950) was made by the acclaimed Japanese director Akira Kurosawa (1910–1998), who is perhaps better known in the West for his epic warrior dramas such as *Seven Samurai* (1954) and *Ran* (1985). *Rashomon* has had its share of Western attention, however, garnering the Grand Prix at the Venice Film Festival (1951) and an honorary Oscar at the 1952 Academy Awards. Rashōmon is the name of the main city gate of Kyoto during the Heian period (794–1185), Japan's glorious and prolonged reign of peace and refined court culture before its long descent into the age of samurai rule. Built in the eighth century, Rashōmon stood at an imposing seventy-five feet wide and twenty-six feet tall, with multiple pillars and a roofing enclosure. By the twelfth century, which is the setting of the film, Rashōmon was in disrepair paralleling the disintegration of Heian imperial rule. At this point, the gate is nothing more than a repository for corpses and, reputedly, ghosts. Thus, it functions as a physical mirror of the social and moral chaos that is the underlying theme of the film. The ruined gate also evokes the immediate post–World War II era of the film itself, which was made a mere five years after the atomic holocausts that brought Japan to military defeat. In the opening scenes at Rashōmon, a Buddhist priest refers to the earthquakes, famine, fire, plague, war, and wind that have ravaged the country—a description that applies to the end of the modern Japanese imperial era as well as to the disintegration of the Heian dynasty.

This multilayered reference to social chaos appears to stage a story about human mendacity and weakness. The main event in question is

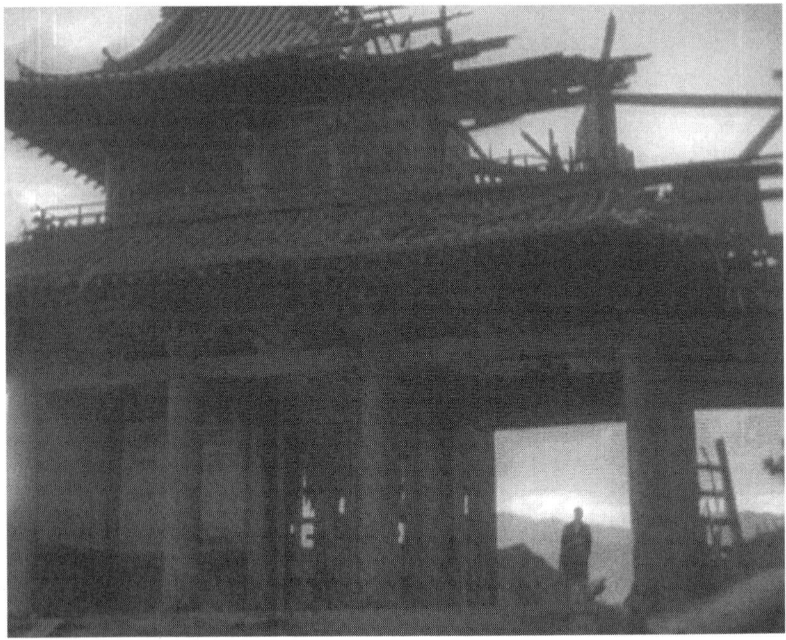

FIGURE 4.1. The Rashōmon gate reflects the social and moral disintegration of the twelfth century and the fall of the Heian dynasty.

the rape of a woman by a bandit and the subsequent death of her samurai husband. The rape is not as central as the circumstances of the husband's death afterward. We get the testimonies of the bandit, the wife, the dead husband (speaking through a spirit medium), and a bystander. The anchor of the film is how much these accounts contradict each other, particularly on two critical points: the character and actions of the wife in the wake of the rape, and the manner and weapon with which the husband was killed. The first three testimonies are given to court authorities, but the actors address the camera as if the film's audience is the judge. This effect is accentuated by the fact that the voice of the interrogator is never heard, and the characters face the camera to respond to the questions that arise in the mind of the viewer, as if they are hearing our thoughts. Maintaining this premise, the film does not conclude by solving the mystery, but rather leaves the question of what actually happened to the audience. Unlike the Western "whodunit" genre, the film does not offer clarity but rather invites second-order reflections on the nature and possibility of truth itself.

Buddhist Origins

Kurosawa based his film on two short stories by the writer Ryunosuke Akutagawa (1892–1927), entitled "In a Grove" (*Yabu no naka*) and "Rashōmon." "In a Grove" is written as a series of testimonies, with no framing narrative, regarding the murder of a samurai in a bamboo grove near Kyoto. The accounts provided by the bandit, the wife, and the samurai form the core of the depositions and they are faithfully reproduced in the film. Kurosawa's adaptation of "Rashōmon," on the other hand, departs more substantially from Akutagawa's story. The original tale focuses on an unemployed servant who takes refuge at the dilapidated gate and contemplates his bleak life prospects: he debates whether to starve or turn to thievery. Quite unexpectedly, he stumbles upon an old woman ripping out the hair from the corpse of her former mistress to make a wig and sell at market. When the old woman justifies her violation based on her need to survive and her mistress's own dishonesty while alive, the servant parlays this rationalization into a justification to rob the old woman in turn of her robes and flees into the night.

In Kurosawa's film, the characters at Rashōmon are changed into a Buddhist priest and woodcutter who narrate the conflicting testimonials about the rape they witnessed at the court. The segments at Rashōmon, then, create the frame narrative lacking in Akutagawa's "In a Grove": it is where the film begins and ends, and it is where each character's story—including the woodcutter's own eyewitness account—is told in a series of flashbacks. These tales are narrated to a commoner who takes refuge at Rashōmon from the pouring rain. In hearing these tales of perfidy, the commoner then justifies stealing the robes of an abandoned baby discovered at the end of the film, reprising the essential element of Akutagawa's "Rashōmon" story.

So far, there is nothing in Kurosawa's film or its source materials that suggest a Buddhist pedigree or intentionality. The Buddhist priest at Rashōmon is not the one who supplies the superlative vision, as in the previous two films. This priest is immobile with confusion and despair, and badgered by the loud opinions of the commoner. To see the Buddhist associations of *Rashomon* requires looking deeper into the film's literary sources. Akutagawa was a modern fiction writer who was interested in vivid articulations of the human condition rather than any religious didacticism. But his short stories are based on much earlier tales, the nature of which merits some attention. "In a Grove" and "Rashōmon" are based on medieval Buddhist *setsuwa* ("tales" or "legends") from the *Konjaku monogatarishū* ("tales of long ago"), which was compiled around 1100 by an unknown Buddhist monk.[1] With 1,039 extant tales in thirty-one books, the *Konjaku* is the largest collection of stories that recount the history of Buddhism, celebrate the miraculous powers of Buddhist images and texts, and preserve didactic tales about karmic cause and effect.

Setsuwa literature is a written record of the oral storytelling that was critical in the broad dissemination of Buddhism in Japan.[2] The ubiquity of these tales is suggested by the thirty major setsuwa collections from the Heian and Kamakura (1185–1333) eras.[3] Setsuwas are marked by their short length, their focus on miraculous or unusual events, and their claim to be historically true. This leads to their frequent characterization as "legends." This kind of storytelling predates Buddhism in Japan and frequently focuses on miraculous occurrences, such as human encounters with native deities and spirits. As Buddhism was introduced to Japan, Buddhist images, texts, and underworlds took the place of native spirits as the subject of miracle tales. In setsuwa, we can see the conversion of native gods to Buddhism and the gradual displacement of indigenous myths and values with Buddhist ones. In this, the setsuwa parallels Indian Buddhist jātaka literature and the way it enveloped native yakṣa and nāga spirits into the Buddhist fold.[4]

"In a Grove" and "Rashōmon" can be found in the "secular" section of the *Konjaku* (Books 21–31), which is given that label by the original compiler because there is no overt Buddhist content to the tales therein. The inclusion of such secular tales may seem puzzling and create the impression of disunity in the *Konjaku* collection. But in fact, the work is characterized by a very purposeful editorial intent to address the social and moral chaos of the times. This explains why Book 29, where the two tales are located, specializes in descriptions of thefts, rapes, and murders. In the words of one *Konjaku* scholar, the compiler-monk sought to "illuminate the nature of the world . . . and to provide specific strategies for coping with [that] world" (Kelsey 1982, 157). This entails, first, providing a systematic account of the history and teachings of Buddhism beginning in India, then moving to China, and finally to Japan. Then the secular tales are added, which serve "to provide practical guidance and teachings for daily life" (Kobayashi 1979, 17).[5] The secular tales probably originated and circulated outside of the Buddhist fold but were included for the purpose of illustrating Buddhist lessons. In medieval China and Japan, Buddhist monks routinely collected unusual stories to add interest as well as fodder to their sermons. Hence, "it is often the case that zealous Buddhist preachers have appropriated stories told originally in totally different context and given these stories a new, Buddhist interpretation in telling them" (Kelsey 1982, 19). Monks across East Asia were important agents in preserving oral literature and turning them to overt Buddhist purpose as well.[6]

Akutagawa was taken with the literary freshness of the *Konjaku* tales, which he developed even further. Along with "Rashōmon" and "In a Grove," his most well-known stories, such as "Nose" (*Hana*) and "Hellscreen" (*Jigokuhen*), are probing exposés of human psychology and perversion.[7] The setsuwa version of "In a Grove" is comparatively tame, consisting of a very brief account of a rape. There are no conflicting narratives offered up by its various dramatis personae, but only some intimations of its emotional aspects. The bandit confesses attachment to his female victim, leading him to spare the husband's life, and the woman in turn expresses impatience with her husband's fecklessness, which led to the rape in the first place. The compiler's only summary comment is that the husband was foolish for entering a grove with a man he barely knew. On the basis of this skeletal account—one of the shortest in the *Konjaku*—Akutagawa's version explores the full gamut of emotional possibilities the situation offers, making each testimony a fully embodied and subjective reality against which the factual details become lost.

It is easy to see Kurosawa's resulting film as a general observation about human deception rather than an overtly Buddhist tale. The commoner in the film voices the theme of human mendacity upon hearing of the testimonies from the priest and woodcutter. The commoner also deduces that the woodcutter stole a valuable dagger from the murder scene, casting doubt on even the latter's innocence and neutrality. Thus, the impossibility of honesty and the ambiguity of "truth" are suggested in contrast to the moral clarity of medieval Buddhist literature. But these themes fulfill the *Konjaku* compiler's desire to address existence as we know it, which is what the Buddha himself claimed to do. What Kurosawa's *Rashomon* cries out for, at this point, is an overt application of Buddhist language and concepts to what it depicts.

The Subjectivity of Perception

In keeping with the setsuwa genre, *Rashomon* is an account of strange occurrences made compelling by its claim to be true. For what can be more true and unsettling than the fact that our stories radically conflict, even when they are about the same event recounted by the principal participants themselves? This insight prompted Kurosawa to some unprecedented and startling filmmaking, by breaking the linear mode of storytelling and depicting the same incident multiple times. The film was greenlighted with considerable reluctance by Daiei studio, whose executives and production staff feared that the unconventional narrative would confuse audiences.

It could be suggested, however, that such radical filmmaking actually reprises a genre of Buddhist literature that David McMahan calls "symbolic fantasy." Mahāyāna Buddhist sutras, such as the *Gaṇḍavyūha* depicted on the third and fourth galleries of Borobudur, are notable for how frequently they depict meditative visions of vast Buddha assemblies and cosmic lands. Two aspects of this literary genre are relevant here. First, it is a translation of Buddhist teachings into visual form, which "imagines the experience of beings who have developed the human technologies of meditation and self-cultivation . . . to their fullest capacity" (McMahan 2002, 131). Second, these visions disintegrate time by depicting a totalistic "Buddha-verse" that is continuous with our own tainted samsaric world. As an enlightened vision, the temporal distance between samsara and nirvana is erased to give us an immediate experience of what the Buddha sees.

At Borobudur, the *Gaṇḍavyūha* panels abandon the prior linear mode and depict meditative visions through a series of "small, clearly realized parts that must be mentally assembled to arrive at the whole panorama" (Gifford 2011, 76). Nineteen panels are used to depict the vision of Maitreya's palace, for example, in which each panel pictures a different decorative embellishment of the exact same setting. One panel depicts the palace with bells, the next with banners, the next with lotus ponds, and so on. These are not different palaces but rather different details of the same scene, painstakingly constructed for our own careful and piece-by-piece visualization. The multiple depictions of *Rashomon* are not of a fantastical Buddha-verse seen through meditative vision, of course. Instead, it is of ordinary beings who seem weak and self-deluded. But with its multiple visions the film offers an equally important Buddhist observation into the nature of the self and the stories we construct. The multiple sequences, like the multiple panels that parse Maitreya's palace, allow us to mentally assemble this vision into a panorama that is not ordinarily available to us. Just as the visions of Buddha-verses are projected by those who have developed the technology of meditation, the technology of film is able to reverse the linearity of ordinary experience into a totalistic and penetrating insight.

In the Buddhist analysis of the self, our mental perceptions arise at the behest of our sensations, and sensations in turn are rooted in our bodies. Being spatially and temporally confined, the perceptions that arise from such bodies discriminate what is good or bad, desirable or undesirable, in an egocentric and embodied manner. Our combined physical and mental apparatus is not conditioned to take in the world *as such,* but rather to assess it relative to our individual wants and needs. The self-interested bidding of our bodies is not just biological in nature. Bodies are also located in social space, which differentiates the values and functions of different bodies. This social differentiation creates diverging and often conflicting demands that can result in radically opposing perceptions of reality.

The social setting of Heian Japan, as with many traditional societies, is particularly discriminating when it comes to the sex and class of bodies. Noblewomen are defined by their virtue, and warriors by their honor. Even bandits aspire to valor and principle, while commoners struggle to survive as supposedly lesser moral beings. Strong social norms add a thick layer of prejudicing perspective in addition to the fact that no two bodies, no matter how alike, can occupy the same place at the same time and perceive the exact same thing. Kurosawa's *Rashomon* depicts the emotions and meanings produced by these differentiated bodies as they interact with each other in the same space. We can briefly recount these diverging experiences in turn.

The first testimony is given by the bandit Tajumaro, who boasts of how the woman he coveted quickly succumbed to his embrace. He had his way with her even without killing the husband, he asserts, who had to helplessly witness the defilement of his wife. The bandit reports that in the wake of the rape, he was ready to take his leave when the wife intervened, demanding that one of them must die as two living men cannot have knowledge of her womanly "shame." This results in a duel between the bandit and the samurai, depicted quite heroically with dramatic music. "We crossed swords twenty-three times," Tajumaro boasts—the most any opponent has gotten of him—before he prevailed and killed the samurai. In the bandit's tale, the duel is honorable and his opponent's death commendably courageous. He confesses no weakening attachment to the woman but admits to the murder of her husband as a matter of stoic honesty and bravado.

In the woman's story, the bandit is far less significant and plays no role in the events that occur after the rape. She testifies that he simply ran off after forcing himself upon her: he literally disappears from the scene. The wife's focus is on the humiliation and pain of her husband, who is helplessly bound in ropes. She ran to her husband to release him, she reports, but was arrested in her tracks by his expression. This is the most consequential and central moment of her story. She sees a chillingly contemptuous stare for *her* on her husband's face that drains her of sentience and reason: his unspeaking coldness drives her to a madness that causes her to faint. When she wakes up, she sees her dagger buried in the body of her now dead husband. In this manner, she confesses to having taken his life. But the woman's tale emphasizes her own vulnerability as a violated woman, and the ensuing ambiguity of her social and personal status. To be turned upon by the person on whom she most depends—her husband—is the greater transgression, tantamount to execution by his lack of mercy.

In the dead man's tale, the victim and victimizer are reversed, demonstrating the quixotic nature of perception, particularly where power is involved. In his eyes, there is a suggestion of conspiracy between his wife and her violator. According to the dead man, the bandit begs the wife to run away with him, and after some inconsolable tears, she suddenly agrees. She looked as if in a trance, the dead man reports, and was more beautiful than he had ever seen her. But his pain does not end there. In his version of events, his abjectness is brought to inhuman proportion through the direct agency of his wife: in mid-flight, she halts, turns back to point at her husband and demand that the bandit kill him before they depart. They were the most hateful and damnable words ever uttered by humankind, the dead man declares, turning even the bandit against her in disgust. She runs off, with the bandit giving chase, leaving the husband to his abandonment. Realizing that the sound of crying he hears is his own, he takes his wife's dagger and stabs himself. After some time in the darkness and silence of death, he feels someone pull the dagger from his body and depart.

The film version of the woodcutter's story is much more elaborate than in Akutagawa's tale, where he simply testifies that he found the body—without a dagger or weapon of any kind on the scene. In Kurosawa's film, the woodcutter stumbles upon the immediate aftermath of the rape, thereby presenting a forth version of events in the guise of the outsider's disinterested perspective. The woodcutter affirms the dead man's claim that the bandit courted the wife, but in his version, her response is markedly different. "How could I, a woman, say anything?" she demands, and cuts her husband's ropes. The bandit takes this as a request for a duel, but the husband refuses to fight, saying the wife ought to kill herself in her shame. The bandit then wavers in his own desire for her, and for a long moment the woman is poignantly and desperately caught between the rejection of both men. At this point, the wife exhibits a ferocious transformation: in a fit of hysterical laughter, she maniacally taunts both men for their weakness, saying the bandit should fight to win her and the husband should fight to keep her. She badgers and shames them into a duel, but this time it is shot as a prolonged, clumsy, and cowardly effort. There is no music, and the whole sequence unfolds in silence except for the sounds of the two men's desperate scrambling and labored breathing. When the bandit finally pierces the samurai, it is in terror of his own act as the samurai piteously begs for his life. When the bandit turns to the woman to claim her, she runs off.

Among all of the discrepancies between the testimonies, the most overtly empirical question concerns the agent and weapon of the samurai's death. Interestingly, the bandit, wife, and husband all implicate *themselves* rather than one another, suggesting that there are matters far more significant than being guilty of murder or suicide. For all three, the primary issue is how they experience and constitute themselves—to be exact, as the valiant fighter, the rejected wife, and the betrayed husband, respectively. All three self-imaginings may be deluded, but they are also socially and emotionally mandated given the identity of their respective bodies. The bandit's career trades on his reputation for fierceness and his own brand of honor. He will willingly hang for murder as long as he can preserve this identity for himself as well as for others. For the wife, the soiling of her sexual virtue is of the greatest import, and to suffer her husband's coldness upon her violation is her worst fear and consequence. It signals the end of her life, compared to which killing her own husband—and admitting to it—adds little of consequence. In the husband's experience, his initial failure to protect his wife is fully and egregiously exacerbated by his fear that she may prefer the coarse but stronger villain, completing his debasement as a man. His suicide merely finalizes his social death.

The jeweled dagger that is the agent of the wife's murder, the husband's suicide, and the woodcutter's theft embodies an important Buddhist image. It evokes the Buddhist notion of the "second dart," or the psychological and conceptual dagger that adds the greater damage to the natural piercings of sensory experience. The metaphor of the dart is ubiquitous in Pāli Buddhist sources, where it usually refers to the additional pain that humans inflict upon themselves through mental operations.[8] In the *Salla Sutta* ("the dart sutta") of the *Sutta Nipāta*, death is a natural sorrow but it is increased by our attachment to death in the form of unreasoning grief. This is the second dart. But, "The man who has taken out the dart, who has no clinging, who has obtained peace of mind, passed beyond all grief, this man, free from grief, is still" (SN 593).

The variability of the characters' stories and the fragility of truth is perhaps most apparent in the portrayals of the young wife. Is she a cold and manipulative conniver, or the powerless and weaker sex? Even in contemporary liberated society, female sexuality provokes the most irreconcilable of subjectivities. Women may be physically and socially weaker, but powerful men—professors, mentors, even presidents—seem to grow witless in their midst. These men might consider themselves bewitched, as if by a cunning spirit, but at the same time they can be accused of abusing their stronger position. The young wife and her husband narrate one such version of the "he said, she said" testimonial, which our own judicial system is helpless to parse. But Kurosawa's inclusion of the woodcutter's account, as the comparatively objective view, suggests a deeper paradoxical insight that perhaps both opposing accounts are equally true. In the woodcutter's perception, the woman's ferocity roars into being at the moment and behest of her greatest vulnerability, when both men are ready to dispose of her. Her weakness begets a strength that is both pitiable and formidable, both victimized and victimizing. The woodcutter's more complex view cannot settle upon a single essence or definition of her personhood. As with the wife in *Nang Nak*, we see that women across cultures are the site of male projections and fears. The social location of women and their female bodies admittedly constrains their possibilities, but even that constraint cannot be exhausted by a single version of their nature.

To be sure, the woodcutter himself does not embody perfect objectivity. His own interested storytelling is divulged in his fib concerning the dagger. In addition, his perception of the inglorious duel between the bandit and the samurai taunts the supposed valor of these men who are supposed to be his physical and social superiors. But his humane and sympathetic view of the wife conveys a sense of subjectivity as something more than self-delusion or outright deceit. Instead, it suggests that the relativity of all perspectives compels us to recognize the humanity of each. But this leads us to a further possibility—that is, the possibility of giving up the distinction between truth and falsity to recognize that we always live in a space between them. What this ultimately recommends is detachment from all views, even as we entertain them. According to Buddhist teachings, as well as the outcome of *Rashomon*, it is only then that moral action becomes possible.

The Perception of No-Perception

The opening scene of the story in the forest begins with a direct shot of the sun filtered through leaves and branches. The shot is dynamic from the beginning, as the moving camera tracks the steady sun against a foreground of flowing branches and trees. The shot then cuts to the axe slung on the back of the woodcutter, who is steadfastly moving deeper and deeper into the forest. This long and continuous sequence cuts back and forth between the quick pace of the woodcutter and the passage of thick forest vistas that measure and mark his movement. The combina-

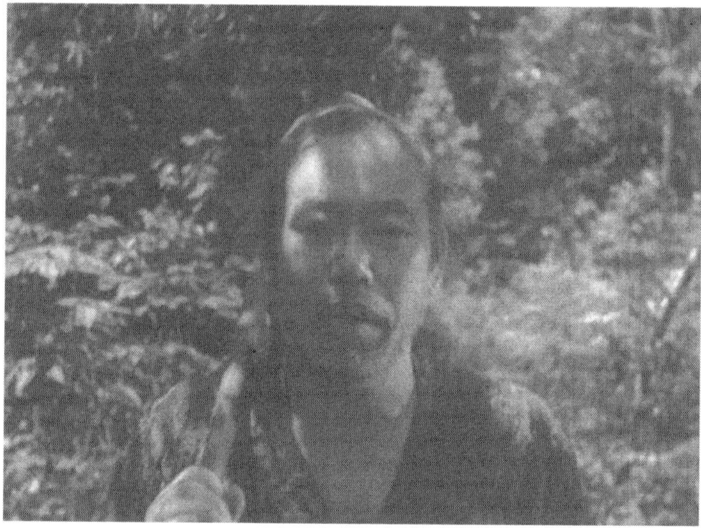

FIGURE 4.2. The woodcutter descends into the woods where light and shadow are inextricably entangled.

tion of sun, forest, and movement creates a remarkable dance of light and shadow that portends the flickering play of human subjectivities to come. The scene halts its pace as the woodcutter comes upon various signs of the crime that took place in the forest, including, finally, the body of the samurai. But the moral of the story has already been told through the visual medium, in which the dappled light intertwines and tangles with the darkness and suggests the impossibility of any clear differentiation between what is true and what is false.

This descent into wilderness reprises the title of the original story, "In a Grove," and both, in turn, evoke the Buddhist metaphor of the "thicket" or "wilderness" of views.[9] These images, among others, are used to characterize the Buddhist notion of "wrong view," which does not refer so much to false doctrines but rather to the *attachment* that human views can foster, and its subsequent ill-effects. A proper understanding of this depends on the proper appropriation of Buddhist doctrine itself. The first component of the eightfold noble path of Buddhism is "right view," which generally refers to the Buddhist teaching that suffering exists, that all is impermanent, and that all things lack inherent existence or substance. Thus, Buddhism has its central tenets and posits an unambiguous set of proper beliefs. But the rightness and wrongness of "views" (*dṛṣṭi*) are defined by their effects above all else: "A view can be doctrinally correct but if, through giving rise to attachment, it distorts the holder's response to the world, it is a wrong-view" (Fuller 2005, 79). The rightness of Buddhist views, then, has less to do with their correctness than the actions encouraged by them.

The *Aṭṭhakavagga* ("chapter of the eights") of the *Sutta Nipāta*, one of the earliest sources in the Theravāda Pāli canon, gives us a clear sense of the actions fostered by right views:

> The noble one who wanders in the world, liberated from views, does not grasp them and enter into arguments. . . . That wise one does not become conceited through views or knowledge, for he is not attached to that sort. . . . There are no ties to him who is free from ideas, there are no delusions to him who is delivered by wisdom. Those who grasp ideas and views, wander about coming into conflict in the world. (SN 845–47)

The significant idea here is that the noble one is liberated from *all views* and therefore does not enter into philosophical disputations. This seems to be at odds with the fact that Buddhism itself preaches essential tenets: without knowledge of suffering, karma, dependent arising, and the insubstantiality of all things, Buddhist enlightenment is not possible. And yet, the *Sutta Nipāta* extols the need to rise above all views. Moreover, this exhortation is made *in tandem* with such propositions about the truth of cause and effect, and the insubstantiality of the self.

In order to make sense of this situation, it is necessary to question the idea that the principle tenets of Buddhism are actually doctrines or statements of metaphysical truth. Instead, they may be understood as observations that induce a particular kind of practice—to wit, the practice of overcoming greed, hatred, and delusion, or the "three poisons" that give rise to suffering. The common denominator of these observations is the empirical insight that nothing in human experience is enduring. Therefore, clinging to any of these transient phenomena only ends in grief. The idea of "no self," as a result, is not a metaphysical assertion that the self or soul does not exist, but rather an exhortation to detach from and be free of the idea of the self as a fixed and singular entity. The "doctrine" of karma can certainly be interpreted as a metaphysical assertion about the truth of rebirth, but it is also the practice-driven observation that a mind submerged in greed, hatred, and delusion perpetuates this experience into the future, thereby prolonging suffering.[10] What Buddhist teachings prompt is the practice of *detachment* from unwholesome mental states. The exhortation to give up all doctrines, then, is not in opposition to Buddhist teachings but rather harmonious with them. The Buddhist concept of right view does not mean believing in the right propositions as opposed to the wrong ones, but rather the freedom from slavish or self-serving attachment to dogmas.

The *Aṭṭhakavagga* chapter of the *Sutta Nipāta* is particularly focused on the dangers of dogmatism. It begins with discourses warning against attachment to sensory delights, which are initially defined as worldly possessions and sexual pleasures. But doctrines and views are also included in what a person "sees and hears" (SN 778), and therefore count as a sensory delight. This may be counterintuitive to our own cultural logic, which separates the mind and body as qualitatively different phenomena. In Buddhist logic, however, the mind is the sixth sensory organ that apprehends its own brand of sensory objects. Akin to visual objects such as beautiful women, and gustatory delights such as tasty food, mental objects such as ideologies and doctrines can engender attachment and self-indulgence. The *Aṭṭhakavagga* observes, "The debaters, having entered into the gathering, start disputes calling each other fools"; they seek praise, which is often frustrated, and, "In defeat he becomes downcast and, seeking for flaws in others, becomes enraged by their criticism." Those who successfully defend their views "thrill with joy" but "elation itself is the ground of his downfall; for still he talks with pride and arrogance" (SN 825–30). Clinging to views, as much as grasping for wealth and other worldly delights, is a "dart of passion" (SN 779). The standard Buddhist image of the dart that wounds evokes the dagger in the rival stories of *Rashomon*, which always functions as the object or agent of each person's attachment. In contrast, the wise and noble person "has ceased to associate with dogmas for he no longer requires the solace that dogmas offer" (SN 801).

A "right view," then, can be defined as a form of action, particularly moral action that comes after giving up the thoughts and rationalizations that inhibit compassionate responses to others. This is clearly depicted in the outer frame tale at Rashōmon, where the woodcutter, priest, and commoner debate the significance of what has happened. The interlocuters at Rashōmon, like the characters in the grove, are also engaged in telling stories. But unlike the stories concerning what happened in the thicket, the interlocutors at Rashōmon tell tales that signal their own actions to come. The woodcutter and the priest form the initial voices in this debate. The woodcutter repeatedly expresses his despair over humanity, while the priest insists that one must maintain faith in the goodness of human beings. He proclaims that he simply cannot live in the hell that would otherwise result. From the opening scene up until the penultimate end, these two dejected and inert figures frame the film with their paralysis—a paralysis that results from their very need to ascertain some grand "truth" about humanity. This irresolvable and futile pursuit renders them hapless and weak.

The commoner, in contrast, confidently proclaims the evil nature of human beings. He declares that "[i]t's human to lie" and that "[g]oodness is only pretend." The cynic essentially holds court in these sequences, badgering the woodcutter and priest with his energetic views. For the casual observer, he might also be taken as the authoritative voice of the film that articulates its lessons and conclusions. What he does during these disquisitions is telling, however. As the cynic speaks, he strips wood from the gate structure to build a warming fire, conspicuously dismantling the civic and moral order that the gate symbolizes. This depiction provides an insight and a caution: the commoner's actions mirror his words, for his assertions about the naturalness of human evil also foster and enact his own immoral actions at the end of the film.

The final act of the film centers on an abandoned baby discovered in a remote corner of Rashōmon. In attempting to fathom how the baby came to be there, the infant functions as a Rorschach that throws into relief the subjectivities of the individuals who encounter it. The cynic, remaining true to his worldview, concludes that its parents simply abandoned their responsibilities after their sexual sport. The woodcutter, on the other hand, divines anguish in this desperate act: "See how they left an amulet to protect the baby!" he counters. These speculations reveal the affective reality of the speakers rather than the reality they presume to describe. Most importantly, interpretation leads to corresponding actions. The cynic uses his story to justify stealing the baby's cloak as his parting act. When the woodcutter calls him evil, he counters that it is the parents who are evil for abandoning the infant. The cynic's action makes the intent of his storytelling clear: the declaration that humans are naturally evil justifies his own selfish actions as morally neutral. He is only living within the rules that others have established, he rationalizes, so his behavior is justified given the precedent of others. He tells the story of human evil in order to mask his own moral agency—an agency that is clearly demonstrated and exercised by his choice of what story to tell.

With this denouement, Kurosawa faithfully captures the essence of Akutagawa's original "Rashōmon," which depicts the way cognition and thought are inexorably linked to actions. Before the impoverished servant discovers the old woman ripping hair from corpses abandoned at Rashōmon, he engages himself in a debate about his own options in the world—whether to starve to death or turn to theft. When he encounters the old woman in her gruesome act, he is initially repulsed and furious to the point of violence. But when she justifies herself by pointing to the evil of others, the servant reaches a turning point: "A new kind of courage began to germinate in his heart," we are told. The servant then exclaims to the old woman, "You won't blame me, then, for taking your clothes. That's what *I* have to do to keep from starving to death" (Akutagawa 2006, 9). Akutagawa's tale revolves around this astute psychological portrayal of how thought enables corresponding behavior.

It is at this point that the woodcutter is able to overcome his own paralysis and take action. Most significantly, his agency is awakened only after his claim to moral righteousness is resoundingly silenced: when he upbraids the commoner for taking the baby's cloak, the latter trumps him by deducing that the woodcutter himself stole the dagger in the grove. The cynic gleefully reveals the woodcutter's own guilt and arrests any further criticism. He taunts the woodcutter with the words, "Do you have anything more to say?" which is met with dejected silence. But this turn is significant in an unexpected way. By having his subjectivity fully disclosed, the woodcutter is freed from the cynic's own conceit of seeing the truth and the self-deception this allows. The woodcutter's awareness of his own limitations paradoxically allows him to act in a morally transformative manner. He decides to take the baby home, observing that one more mouth to feed in his large family is of no matter. This turn comes about after he gives up the quest for understanding: He observes, "I don't understand my own heart." This admission of ignorance is a liberating confession that frees him from both self-deception and debilitating words.

The scene at the end of the film is particularly striking in depicting this transformation and forms an explicit bookend to the long sequence of the woodcutter descending into the woods at the beginning. In this early segment, the woodcutter strides at a rapid pace into the woods and forms a part of the tableau of light and shadow that parallels the lack of narrative clarity in the film. At the end, after the cynic has exposed the woodcutter's secret and fled with the baby's cloak, the woodcutter and priest are shown standing in both physical and intellectual paralysis against the wall of Rashōmon. Their absolute stillness is in stark contrast to the woodcutter's rapid movement at the beginning, and accentuated by a series of cuts that hone in on the silent and unmoving figures. The actions have moved from energetic debates to a stillness of both body and mind. This hiatus is suddenly broken by a sharp cry from the baby, which galvanizes the priest to pace back and forth in an attempt to soothe the infant. At this point, the woodcutter moves to take the baby from the priest. The priest initially mistakes the woodcutter as intending further harm to the child but is disabused of his confusion by the woodcutter's words. The cry of the baby, like the physical blows that Zen masters are renowned for dispensing on their followers, functions as the non-semantic wake-up call—or "sudden enlightenment" in Zen parlance—that signals movement from paralyzing thought to awakened action.

At this point, the moral resolution of the film is reached. The priest declares that his faith in humankind has been restored. The fact that the common woodcutter rather than the Buddhist cleric enacts the resolution is also very Zen in flavor, with its view that institutional religion tends to ossify into dogmatic formulations that are inattentive to the present. The priest has not been able to draw on his career to gain any true understanding and presents as a particularly helpless figure. It is the simplicity of the woodcutter, perhaps, that enables him to move more quickly to right action. This transition is signaled by the sudden halt in the incessant rain right before the baby's cry. The breaking sun and woodcutter's beatific expression as he carries the infant away is the final image of the film and the only sense of certainty it offers. His ability to act obliterates the specter of innate human corruption that has been entertained and enacts a very different reality.

The conclusion of *Rashomon* demonstrates that the ability to take moral action is quite separate from—and perhaps even contrary to—adherence to grand abstractions and conceptual constructions. The conflicting stories told by the bandit, man, and woman in the grove cannot be resolved by themselves alone, and, furthermore, they cannot be resolved by those who debate them. Such debaters may be removed from the bias of the original three, but their attempts to illuminate

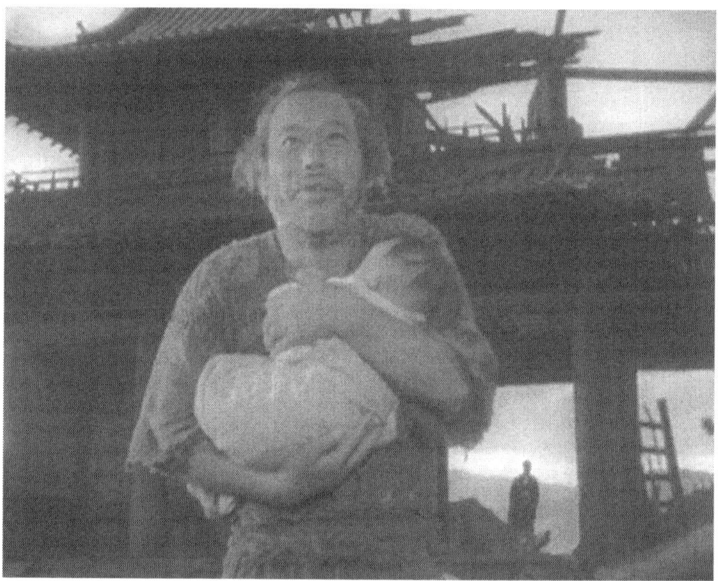

FIGURE 4.3. The woodcutter emerges from the Roshōmon gate into the clear light of moral action.

the situation are only trapped in further bias. We are all caught in an endless chain of limiting perspectives. But *Rashomon* insists on making us, the viewers, the final arbiters. In doing so, it does not invite us to further declaim on the nature of the world or the inherent morality of human beings. The *Sutta Nipāta* informs us that "There is a state where form ceases to exist. . . . It is a state without ordinary perception and without disordered perception and without no perception and without any annihilation of perception" (SN 874). That is to say, it is possible to attain a state beyond ordinary perception that neither obliterates nor succumbs to it. All of us cannot help standing *somewhere,* but it is our attachment to our own perceptions that hinders our awareness of the very limited places on which we stand. This is what inhibits our ability to act correctly. The moral resolution of the film suggests that appropriate actions can come only when we set aside the impulse to elevate our limited view of things, and attain the perception of no-perception.

The Emptiness of Being

A Hollywood screenplay manual plainly states the norm of cinematic storytelling: "In the beginning of the motion picture we don't know anything. During the course of the story, information is accumulated, until at the end we know everything" (Vale 1972, 64). Omniscience is a pleasure afforded by narrative, and its clarity about the world has the power to move people to action. It is this very same capacity, however, that raises controversy over Mel Gibson's *The Passion of the Christ* (2004), whose clarity of vision tells people that Jews should be treated as the enemy of Christianity.

The Buddhist conception of karma, with its emphasis on actions that create merit and demerit, is easily taken to differentiate between good and evil. In fact, karma pivots on the concept of *kusala,* translated as "wholesomeness" and "skillfulness," and its opposite *akusala,* "unwholesomeness" and "unskillfulness." *Kusala* is difficult to render in terms of positive content, for "far from denoting a static good or a generic wholesomeness or skill, it denotes acutely context-sensitive movement in the direction of increasing good . . . [which] implies situationally apt, intensifying excellence" (Hershock 2007, 190). Our examinations of karma in the previous chapters testify that this "context-sensitive movement" happens when insight into the inherently formless nature of being makes it possible for actions to become their own natural reward, and our perception of suffering enacts compassion rather than condemnation.

The root of *akusala*—unwholesomeness and unskillfulness—is consistently identified as something that runs deeper than the usual immoralities of greed, hatred, and the like. These roots of suffering have their own root—*prapañca* (Pāli: *papañca*)—which is the process of mental proliferation instigated by conceptual discriminations (D II.277). The idea of proliferation is consonant with the image of a "thicket" of views, and it connotes the natural tendency of the mind and mental constructions to self-enlarge and multiply. This proliferation of mind becomes the impediment to the moment-by-moment awareness of which wholesomeness consists. Cinema is considered escapist at times because it supplies the comforting clarity that lived experience often lacks. But *Rashomon* demonstrates that film can also move in a different direction toward a different kind of excellence. Such excellence is difficult to appreciate from a narrative sensibility that strives toward a finality in which all is revealed and all is resolved. For this reason, to see the Buddha and the nonlinear and interpenetrating reality that is attributed to his vision, one must ultimately move to an aesthetic modality, to which we turn next.

CHAPTER 5

The Depth of Shadows in *Maborosi*

Maborosi (1995) is the first feature film of Hirokazu Kore'eda, who began his career as a documentary filmmaker. The cinematography of this film has elicited comparisons with the iconic Japanese director Yasujiro Ozu (1903–1963), particularly in its limited use of the camera: *Maborosi* has almost no panning or tracking shots, and no close-ups or zooms. Another point of similarity is the "still life," or scenes of everyday objects that in Ozu's case, "serve not to symbolize but to contain emotions" (Richie 1974, 136). Kore'eda pays overt homage to Ozu by replicating his signature shot of a steaming water kettle, but *Maborosi* is particularly notable for non-diegetic scenes of people engaged in ordinary activities—cleaning, napping, mending a fence, washing dishes, and looking out a window. The high frequency of such shots reflects the fact that *Maborosi* does not offer much in the way of dramatic action or plot development—again, much like the films of Ozu.

Maborosi tells the story of a young woman named Yumiko whose husband commits suicide on the train tracks when their baby is only a few months old. Some years later, Yumiko marries again and relocates to her new husband's seaside town. The dramatic height of the film comes at the end, when a visit back to Osaka triggers depression over the unintelligibility of her first husband's death. She finally voices her incomprehension to Tamio, her second husband: "Why did he do it?" she asks. "It just goes around and around in my head." Tamio replies that the sea has the ability to beguile. His own father has seen a beckoning light far out in the water when he was a fisherman. It can happen to all of us, Tamio concludes. His reference to the sea may be triggered by the fact that both of them are standing on an ocean jetty during this conversation. But the dominance of the images and sounds of water in the second half of the film makes Tamio's allusion to the sea much more significant. William LaFleur suggests that it paints "a contrast between an ever widening visual spaciousness on screen and what we cannot avoid perceiving as the protagonist's narrowly focused mind" (2002, 160). The spaciousness of the ocean provides a visual alternative to the inevitably limited vistas of human perception.

The emotional center of *Maborosi* lies in human incomprehension and the frustrated desire to know—both for Yumiko as well as for the audience. This is triggered by the fact that the suicide is never explained or resolved in the film. Instead, we have references to the depth and vastness of the sea, whose unfathomability has the power to beguile and draw us in. The artistry of *Maborosi* as a film lies in the way it renounces explanations, which merely feign comprehension and light, in favor of an aesthetic appreciation. There is an overt similarity between *Maborosi* and *Rashomon* in that both refuse to tell us what happened. But whereas *Rashomon* provokes philosophizing about the nature and possibility of truth itself, *Maborosi* relinquishes debate for the task of *looking* at things that becomes possible only after we unburden ourselves of the strain of intellectual understanding. This aesthetic attitude, then, is supported by the Buddhist one that says, "Just as we cannot physically hold in place or in stasis that which is passing away, so too we cannot *hold in mind* that which ultimately runs far beyond our mental grasp" (LaFleur 2002, 159).

In LaFleur's telling, it is the film's "complex play of light" that promises an "intense epiphany of things" (2002, 161). The full Japanese title of the film is in fact *maboroshi no hikari*, which translates as "illusory light" or "phantom light."[1] LaFleur suggests that an intense experience of "the seductive power of light" that is film itself is what *Maborosi* ultimately gives us (164). But, in fact, the dominant visual characteristic of this film is the way it favors shadows. This results partly from the fact that Kore'eda shot the movie with no artificial lighting. But his choices to set his scenes so frequently at night and to clothe his actors in black also contribute to the darkness. Of course, light and shadow necessarily arise together, and one cannot exist without the other. This fact is displayed through brilliant visual compositions in scene after scene. In one striking vignette, we see Yumiko engaged in the mundane task of washing the basement stairs. The darkness of the room showcases the almost tangible and thick shafts of light that pour in from the open trapdoor above. In another scene, a pitch-black room is pierced by the grey light of the early dawn when Yumiko opens the solid wooden window. The brilliance and beauty of the light we see in *Maborosi* is enabled by the shadows, just as the glint of sun on ocean water is offset by the darkness of its depths.

This essay focuses on the shadows, because our natural attraction to the light often leads us to overlook the darkness that is the prerequisite of light. The choice between light and shadow is not just an aesthetic one, and the Buddhist tradition at play here moves purposefully from the light to the shadows to make a philosophical as well as artistic point. The focus on shadows, as we shall see, is paralleled by an injunction to relinquish discursive meaning in favor of mystery. These values are embodied in the Buddhist-derived aesthetic concept known as *yūgen*. This chapter will trace the medieval origins of this concept and bring it into the contemporary world of *Maborosi*. Giving up the explicit signs and symbols of discursive meaning also allows us to transition from overtly Buddhist figures to the potential of secular signs to function in a Buddhist way. The ultimate trajectory is to go beyond *Maborosi* into non-Asian cinema, where the next chapter will take us. It is this link between Buddhism and aesthetics that creates the ability to see the Buddha without any overt religious icons. The fecundity of the shadow, with its absence of light and forms, opens up the potential for endless forms to function religiously.

The Preference for Shadows

The ubiquitous shadows that appear in *Maborosi* are the results of the film's cinematography. The use of long shots frequently turns the characters into dark silhouettes, as in the penultimate scene of Yumiko and Tamio on the jetty. Another striking example is when their children run along a lake and are reflected into mirror images in the water that are brighter than the silhouettes formed by their physical bodies. Whereas close-ups of faces require sufficient lighting, long shots need not worry about illuminating visual expression or emotion. Humans become one part of the scene rather than its center, often moving in and out of the frame of the stationary camera. We are made to look at places well before and long after people occupy them, which calls attention to the larger patterns of darkness and light that compose the world. In the absence of the anthropocentric focus, the screen turns into a play of chiaroscuro

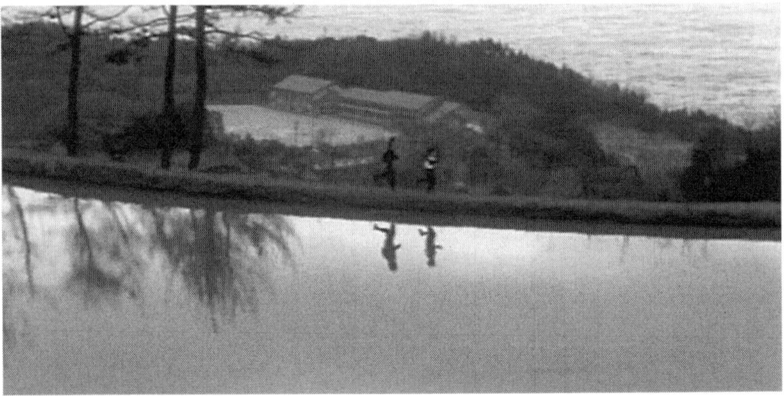

FIGURE 5.1. The running children are more distinct as shadows reflected in the bright surface of the water.

in which humans meld into the darkness and are obscured by the light coming in through a window, reflecting off the water, or illuminating the sky.

To a certain degree, the merging of person and shadow reflects a somberness of mood, particularly in the case of Yumiko. When she dislodges from the bus that takes her to the ocean in the penultimate scene, it takes a while for the viewer to locate her in the depth of the shadows

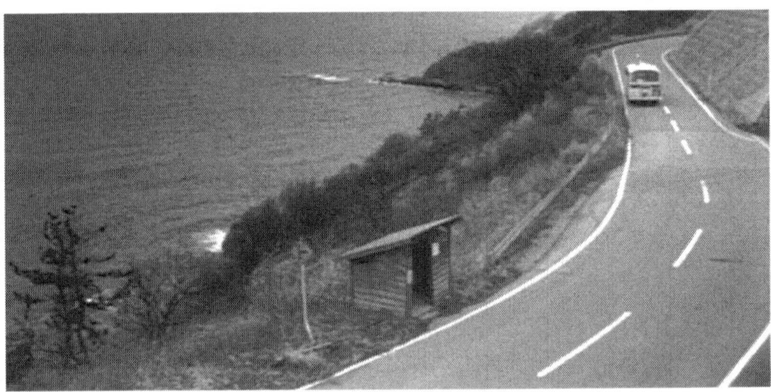

FIGURE 5.2. In this long-distance shot so typical of *Maborosi*, Yumiko's figure is hidden in the bus stop enclosure as the bus slowly winds its way out of the still camera frame.

of the bus stop enclosure. Her immersion in darkness very much mirrors the abyss of her depression. Kore'eda acknowledges the somber cast of the film as a whole in his statement that "[f]or my generation, there is a feeling of a lack of certainty about anything—a universal undefined feeling of loss" (DVD special features interview). But the descent of humans into the shadows of the space they occupy is also noticeable in scenes of intimacy and connection. In perhaps the warmest depiction of conjugal happiness, Yumiko and Tamio sit entwined after lovemaking on a hot summer afternoon in the coolness of the dark beneath a window. Although the scene is shot at medium range, they are too enveloped in darkness to be clearly discernable from the shadows or from each other. Intimacy is suggested by this use of shadow to blend husband and wife together. This technique echoes a much earlier scene of Yumiko and her first husband Ikuo riding astride a single bicycle, which is filmed in a rare tracking shot. This time, nighttime provides the cover of darkness so that it is difficult to distinguish where one person ends and the other begins. In both scenes, the warmth of the conversation reinforces the impression of interconnectedness.

Overwhelmingly, however, *Maborosi* does not create a sense of connectedness and identification for the audience. The literal distance of the characters from the camera distances the viewer from the human action, which does very little to make one feel a part of it. The length of time that is expended on the scenes, which contain minimal human movement, encourages the eye to wander all over the screen—partly because one is not sure of the location of the narrative focus, and partly because there is nothing else to do. The effect is voyeuristic and depersonalizing. We are given a vista into the lives of others without being told what any of it means. William LaFleur suggests, quite rightly, that there is no attempt to explain the death at the center of the story because any intellectual rationalization of suicide is ultimately inadequate and unsatisfying. Instead, the camera induces a contemplative stance that "respects and relishes what may forever remain *unknown* in things" (2002, 159). The humans in *Maborosi* are defined by the spaces and objects around them, which have the effect of decentering them and their questions. They are small and distant within this framing, and both literally and figuratively covered in darkness.

In the evolution of his own interpretation, however, LaFleur focuses on images of light to ultimately offer an explanation of the suicide. He does so by turning to a piece of Buddhist history to float the possibility of being attracted to the moment of death. This is quite different from the desire for nonexistence. Rather, LaFleur focuses on the moment right before death "as possibly providing an absolutely unparalleled experience of being connected to the panoply of things" (2002, 162). LaFleur alludes to medieval accounts of Japanese Buddhist devotees who set sail for the island of Fudaraku (Sanskrit: Potalaka), which is the legendary abode of the Bodhisattva Kannon (Sanskrit: Avalokiteśvara). Between the ninth and eighteenth centuries, there are accounts of people who sailed off and never returned, having drowned themselves for the purpose of being reborn on the other shore of Fudaraku.[2]

Some are said to have been prompted by sightings of a wondrous light far out in the ocean, which is perhaps the precedent for the *maboroshi no hikari* to which Tamio refers. LaFleur suggests Ikuo experiences a version of such alluring light in an early scene when he stops at a railroad crossing. He looks up to see the flashing interior lights of the passing train lit against the nighttime sky. The scene offers a striking image of light, again enabled by the enveloping darkness. This is Ikuo's experience of *maboroshi no hikari,* in LaFleur's view, and it culminates in his death. *Maborosi* itself never suggests this, of course, and LaFleur concedes that most viewers are apt to miss the film's possible allusion to the Fudaraku suicides. As previously noted, the film does not operate in an explanatory mode but rather creates an experience. In LaFleur's reading, *Maborosi* itself duplicates the experience of *maboroshi no hikari* for the viewer. To watch the film leads to the possibility that "we too could find ourselves caught in the powerful grip of an amazing, alluring play of light" (2002, 164).

The beauty of the light in *Maborosi* has an indisputable power to draw the viewer in. What is less clear is the degree to which this beauty can be associated with a call to death. To be sure, LaFleur emphasizes the attentiveness with which we might experience the world if we were to choose to die. We might see the world at that moment with an intensity that the images of *Maborosi* provide. But LaFleur's detour through the Fudaraku episode rather distracts from this idea because it suggests an explanation for Ikuo's death rather than training our attention on the experience of the film. Furthermore, the religious incentive to end one's life for the sake of rebirth in Kannon's Fudaraku or Amida's Pure Land does not automatically produce a beatific vision at the moment of exit. Medieval accounts of religious self-immolation attest to the problem of botched attempts because of an all-too-common loss of nerve.[3] Suicide is not usually conducive to contemplative attention, and for this reason, it is prohibited in Buddhist teachings.

LaFleur is prompted by the invocation of light—the *hikari* of the title—and is thus led to a particular episode in Japanese Buddhist history connected with the embrace of death. However, the other half of the title—*maboroshi*—conveys a more pervasive Buddhist meaning that also has a substantial aesthetic dimension. The meaning of *maboroshi* is "illusion" and "phantasm," which is what Buddhists are in the habit of calling our world of sensory experience. Both light and shadow create the phantasm of experience and *Maborosi* invites us to marvel at its own celluloid instantiation of it. Any diegetic approach to Ikuo's death, on the other hand, negates the space to simply contemplate this play of light and shadow. This aesthetic approach is also religious, and derives from the medieval Japanese concept known as *yūgen*. This aesthetic concept can be traced to Buddhist and Daoist sources that explicitly invoke darkness to suggest a depth to things beyond intellectual explanation. Through this concept, the link between the religious and the aesthetic becomes quite overt.

The Religious and the Aesthetic

The reference to light and shadow makes its earliest appearance in the Chinese cosmological terminology of Yin and Yang, which literally mean shadow and light, respectively. As cultural rubrics they signify considerably more, however, being associated with an endless list of opposing yet correlative concepts. "Female" and "male" is a prominent example, but more abstractly, Yin is the negative principle whereas Yang is the positive. Above and beyond any particular instantiation, the most important idea is an aesthetic one about the phenomenological patterns into which our sensory and social worlds are organized. Light and shadow are complementary pairs, as demonstrated by the constant succession and alternation of heat (summer) and cold (winter) in nature. The human order is thought to follow this pattern with a string of complementary pairings such as male and female, parent and child, ruler and follower, and so forth. This seguing from the natural to the human order integrates aesthetic patterns to moral ones. Just as the mutuality and interdependence of Yin and Yang are evident in nature, it is believed that they must be respected and nurtured in human society. This patterning of morality on the model of the sensory world is key to the blending of aesthetics and religion.

In the Daoist text of the *Daodejing*,[4] a concerted preference is expressed for the negative principle of Yin. It emphasizes what is ordinarily overlooked in sensory attention, which is typically drawn to overt forms. In response, the *Daodejing* reasserts the absent and negative side of things as the necessary condition for what is present:

> Knead clay in order to make a vessel. Adapt the nothing therein to the purpose in hand, and you will have the use of the vessel. Cut out doors and windows in order to make a room. Adapt the nothing therein to the purpose in hand, and you will have the use of the room. Thus what we gain is Something, yet it is by virtue of Nothing that this can be put to use. (Laozi 1963, 67)

For the *Daodejing*, this insight also applies to the political and religious realms. To accomplish human purposes, the negative principle of Yin is again favored as superior to the overt forms of Yang. Therefore, in getting things done, one should adhere to "the deed that consists in taking no action," and for leading others, one should utilize "the teaching that uses no words" (Laozi 1963, 58). This is the Daoist path of *wuwei,* which is often translated as "non-action." More accurately the term signifies an effortless action that becomes possible only after one has overcome the concern with overt forms and rules. In this schema, preoccupation with forms is a sign of amateurism that has yet to attain true creativity and skill. Therefore, "The five colours make men's eyes blind; the five notes make his ears deaf; the five tastes injure his palate" (1963, 68). The five colors, notes, and tastes refer to sensory perceptions but they represent social values as well as because they are "the particular colors, tones, and flavors that are selected out of the total spectrum and assigned special values and 'names'" (Ziporyn 2012, 148). With aesthetic and moral practice alike, attaining "the Way" (*Dao*) means transcending such distinctions and tapping into the original emptiness that is the fertile cradle of all recognizable forms. "The way is empty, yet use will not drain it," the *Daodejing* observes, "Deep, it is like the ancestor of the myriad creatures" (Laozi 1963, 60). The Yin, then, is the emptiness that is prior to and the precondition for all forms. It is hard to describe because it is itself shapeless and formless. Nevertheless, it is characterized as the fertile "mysterious female" and paired with images of dark and empty spaces such as the valley.

The language of the Yin principle produced an immediate synergy between Daoism and Mahāyāna Buddhism's own concept of emptiness—particularly the emptiness philosophy of Nāgārjuna and his Madhyamaka ("middle way") school. This version of emptiness extends the earlier teaching of *anātman* and dependent arising to all phenomena and avers that everything is empty of an intrinsic essence and existence. Despite this negation of substance and essence, Buddhist emptiness signifies the innate condition that allows the myriad phenomena of the world to arise at all. Buddhist thought does not render this emptiness into a cosmogonic fountainhead in the manner of the *Daodejing*, which talks about the "valley" as the literal root of heaven and earth. Mādhyamika philosophers were in fact keen on preventing the reification of emptiness into a metaphysical entity or realm. But this entailed the similar strategy of deconstructing the world of overt forms in order to look more deeply at it. Daoist thought does this by *subsuming* the "myriad creatures" (all phenomena) into the infinite potentiality of absence—all things are born from the void and ultimately return back to it. Buddhist thought focuses on the intrinsic absence (of essence and substance) *within* each form, which makes emptiness the causal condition and source of all phenomena. The absence of an intrinsic identity at the center of each and every thing allows for their constant coming-to-be. Both Daoist and Buddhist thought points to absence as the source of everything that is present to us. The *Daodejing* directs us to look literally *at* the absences with its preferential Yin images, whereas Buddhist thought looks beyond the illusion of substance and essence in all things to see the emptiness with*in*.

These religious ideas are combined and appropriated in Japanese discourses on the purpose of poetry and drama, particularly through the aesthetic concept of yūgen. The term was originally used in China to refer to the depth of Daoist and Buddhist teachings.[5] The first character for "yu" (幽) means "dark" and "dim," and suggests something hidden. The second character for "gen" (玄) refers to a dark color, and connotes something silent, subtle, and profound. The Chinese usage was imported into Japan and around the tenth century the term surfaced in poetic theory to refer to the profundity that poetry can capture. In terms of actual poetic practice, this meant a subtle evocation of feeling rather than explicit descriptions: "Yūgen—a sense of profundity—emerges paradoxically from incomplete expression" (Konishi 1991, 183). Fujiwara Shunzei

(1114–1204)[6] discusses yūgen in his *Korai fūteishō* ("notes on poetic style through the ages") by invoking Tendai Buddhism and its articulation of emptiness (Japanese: *kū*) to describe a "dimension of depth" in poetry.[7] But echoes of the *Daodejing* are sounded in his emphasis on subtlety. This depth cannot be overtly described through words but merely *evoked* through the surface reality of what is depicted. The surface reality, or the overt subject of the poem, is important because the depth of yūgen does not consist of a hidden meaning that is somewhere *beyond* the overt phenomenon or sign. The yūgen aesthetic adheres to Madhyamaka Buddhist teaching—mediated by Chinese Tiantai and Japanese Tendai Buddhism—that emptiness paradoxically resides *in* apparent forms rather than beyond and apart from them.

The favored technique to evoke the depth of yūgen is typically the Daoist "less is more" approach. Kamo no Chōmei (1154–1216)[8] articulates this by describing the power of spareness in his *Mumyōshō* ("nameless notes"): "On an autumn evening, for example, there is no color in the sky, nor any sound, and although we cannot give a definite reason for it, we are somehow moved to tears" (Chōmei 1968, 408). The preference for the colorless and the soundless is in direct lineage with the *Daodejing*, and Chōmei applies it explicitly to poetry:

> Completely to display your feelings in words by saying of the moon that it is bright, or by praising the cherry blossoms, declaring that they are pretty, how can that be difficult? Where would there be the virtue of the uta [song], which is to be more than an ordinary statement? (Chōmei 1968, 409)

Singing about what is colorful and bright is to produce ordinary conversation, which focuses on what is immediately engaging and overt to the senses. In order to attain the deeper level of poetry, one is again advised to look at the absences, or at least at the subdued and the commonplace. Then one can "exhaust your mind in all its depth," according to Chōmei, in the moment when "thinking does not lead anywhere and words are inadequate" (1968, 409). Shunzei's own son, the poet Fujiwara Teika (1162–1241), created subtlety in his own distinctive manner and is considered a master of the yūgen style. He subverted the poetic demands of *kokoro* ("heart") and *hon-i* ("essence"), which conveyed conventional meanings for set poetic topics, and used understatement to suggest an essence that deviated from standard understandings. For this reason, his poems were often judged to be incomprehensible by other poets. Teika described his own verses as "Zen nonsense poetry" (*daruma-uta*) because for him, "the essence of a topic could only be grasped at a deep mental level" (Konishi 1991, 196).

Suggestiveness and restraint are also promoted by Zeami Motokiyō (1363–1443) in his treatises on the Nō masked drama. Zeami and his father Kannami Kiyotsugu (1333–1384) are credited with transforming a humble folk tradition into "an experience of profundity and almost religious exhilaration" (Rimer and Masakazu 1984, xvii). Nō evolved from *sarugaku* ("monkey entertainments"), a combination of comic mime, song, dance, and acrobatics that originated in China. In the thirteenth century, a strand of *sarugaku* dramas developed with plots borrowed from Buddhist temple performances known as *shushi*. *Shushi* died out as an independent art form but was absorbed into *sarugaku* dramas, giving them the solemnity that is the hallmark of what became Nō in the fourteenth century.[9] Zeami's treatises theorize this newly elevated art now patronized by shoguns, and Zeami's work is filled with references to yūgen as Nō's highest achievement. In *Kakyō* ("a mirror held to the flower"), Zeami channels the ethos of the *Daodejing* by writing about the power of the moments when the actor is still, in the interstices between two physical actions:

> The actor must rise to a selfless level of art, imbued with a concentration that transcends his own consciousness, so that he can bind together the moments before and after that instant when "nothing happens." Such a process constitutes that inner force that can be termed "connecting all the arts through one intensity of mind." (Zeami 1984, 97)

References to mind and concentration regularly appear in expositions of yūgen, reflecting its close association with Buddhist meditative discipline and insight. Shunzei compares the depth of yūgen to Buddhist meditation in which one first brings ordinary thoughts to a standstill, which then enables insight into the truly empty nature of things.[10] Zeami's reference to "a concentration that transcends his own consciousness" is actually *mushin* (無心) in Japanese, which is the Zen concept of "no mind." Mushin refers to a deep level of consciousness distinct from ordinary awareness, which overcomes the conventional meanings and values attached to the identification of "names" and forms. Attaining "no mind" is to "see" the un-seeable emptiness that is present in these very same forms.

Throughout the medieval period, poets and dramatists consciously fused together Buddhist and aesthetic practices. Zeami claims that the Nō drama originated in India when the Buddha himself staged performances of flute and drum music during the dedication of the Jetavana Monastery.[11] Zeami adds that the Japanese Prince Shōtoku (574–622) confirmed that the "wild words and embellished phrases" (*kyōgen kigo* 狂言綺語) of the drama "will serve to praise the Buddha and provide the means to spread his teachings" (Rimer and Masakazu 1984, 34–35). *Kyōgen kigo* is a stock phrase that originated with the Chinese poet Bo Zhuyi (722–846) to refer to his poetry, which he said might function to honor the Buddhist Dharma in spite of its apparently frivolous nature (LaFleur 1983, 8). The impact of this idea on Japanese aesthetics was immense. Shunzei defends the *kyōgen kigo* of poetry in the *Korai fūteishō*, stating, "It is exactly here that the profundity of things is demonstrated. This is because there exists a reciprocal flow of meaning between such things [as poetry] and the way of Buddhism, a way that maintains the interdependence of all things" (quoted in LaFleur 1983, 90). In the *Yūgaku shūdō fūken* ("disciplines for the joy of art"), Zeami also affirms that the art of Nō arises from the Buddhist truth of emptiness, here glossed in the Zen language of *mu* (無), or "non-Being":

> Being might be said to represent an external manifestation that can be seen with the eyes. Non-Being can be said to represent the hidden, fundamental readiness of mind that signifies the vessel of all art [since a vessel is itself empty]. It is the fundamental Non-Being that gives rise to the outward sense of Being [in the Nō]. (Zeami 1984, 118–19)

Zeami invokes the empty vessel that we originally saw in the *Daodejing*, using it to understand art as a wellspring for the forms and configurations that arise from emptiness. Zeami unites this image with the Buddhist language of *mu* to add the idea that art cultivates the mind that can look directly at this original source of all things. The unity of aesthetic and religious experience is affirmed.

From the Medieval to the Modern

The medieval Japanese world self-consciously affirmed the nondualism of Buddhist and aesthetic pursuits, fusing the contemplative life of the monastic with the worldliness of poetry and drama. This effort came from both Buddhist clerics and secular literati because of how frequently and easily these social realms overlapped in the progression of individual lives: literati often entered the monastic order at some point and fulltime monks were addicted to the cultural practice of poetry. As Bo Zhuyi wrote in 817:

> Since earnestly studying the Buddhist doctrine of emptiness,
> I've learned to still all the common states of mind.
> Only the devil of poetry I have yet to conquer—
> Let me come on a bit of scenery and I start my idle
> droning. (2000, 88)[12]

Taking their cue from Bo Zhuyi himself, Japanese theorists decisively affirmed the indivisibility of aesthetic and religious practice until it became a truism. Hence, the haiku poet Bashō (1644–1694) could speak unself-consciously of himself and others who "had given over their whole lives to the search for truth in art" (2000, 69), and the Zen poet-monk Ryōkan (1758–1831) versified that "[t]he mind of poetry, the mind of Zen; Come together effortlessly" (1996, 110). As a direct result, overt references to Buddhism and Zen were gradually erased and rendered unnecessary in discussions of art. This cultural trajectory faithfully follows what Buddhist emptiness doctrine overtly demands: the collapse of the nirvana and samsara distinction, particularly through a reversion to ordinary, nonreligious forms. In East Asia, this process was abetted by strident Zen iconoclastic rhetoric against Buddhist religious signs and institutions as actual hindrances to liberation. This self-erasing impulse of Buddhist teachings has historical significance and impact. William LaFleur makes a trenchant observation in this respect, particularly regarding the advent of the modern era:

> Because the critique of the Buddhist symbol-system came
> in part from Buddhism itself, the clash of rival systems as
> Japan moved into the modern era was much less overt than
> that which characterized Europe's torturous move from the
> Catholic medieval epoch to the "secularized" modern one.
> This is to say that a move toward the secularization of
> Buddhist symbols may have taken place fairly early in Japan,
> coming out of the heart of Buddhist philosophy itself.
> (1983, 25)

LaFleur's chronological narrative here parallels the spatial progression of the temple Borobudur, which in turn serves as the model for the sequence of films in this book. In all three cases, the more successful one is in seeing the Buddha, the more one does not need to see him at all. *Maborosi*, needless to say, features no overt images or other signs of the Buddha, demonstrating instead the cultural practice of painting (in words, actions, or imagery) what disciplined contemplation of the world is thought to perceive—a seeing in the manner of the Buddha himself.

In the twentieth century, this goal is often translated into "secular" aesthetic practices, reflecting the so-called modernization of Japan. The aesthetics of *Maborosi* might be linked to the novelist Jun'ichirō Tanizaki's 1933 essay, *In Praise of Shadows*, for example. This work is the product of the early modern era in which the nativist thesis of "Japaneseness" (*nihonjinron*) opposed Western claims of cultural superiority with its own rhetoric of uniqueness and justified political ambitions. Tanizaki's essay displays the essentializing idioms of the "Oriental" versus the "Western," which creates the temptation to dismiss his observations as a mere exercise in counterhegemonic rhetoric. It would be regrettable, however, to allow the politically chauvinistic framing of his essay to blind us to the value of its cultural and semiotic observations.

Tanizaki echoes the flavor of *Maborosi*'s visual aesthetic when he states, "We Orientals tend to seek our satisfactions in whatever surroundings we happen to find ourselves, to content ourselves with things as they are; and so darkness causes us no discontent" (1977, 31). Tanizaki traces this preference for shadows to the architecture of traditional Japanese homes, with their deep overhanging eaves that block the sun. He explains how this practical feature was parlayed into an aesthetic preference and a kind of moral value. The basic elements of Tanizaki's secular-aesthetic disquisition reflect the traditional values of yūgen but the "East versus West" scaffolding politicizes it by bringing it into a modern global and comparative discourse. Tanizaki sees the West as representative of a will-to-power over nature and fellow humanity, which he distills into an aesthetic penchant for everything that gleams and shines with light. Tanizaki adduces the example of the modern Western bathroom clad in shining white tile as a testament to this cultural desire to triumph over nature. Tanizaki then presses home the difference in the "Oriental": "The quality that we call beauty, however, must always grow from the realities of life, and our ancestors, forced to live in dark rooms, presently came to discover beauty in shadows" (1977, 18).

Tanizaki's polarization of cultures reflects the discourses of his day and displays a reverse-Orientalist strategy that seeks to transform the image of the passive and fatalistic Oriental into the hallmark of another kind of virtue. This is willfully blind to the intracultural diversity of both East Asian and European American societies, to be sure, but the comparative framing offers an interesting taxonomy of aesthetic-moral orientations. The aggressive economic and infrastructural development current in China and the growing ecological movement in Western nations negate the idea that Asians always embrace the "less-is-more" way of nature, and that Western societies always seek to impose their will on the environment. But it is also true that Zen Buddhism and Daoism now function as resources and inspiration for contemporary Western ecological movements. Not all quarters of East Asian society practice Zen and Daoist values but these Asian traditions serve as icons of a now-global ideal of ethical living. This too reflects the relative ease with which Buddhist practices have moved into the modern age. Their aesthetic and moral sentiments easily shed traditional religious trappings—for better or for worse—and readily integrate into secular worldly activities.

Before we turn to the implications of this secularization process in seeing the Buddha, let us examine a still later instance of comparative observation. Roland Barthes's *The Empire of Signs*, which is a collection of short essays on Japan, comes decades after Tanizaki and exhibits an evolution in critical consciousness. Originally published in 1970, Barthes is careful not to reify the actual country of Japan into an essence. As a semiologist, he is aware that this is often the effect of language and discourse, and so he begins by admitting to the fact that he is constructing a fantasy by isolating certain notable features in order to "deliberately form a system" called "Japan" (1982, 3). And what Barthes constructs is noticeably familiar. One exemplary case should suffice for our purposes. In his examination of the city of Tokyo as a sign—particularly its physical layout and the way it directs the movement of bodies—Barthes notices the conspicuous emptiness of its center. It is not literally empty, of course, for the Imperial Palace occupies this space. But for that very reason, the sizable area of one-and-one-third square miles in one of the most densely populated cities in the world is off-limits to the public and empty of people except the emperor, who is rarely seen. Ringed by moats and walls, traffic is forced to make perpetual detours around it, and so "the system of the imaginary is spread circularly, by detours and returns the length of an empty subject" (Barthes 1982, 320). As with the empty stūpa at the center of Borobudur, one is forced to return to the periphery of the world and its panoply of signs. Nirvana mandates the return to samsara. This recursion, Barthes helpfully notes, resists both the structural and metaphysical logic of the idealized Western city, where "the center is the site of truth":

> [T]he center of our cities is always *full*: a marked site, it is here that the values of civilization are gathered and condensed: spirituality (churches), power (offices), money (banks), merchandise (department stores), language (agoras: cafés and promenades): to go downtown or to the center-city is to encounter the social "truth," to participate in the proud plenitude of "reality." (1982, 30)

What Barthes conveys in his own comparison of cultural signs is yet another version of the Yin/Yang dynamic, in which systems can be readily classified into coherences based on the empty or the full. The *Daodejing* originally applied the distinction to Chinese schools of thought: it recommends the virtue and power of the way of Yin as that which subsumes and engenders the overt Confucian path of Yang. Given this original usage, it is manifestly silly to characterize all of Asia as inherently Yin and Western civilization as Yang. But the human use of signs such as "Yin" and "Yang" always abstracts imagined systems from the messiness of lived experience, as Barthes does, and creates intelligibility by helping to focus our attention. The way Barthes expands the sense of this organizing sign system suggests substantial and important differences in what Yin and Yang convey—at least to the human intellect. It also suggests that the "intelligibility of non-intelligibility" and the Yin sensibility expressed by Buddhist and Daoist systems can appear beyond these original religious sites. We can then look forward to the possibility of seeing this aesthetic in other cultural contexts, including the contemporary West.

From National Cinemas to Buddhist Cinema

Maborosi is our transition point from Asian cinema to Buddhist cinema, meaning a cinema that is not bound by any particular cultural location. The movement from the empty center to the signed periphery means encompassing multiple cultural sites. Film studies itself has recently turned away from the idea of national cinemas, which has produced some rethinking about Japanese cinema within a global context:

> The paradigms of Orientalism have tended to emphasize the Japaneseness of Japanese cinema at the expense of its modernity. The framework of vernacular modernism, however, enables us to move beyond the binaries of East and West to recognize the modernity of this cinema as a discourse of mass culture, (Russell 2011, 3–4)

This trend is reflected in Christine Marran's reading of *Maborosi*, of which she claims that "there is nothing that marks this film as aesthetically related to anything Japanese except for a kind of obeisance that it seems to pay to Ozu who is consistently, and erroneously, framed specifically as a 'Japanese' director" (2002, 167). Catherine Russell agrees, stating that Ozu "captured an ideal of Japanese identity that doesn't quite hold up to scrutiny. Not only can Westerners understand these films, they can be moved by them" (Russell 2011, 20). All fifty-three Ozu films, which are domestic dramas (*shomin-geki*) about ordinary people, do nothing more than face the inevitability of transition and change—particularly death, marriage, and the distancing between generations. These are uneventful stories that provoke us to see the intense drama in the ineluctable passage of time. The events are universal by virtue of their ordinariness. Turning to *Maborosi*, Marran suggests that reading it through Buddhist lenses unnecessarily "Japanifies" it, thereby "leading us away from the underlying trans-existentialist and minimalist tone of the film" (2002, 167).

It is also worth noting that the penchant for depicting shadows is not a monopoly of the East. The Hollywood tradition of film noir is too diffuse to be called a genre, but it is readily identifiable as a visual style that favors darkness, chiaroscuro, and patterns of light and shadow. This look goes along with a characteristic bleakness of mood and subject matter. The hardboiled detective and femme fatale are the typical leads, but more broadly the focus is on crime, corruption, and cynicism. Paul Schrader notes a particular parallel between lighting and tone:

> The actors and setting are often given equal lighting emphasis. An actor is often hidden in the realistic tableau of the city at night, and, more obviously, his face is often blacked out by

shadow as he speaks. . . . When the environment is given an equal or greater weight than the actor, it, of course, creates a fatalistic, hopeless mood. There is nothing the protagonist can do; the city will outlast and negate even his best efforts. (1996, 57)

Flourishing from the 1940s to early '50s, film noir is interpreted as a reflection of postwar disillusionment, with its depictions of the underside of modern American life. Schrader deems film noir to be first and foremost a visual style rather than sociological commentary, however, which for him explains why film critics—in their preference for theme over style—have neglected it. If this is the case, then perhaps the depiction of shadows is not inherently indicative of a "fatalistic" and "hopeless" mood. The look of film noir is somber by Hollywood standards, to be sure, and owes its largest aesthetic debt to German expressionism, which was brought to the American screen by expatriate directors such as Fritz Lang, Otto Preminger, Billy Wilder, and Robert Siodmak. But the phrase "film noir" is used to describe the visual look of films well beyond this era of filmmaking, and it is perhaps possible to put the lens of the yūgen aesthetic to cross-cultural use.

Ridley Scott's *Blade Runner* (1982) is a cyberpunk tale about a near-future dystopia that is heavy in the ambiance of film noir (Doll and Faller 1986). Set in Los Angeles in the year 2019, the city is beset with urban decay and density, as well as a perpetual rain and haze. Nighttime appears to be the ubiquitous hour. The drama centers on Deckard, a Blade Runner, or special cop who "retires" illegal androids made for labor and entertainment in off-world colonies in outer space. These "replicants" look like humans and have emotions, but their superhuman strength makes them a threat and they are banned from Earth. Deckard is forced out of retirement to hunt down and kill four replicants who have escaped to Earth in order to find their creator—the founder of the Tyrell Corporation—and demand an extension of their four-year lifespan. Deckard eventually succeeds in his mission of retiring all four, although his life is spared during the confrontation with the last remaining android—Roy, the leader of the outlaw posse. Deckard is no match for Roy's superior strength, but the latter spares him moments before he expires from his own exhausted lifespan. Deckard narrates:

I don't know why he saved my life. Maybe in those last moments he loved life more than he ever had before. Not

just his life—anybody's life; my life. All he'd wanted were the
same answers the rest of us want. Where did I come from?
Where am I going? How long have I got? All I could do was
sit there and watch him die.

The ambivalence expressed in these sentences matches the moral
ambiguity of Deckard's assignment. The replicants' desire to live makes
them difficult to distinguish from humans, and killing them seems like
plain murder. This is particularly the case with the replicant Zhora, who
hides by working as a dancer in a nightclub. Deckard flushes her out and
guns her down in the streets, where she comes to a dramatic end by crash-
ing through the layers of store plate glass windows. Her death is poignant
and the regret on Deckard's face is plain to see. Deckard's compromised
sentiment is abetted by the fact that he is falling in love with another
female replicant named Rachel, who works as Tyrell's personal assistant.
Rachel is special because as the latest and most advanced of androids, she
has been implanted with childhood memories and initially does not even
know she is a replicant. When she kills another replicant who is about
to take Deckard's life, their relationship is sealed. At the end of the film,
Deckard tells his handler Gaff that he will no longer work as a Blade
Runner. Gaff responds, "It's too bad she won't live; but then again, who
does?" referring to Rachel. In the conclusion of the theatrical release, we
see Deckard and Rachel driving off into the mountains and Deckard's
voiceover stating that Tyrell informed him that Rachel has no automatic
termination date. This upbeat and hopeful ending was undoubtedly a
concession to mainstream audiences, but the Director's Cut does not
contain this coda, ending instead with Gaff's final line: "It's too bad
she won't live; but then again, who does?" This might strike a fatalistic
tone for some, but its honest observation of the human condition also
reveals what makes life valuable. Deckard understands that this is the
reason why Roy spared him, the very man who killed his compatriots
and sought to eliminate him as well.

Film noir may very well demonstrate, then, the global span of the
yūgen aesthetic. This raises the question of how to adequately describe it
beyond the language of national cinemas. In addressing the accessibility
of Japanese cinema, critics use the terminology of "modern" and "existential," but the applicability of these terms is questionable. These concepts
emerge from Western cultural history and have meanings foreign to the
Japanese and East Asian context. To be sure, the structures of modernity
are fully integrated into Asian societies when it comes to economic,

demographic, and social organizations. Hence, the idea of modernity does have traction on the global scale. But the notion of modernity also connotes a kind of secularism understood as an explicit alienation from the traditional religious episteme—particularly with the advent of scientific rationality. The philosophical movement of "existentialism" follows suit as a response to the loss of traditional faith and the ensuing quandary over the absurdity and meaninglessness of human existence. Like modernity, existentialism implies an epistemic break with the past, and the resulting predicaments of that rupture.

This "before and after" structure does not compute in Japanese society, as William LaFleur notes, where the "religious" realm of Buddhism and the "secular" realm of aesthetics were merged long before modernity. Modern Western art frequently purveys itself as an alternative to traditional religion, but this has been a *traditional* idea and practice in the East Asian Buddhist world. For that reason, the term *Buddhist* better captures the global resonance of *Maborosi*. The origins of Buddhism may be Asian, but Buddhism itself negates the idea that it must be embodied in any particular historical and cultural form. This is the only way of seeing the emptiness inherent in all forms. The French film *Amour* (2012), by writer and director Michaël Haneke, quietly follows an octogenarian couple and the space in which the husband nurses his wife through a stroke, gradual decline, and death. The cinematography is replete with views of empty rooms and feature many moments of nonaction and nonnarrativity. It could very well be described as Ozu-esque. But one can concur with Russell and Marran and deny that this invokes "Japaneseness"—the film is French, after all. On the other hand, "modern" and "existential" are much too bland and inadequate as descriptors. "Buddhist" is better, paradoxically, because the label means that we are *supposed* to let go of visions of the Buddha. A Buddhist reading of *Maborosi*, far from "Japanifying" it, helps us to transition away from Japanese and Asian films altogether.

CHAPTER 6

The Visual Cinema of Terrence Malick

American filmmaker Terrence Malick (b. 1943) can be described as a classic "auteur" in that his body of works conveys a consistent and distinctive vision.[1] Malick's first film as writer and director, *Badlands*, was released in 1973. In the forty subsequent years to date he has produced five more under his complete artistic control: *Days of Heaven* (1978), *The Thin Red Line* (1998), *The New World* (2005), *The Tree of Life* (2011), and *To the Wonder* (2012).[2] Each film sports a lineup of A-list Hollywood actors such as Christian Bale, Brad Pitt, Jessica Chastain, and Sean Penn. Malick pairs highly recognizable faces with a beautiful visual style, philosophical voiceovers, and a barely-there narrativity that sacrifices the usual conventions of storytelling. Twenty minutes into *The Tree of Life*, for example, the film shifts abruptly from its 1950s suburban Texas setting to a visual narration of the creation of life on both cosmological and microscopic levels, including the formation of galaxies and planets, and the evolution of dinosaurs and human life. Then we return to Texas. The narrative structure of Malick's films becomes increasingly diffuse over the progression of his work until even dialogue is purely incidental in *To the Wonder*. In his *New Yorker* review, David Denby complains: "A Malick sequence has now become a collection of semi-disconnected shots, individually ravishing but bound together by what feels like the trivial narcissism of Caribbean-travel ads on TV" (2013).

To be sure, images are everything in a Malick film, but not all of them are pretty—each film features shots of environmental degradation, pestilence, as well as animal and human suffering. More importantly, the visuality of Malick's cinema never functions as mere aesthetic embellishment but rather says things that language cannot articulate. In a rare and early interview after the release of *Badlands*, Malick recounts his one-year stint teaching philosophy at M.I.T. Malick was a Rhodes Scholar who started but never finished a thesis on Martin Heidegger at Oxford University, and he reports that he was also a bad teacher (Walker 1975). So he decided to turn to filmmaking. It seems that Malick finds the visual language of film more capable of expressing what he was unable to say through academic discourses.

The centrality of images in Malick's films also sacrifices many norms of cinematic storytelling, which predictably leads to viewer dissatisfaction. David Denby thinks the scenes in *To the Wonder* are as "insubstantial as the wind" and add up to nothing (Denby 2013). Other critics, however, are more appreciative of what can be gained by the minimal style. Roger Ebert reports, "As the film opened, I wondered if I was missing something. As it continued, I realized many films could miss a great deal" (Ebert 2013). More than a decade earlier Ebert's assessment of *The Thin Red Line* had a similar conclusion: "But the audience has to finish the work: Malick isn't sure where he's going or what he's saying. That may be a good thing" (Ebert 1999). Emmanuel Lubezki, Malick's cinematographer for *The New World*, *Tree of Life*, and *To the Wonder* confirms that this open-endedness is deliberate. He says of *To the Wonder*:

> The movie has very little plot; it's more of a contemplation, and we're always looking for the moments that editors normally throw out. In many cases they're the moments before and after the dramatic scenes that make up most movies. I don't want to say that those moments feel more real, but they affect me and I relate to them as an audience member. By leaving out the conventional scenes that explain things, the film invites the audience to create some of the story themselves, and I like that. (Hemphill 2013)[3]

These references to incompleteness and insubstantiality render Malick's corpus of films an ideal analogue to the empty stūpa at the center of Borobudur. The underdetermined quality of Malick's cinema invites the viewer to complete the process of narration for himself, just as the absence of a Buddha image at the apex of the monument turns away from seeing the Buddha to put the focus on the nature of our own perceptions. Malick depicts both the misery and glory of existence in a totality that poses the question of what each of us is capable of seeing in the world. For these reasons, Malick's artistic vision is about vision itself. The following analysis will focus primarily on *The Thin Red Line* as representative of Malick's oeuvre, with briefer references to *The Tree of Life* and *To the Wonder* as more recent works.

The Nonnarrative Language of the Visual

Malick's films have overt spiritual and philosophical concerns that reviewers often discuss by bringing up the Christian symbolism and themes in his work. One film critic formulates this as the tendency "to urgently question, yet also accept, the presence of God in a fallen world" (Chang 2011). This observation refers to *The Tree of Life* specifically, but it is characteristic of Malick as an auteur and embodied in the man or woman of grace that seems to appear in every movie. This figure—Private Witt in *Thin Red Line*, Mrs. O'Brien in *Tree of Life*, Father Quintana in *To the Wonder*—embodies and articulates the possibility of another world even in the presence of human pain.

This general framework is assisted by direct Christian textual and literary sources. *Tree of Life* begins with a Biblical passage from The Book of Job: "Where were you when I laid the foundations of the earth? . . . When the morning stars sang together, and all the sons of God shouted for joy?" The conclusion of *Tree of Life* features a resurrection scene in a naturalistic heaven—a beach—where the child and adult versions of the main character are reunited with the members of his family, including his brother who died at the age of nineteen. *To the Wonder*'s Father Quintana is a Catholic priest who struggles to see God in his abject parishioners and the suffering that he works to alleviate. "Teach us where to seek you," his voiceover says, followed by passages from the prayer of St. Patrick: "Christ with me, Christ before me, Christ behind me, Christ in me, Christ beneath me, Christ above me, Christ on my right, Christ on my left, Christ in the heart." Hubert Cohen carefully documents the Biblical references in *Days of Heaven*, the title itself being taken from Deuteronomy (11:21) where it states that God's people will live in the land of milk and honey and their lives will be "as days of heaven upon the earth" (Cohen 2003).

Given the explicit Biblical and Christian language, some understandably see the visuality of Malick's work as representing the "omniscient presence" of God (Cohen 2003, 59) and "the slippery viewpoint of God" (Feeney 1999). Many recognize Malick's cinema to be religious and meditative in that it "put[s] us in touch with eternal rhythms and spiritual questions underneath [the] melodramas of survival" (Lopate 1999). But Malick's meditations can be described equally well in the language of Buddhism without, at the same time, displacing or contesting that of the Bible. To the degree that Malick "puts us in touch with eternal rhythms," he is also capable of accommodating a plethora of historical and imaginative filters to parse such experience. Wendy Doniger's notion of the "mythical method" in which traditional myths, novels, and films can move us from the personal to the cosmically abstract is helpful here. All stories must speak in a particular vernacular about particular people and events but it is in the nature of mythical narratives to say, "This could happen to anyone" (Doniger 1998, 7). If that is the case, then the language, place, and time can be changed without losing the force of the story.

By happenstance, Doniger elucidates this via the passage from the Book of Job with which *Tree of Life* begins—"Where were you when I laid the foundations of the earth? . . . When the morning stars sang together, and all the sons of God shouted for joy?" Doniger focuses on how this response from God to Job's complaints is an example of the Bible's own practice of the mythical method because God's response "whips the microscope of self-pity out of [Job's] hand and gives him, in its place, a theological telescope" by invoking the overpowering riddle of creation (Doniger 1998, 12). When a story reaches in this way beyond the personal to the abstract, "myth is cross-culturally translatable, which is to say comparable, commensurable" (Doniger 1998, 9). This commensurability exists in the fact that different cultures address the same questions, and these questions are not bound to any single system of articulation. One movie critic expresses this understanding in observing Malick's own Christian references: "Malick does not mean to be clever or literary: he is simply trading on the texts and traditions we have long relied on to formulate our understanding of the nature of things" (Cohen 2003, 47). For that reason, it is possible to read Malick through Buddhist (and other religious) lenses—to the degree that they too access eternal rhythms and raise spiritual questions.

If we apply a Buddhist filter, the force of Malick's filmmaking is to go beyond the desire for a clear and final pronouncement about what things mean. Its preference for images over storytelling deliberately sacrifices the normal tropes of cinematic meaning and strives for a different kind of language. This sometimes includes novel uses of ordinary language. Malick's trademark voiceover technique, for example, is to have many narrators in order to multiply perspectives rather than creating the clarity this technique normally affords. This is particularly evident in *The Thin Red Line* because of its large ensemble cast. Rather than privileging one character's experience, competing and multiple voices are heard as if the point is multiplicity itself. It is difficult to identify who is speaking at any given moment, and individual characterization is secondary to this panoply of perspectives. Voiceover is even used to splinter what an individual character feels. When Lieutenant Doll shoots a Japanese soldier during battle he yells triumphantly "I got 'em! I got 'em" but his internal voice layers the scene and bemoans: "I killed a man! Worse thing you can do. Worse than rape. I killed a man and nobody can touch me for it." There is no perspicacity evident in human actions, let alone in the totality of existence. It is no coincidence that most of the voiceovers are in the form of questions rather than pronouncements, as we shall soon see.

It is the language of images that stars in Malick's oeuvres, however, and it speaks in a very particular way. Lubezki states, "Photography is not used to illustrate dialogue or a performance . . . we're using it to capture emotion so that the movie is very experiential. It's meant to trigger tons of memories, like a scent or a perfume" (Zeitchik 2011). Malick typically shoots hours upon hours of footage in order to capture spontaneous and accidental moments. Lubezki reports, "The key is to react quickly to an unrehearsed moment in the acting or in the weather. We're all looking for those ephemeral moments, and they're what end up in the film" (Hemphill 2013). Malick then crafts his movies in the editing room, paring raw footage into a final product that often takes years to finish. The priority given to the unrehearsed and nonnarrative moments often cuts actors entirely out of the final product. The final cut of *The Thin Red Line* pared down one hundred hours of film and left every scene with Gary Oldman, Mickey Rourke, and Martin Sheen on the editing room floor. Likewise, the scenes with Jessica Chastain and Rachel Weisz were cut entirely from *To the Wonder*.

The way actors are treated in a Malick film is also a result of its visual emphasis. Roger Ebert suggests that Malick uses his actors like "models" in spite of their marquee status (Ebert 2013). Cast members of *To the Wonder* report that Malick would push them to move around, "telling them to ignore their lines and simply move where the spirit took them" (Zeitchik 2012). Human actors function as prompts for what one might see and capture in the moment rather than as the center of a story. Olga Kurylenko notes that they shot scenes with dialogue but most ended up on the cutting-room floor: "They might have simply been intended as a way for the actors to feel out their characters, rather than sequences audiences were meant to see" (Zeitchik 2012). Ben Affleck also describes the disconcerting experience of being displaced in the middle of a shoot: "I'd see the camera start out on me and then move up the branches and think 'Maybe I should climb up the tree?'" (ibid.). Janet Maslin complains that in spite of the lineup of stars in *The Thin Red Line* "no one here has a role with much continuity, since the film's editing shows off the performers to such poor advantage" (Maslin 1998).

The normal movie viewing process, in fact, puts the Malick film at a disadvantage because it does not reward the usual expectations of star performances and compelling storytelling. To fully appreciate a Malick film it is best to discard the expectation of linear movement, which only suffers constant interruptions from "nature photography as exquisite as it is redundant" (Maslin 1998). The more rewarding approach is to rewatch individual segments repeatedly, in no particular order, and to take in the visual language of this cinema that can sustain the viewer's gaze in the manner of a masterful painting. Being cinema, however, Malick's creations also include the enriching elements of movement, music, and words. Although the stillness of painting is useful for describing the contemplative mood of Malick's films, the dynamism that cinema allows is fully exploited. The movement of the camera features in particular nature and the broader landscape that are the only nonnegotiable stars of Malick's moviemaking.

The Seeing of Nature

As suggested through the film *Maborosi*, seeing like the Buddha entails putting human experience into perspective by decentering it. A visual way to accomplish this is to integrate characters into the natural world so that human actions are simply part and parcel of natural events. Regardless of the setting—the war-torn hills of Guadalcanal, the ancient abbey of Mont St.-Michel, or the large and barren housing subdivisions of Oklahoma—each location is bathed in glowing light and caressed by the camera into an ethereal beauty. As Janet Maslin notes of *The Thin Red Line*, "The way light filters through the canopy of the rain forest means at least as much here as the specifics of battle" (Maslin 1998). Like Kore'eda, Malick shoots in natural light and is inclined to capture wide-open spaces and integrate the human actions therein. Human dramas are not disregarded but neither are they front and center. The vagaries of what people do are offset by the grandeur of nature, which is vaster than passing human events. But nature is not romanticized in Edenic fashion either—we see predation in the opening shot of an alligator slowly submerging into water in *The Thin Red Line* and wildlife is just as prone to suffer as human beings. The lack of narrative clarity in human dramas extends to the larger environment and nature too presents a canvas for the relentless question that drives Malick's filmmaking—the question of what it is that we can see.

The Thin Red Line is set during the Battle of Guadalcanal in the Solomon Islands (1942–43) during World War II. The campaign centers on wresting control of the island and its landing strip from the Japanese in order to safeguard American supply and communication routes in the Pacific. The film's focus is on the men of C Company of the 25th Infantry, whose initial action entails storming a hill while taking heavy fire from the Japanese-held bunker above. They eventually take the bunker and the Japanese stronghold in a Pyrrhic victory entailing heavy casualties. The company is given a week's leave, but then is confronted by advancing Japanese artillery fire. Three soldiers are sent up a river to scout for the Japanese position. Two are killed during this mission but one makes it back to warn his company of the advancing force. As the film ends, we see a new Captain arrive on Guadalcanal to replace the one that has been sent home, and some of the soldiers of C Company are shipped out.

The Thin Red Line was released in the same year (1998) as Stephen Spielberg's *Saving Private Ryan,* another World War II film that features a beach landing and a ruinous assault on a hill commanded by enemy bunkers—this time, in the Battle of Normandy against Nazi German forces. Spielberg's film is about heroic men in the midst of a punishing campaign and it earned him an Oscar for best director. The camera trains steadily on the soldiers, who are cut down with unrelenting frenzy in the extensive battle sequence at the beginning of the film. From the start, the story focuses on the character of Captain Miller and then on Private Ryan. Miller is the fatherly and capable leader who earns the devotion of his men, and Ryan is the committed soldier who opts to stay in the battle despite being given the chance to go home. *Thin Red Line* also features a paternal and humane commander in the figure of Captain Staros, but he is only one character in a large ensemble of many voices that take turns narrating their thoughts and experiences. It is hard to discern the identities of the voiceovers and the army uniforms visually blend the men together so that it is difficult to distinguish between them. Spielberg's focus on key heroic figures, on the other hand, separates the stars from the supporting cast.

The soldiers in *Thin Red Line* are like fish in a barrel during their upward assault, where the lush and waving grass of the hills feature as largely as the human beings. In some places the grass is taller than the soldiers, engulfing them; in others, their heads and torsos emerge from the greenery as if they are outgrowths of the vegetation. When men fall from gunfire, they disappear instantly into the undulating flora as if being swallowed back into the earth. Sometimes the camera's point of view slithers low through the grass, much as the men do, and at other times it offers a wide vista on this landscape, turning the lines of soldiers into marching ants. The way humans are welded to the land is poignantly articulated by Sgt. McCron, who loses all twelve of his men during the battle for the bunker. At nightfall, the sergeant inveighs against the hills—or perhaps God—asking, "Who decides who's going to die?" Tearing at the grass, he observes, "That's us. We're just dirt."

That may be so, but the dirt and what it breeds is shown over and over again in glorious splendor. Malick takes the time to look at

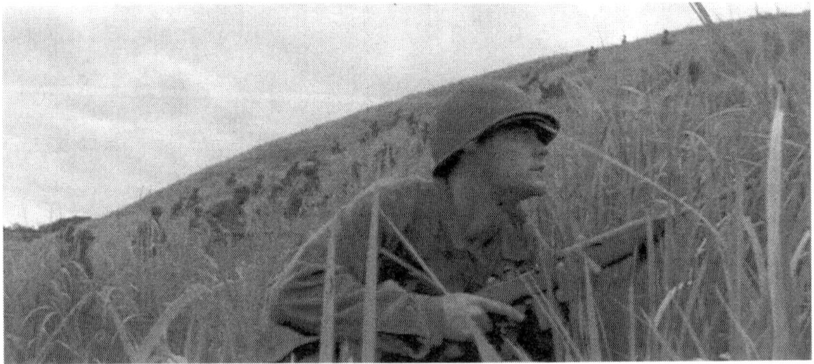

FIGURE 6.1. The men of C Company are outgrowths of the foliage and return to the landscape in death.

these things—panning up the sides of trees and walls to see the sky, and moving away from the main action to train upon the birds, reptiles, and butterflies that coexist with human preoccupations. The film takes time during battle scenes to examine the strange and beautiful behavior of leaves that shrink upon physical contact or repel water droplets like oil gliding off Teflon. After the first two soldiers are mowed down by gunfire at the start of battle, a wide-angle shot of the shadowed hills captures the rippling sunlight that crosses the land and reveals it like an epiphany. With this breaking of light, the fighting erupts in a fury.

A Christian filter naturally evokes Eden or the Promised Land, with its attendant notion of sin and eviction from paradise. Private Witt is an AWOL soldier at the beginning of the film who lives and plays with the Solomon Islander children in a pristine and heavenly land. When Witt returns to the same village after the battle for the bunker, he sees signs of disease, strife, and death. In the eyes of one viewer, "Clearly, Malick wants us to acknowledge that war inherently has the power to make us see the world as it really is—not as our self-imposed innocence has made it seem to be" (Cohen 2003, 47). Witt's certainly sees another side of the Melanesian community, perhaps as a result of his own recent experience. But a linear before-and-after fall from innocence is not so evident. For one thing, the camera's digressions to the flora, fauna, and sky occur in the *midst* of the battle scenes, juxtaposing death and beauty rather than segregating them. Private Witt himself is not irreversibly disillusioned by his darker perception of the Melanesians but goes back to his characteristic state of grace, particularly at the moment of his own death near the end of the film.

The world seen through the lenses of *The Thin Red Line* might be described as indifferently gorgeous in the face of human carnage. The film contemplates beauty in a manner quite absent in *Saving Private Ryan*, which focuses on the grit and chaos of battle in a highly realized rendition of the "war is hell" genre. But to consider such beauty callous to human pain demonstrates a myopia that Malick's landscapes actually defy. The point is not that human suffering is trivial in the grand scheme of things: it may very well be that beauty and pain are inextricably and paradoxically the same. The first voiceover in the film has Witt talking about his mother's death, ostensibly to his fellow deserter during their idyll among the Melanesian natives:

> I couldn't find nothin' beautiful or uplifting about her goin' back to God. I heard of people talk about immortality, but I

ain't seen it. I wondered how it'd be like when I died, what it'd be like to know this breath now was the last one you was ever gonna draw. I just hope I can meet it the same way she did, with the same calm. 'Cause that's where it's hidden—the immortality I hadn't seen.

Witt echoes a perspective on death that William LaFleur finds in *Maborosi*: "as possibly providing an absolutely unparalleled experience of being connected to the panoply of things" (2002, 162). Witt's own death is depicted as realizing the hope he expresses here. He is the soldier who diverts the Japanese troops so that his comrade can backtrack and warn their company about the enemy advance. As he is encircled by the Japanese troops, he looks around and settles into a state of stillness and acceptance, unfazed by the enemy demands for his surrender. He is clearly aware that he is drawing his last breath. He raises his gun in order to draw fire and is shot dead. The next scene immediately cuts to an underwater sequence of Witt swimming in play with the Melanesian children, which replicates an opening scene of the film. His "immortality" has him reintegrated into this world in its blissful version. There are no separate worlds but rather different perspectives on the same single world.

This dynamic is embodied in the interplay between Witt and Sergeant Welsh, his squad leader. Welsh proclaims, "In this world, a man himself is nothing, and there ain't no world but this one," to which Witt replies, "I've seen another world." But most significantly, Witt seems

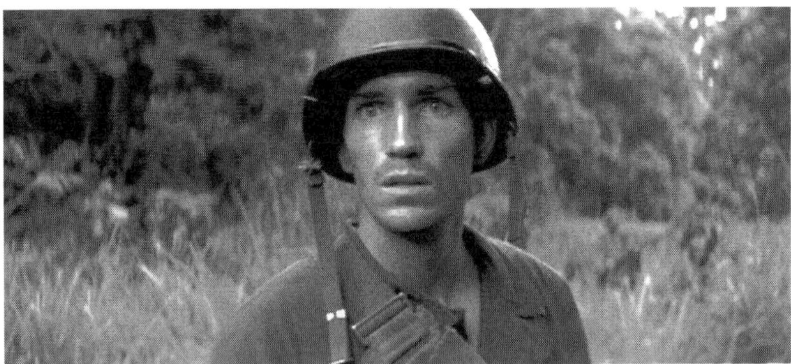

FIGURE 6.2. Private Witt is surrounded by Japanese soldiers in the moment before his death.

to be in this other world precisely at the moments of suffering and degradation. Witt's ability to be with pain is repeatedly displayed—as a stretcher-bearer attending to the wounded, in attending to the dying moments of his comrades, even in his presence with the half-starved, terrified, and deranged Japanese soldiers after their capture. In a later exchange, Welsh taunts Witt: "You still believin' in the beautiful light, are you? How do you do that? You're a magician to me." Witt replies, "I still see a spark in you." This conversation is followed by a voiceover that reiterates this duality of perspective. The voice of Private Train, who also provides the opening and closing narrations, observes: "One man looks at a dying bird and thinks there's nothing but unanswered pain, that death's got the final word. It's laughing at him. Another man sees that same bird, feels the glory, feels something smiling through it."

These opposing perceptions and experiences are further expressed as the views of different characters. Colonel Tall states: "Look at this jungle. Look at those vines, the way they twine around, swallowing everything. Nature's cruel." This sentiment reflects Tall's own embittered experience of the army, which has passed him over for promotion. Tall uses the Guadalcanal campaign as a personal battle for political advancement, disregarding the cost in his soldiers' lives. Tall appeals to nature's cruelty as justification when he relieves Captain Staros of his command for being "too soft" and unwilling to sacrifice his men. Nature is the canvas Tall uses to paint Staros as weak, but the competing perspectives of Tall and Staros, as of Welsh and Witt, suggest the nonintrinsic essence of the world, which always awaits interpretation. As Staros ships out, we hear his voice defining his experience of command for himself. He addresses his men in his mind, saying: "You are my sons, my dear sons. You live inside me now. I'll carry you wherever I go."

Malick's tendency to juxtapose alternative perspectives on the world is pointedly embodied in the figures of Mr. and Mrs. O'Brien in *The Tree of Life*. The opening voiceover by Mrs. O'Brien lays out the options quite plainly:

The nuns taught us there were two ways through life—the way of nature and the way of grace. You have to choose which one you'll follow. Grace doesn't try to please itself. Accepts being slighted, forgotten, disliked. Accepts insults and injuries. Nature only wants to please itself. Get others to please it too. Likes to lord it over them, to have its own way. It finds reasons to be unhappy when all the world is shining around it and love is smiling through all things. They taught us that no one who loves the way of grace comes to a bad end. I will be true to you, whatever comes.

Mrs. O'Brien is the indisputable figure of grace, raising three boys in Waco, Texas, in the 1950s. Mr. O'Brien, on the other hand, embodies the way of nature with a bullying love that wants to toughen his sons to survive in the world. Malick proffers suburban domesticity as more than equal to the drama of world war: a non-diegetic interlude twenty minutes into the film depicts cosmic gas and dust forming galaxies and microorganismic processes forming human life. The cradle of the family is made the pinnacle in the drama of creation itself because that is the place where our habits of perception are formed. This is made explicit in the oldest son Jack, whom we see ricocheting between his parents as a child and whose influences he struggles to reconcile as an adult.

What the O'Brien family faces is no less momentous than the question of life and death endemic to war. There is the death of Jack's friend at the local swimming pool, but the central event is the death of Jack's younger brother R. L. even though it is not depicted in the film. We merely witness Mrs. O'Brien receiving the news via a telegram. Again, narrative is sacrificed in favor of the primacy of experience. In the final resurrection sequence, the family is reunited on a shoreline crowded with people ambling to a majestic operatic soundtrack. Here Mrs. O'Brien and the rest of the family encounter R. L. as the child we have seen in the bulk of the film. Mrs. O'Brien takes him in with wonder and adoration, but in the end raises her hands to the sky and whispers, "I give him to you. I give you my son." In the next scene, the adult Jack wakes up from his dream. The resurrection, it is implied, was his reverie and his own realization of the way of grace and acceptance modeled by his mother.

Cinematic images of children at play feature heavily in *Tree of Life*, which again pairs the idyllic and the menacing, such as the scene of ecstatic boys running through the billowing spray of the insecticide DDT that was widely and indiscriminately used before its toxicity was documented. The specter of the present play in tandem with the future harm it presents makes for a rather ambiguous vista. The vignettes of Jack's own sport begins with the enchantments of childhood play, under the guidance of his mother, but matures into adolescent episodes of vandalism, cruelty, and sexual aggression in the company of like-minded boys. The influence of Mr. O'Brien's way of nature and the way Jack is also beholden to it is suggested here. But the progression from innocent play to unintended malevolence is also a seamless transition. Life flows from one thing to the next until it becomes difficult to separate things in any stable way. This sense of movement is repeatedly visualized in Malick's filmmaking, which creates a visual analogue to the ultimate nonduality of the ways of grace and nature.

Movement and Flow

The Thin Red Line is a meditation on good and evil that goes beyond jingoistic distinctions between good guys and bad guys, and even beyond the ideals of heroism and sacrifice that seem to be the only virtuous possibilities when faced with the senselessness of mutual human destruction. Ethical questions about the origins of good and evil are trumped by meditations that dissolve the boundaries between them. When the battle climaxes with the American takeover of the Japanese position, the din of gunfire and screams fade in volume while the following questions layer over the scenes of rampage and death:

> This great evil. Where does it come from? How'd it steal into the world? What seed, what root did it grow from? Who's doing this? Who's killing us? Robbing us of life and light. Mocking us with the sight of what we might've known. Does our ruin benefit the earth? Does it help the grass to grow, the sun to shine? Is this darkness in you, too? Have you passed through this night?

This climactic sequence offers our first glimpse of Japanese faces and bodies, in contrast to their previous incarnation as the barrage of gunfire that cuts down the American soldiers during their assault on the hill. The enemy that is finally subdued is a ragtag band of half-starved, delirious, and broken humanity that robs the viewer of any sense of victory. The question, "Who's doing this? Who's killing us?" is asked over the slaughter of Japanese soldiers, raising the "us" to a mutually inclusive if not universal category, just as the questions "Is this darkness in you, too? Have you passed through this night?" seem to address us all equally.

"Us" and "them" do not have stable referents as the identities of killer and victim continually exchange and evolve.

The protean dynamics of love is an equal focus of meditation in *The Thin Red Line*. Private Bell's reveries of his wife intersperse the film, shot as his memories of the dance of their lovemaking and intertwining bodies. The voiceover wonders in amazement at its source, and they pose parallel inquiries to the film's questions about evil: "Love. Where does it come from? Who lit this flame in us? No war can put it out, conquer it. I was a prisoner. You set me free." Bell is sustained by the anticipation of returning to his wife even though three years have passed. His voice intones, "My dear wife, you get something twisted out of your insides by all this blood, filth, and noise. I want to stay changeless for you. I want to come back to you the man I was before." Bell's desire for stasis is contradicted by the imperative of movement, however. During the lull between battles, Private Bell receives a letter from his wife informing him that she has fallen in love with another man and wishes to divorce. "I just got too lonely," she explains. The impersonal nature of her explanation tells us both everything and nothing at all. The mystery of love's beginnings is equaled by the mystery of its disappearance.

Of course, there is no serious attempt to offer answers to these questions about the source of love and strife. Instead, Malick turns to movement such as images of flowing water to suggest that these events are the rhythms and patterns of human experience. In the final voiceover, we see Private Train standing in the back of the transport ship leaving the island. Over the image of flowing water, we hear his voice say:

> Where is it that we were together? Who were you that I lived with? The brother. The friend. Darkness, light. Strife and love. Are they the workings of one mind? The features of the same face? Oh, my soul. Let me be in you now. Look out through my eyes. Look out at the things you made. All things shining.

This is not the first time we hear the suggestion of a fundamental oneness. In an early scene when Private Witt attends to a wounded soldier during his duties as a stretcher bearer, we hear him say, "Maybe all men got one big soul everybody's a part of, all faces are the same man. One big self." We see flowing water here as well, in the stream where Witt pours cleansing water over the head of a wounded man in an act

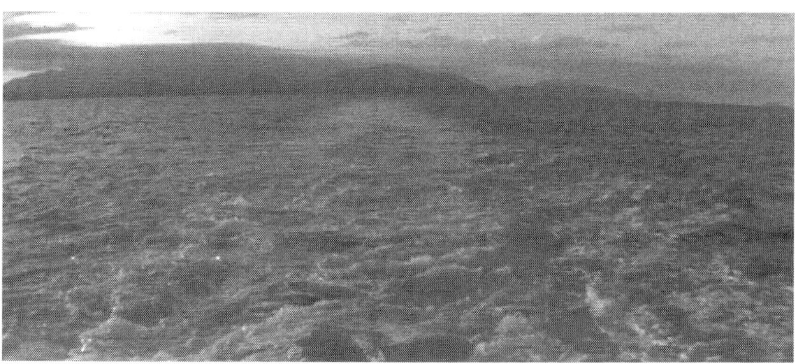

FIGURE 6.3. The image of flowing water sustains Private Train's reflection: "Darkness, light. Strife and love. Are they the workings of one mind? The features of the same face?"

that reads equally well as Christian baptism and Bodhisattva compassion. Water is also metaphorically invoked to speak of a fundamental unity. Private Bell reflects on his wife and intones, "We. We together. One being. Flow together like water. Till I can't tell you from me. I drink you. Now. Now."

The malleability of water reveals its intrinsically empty nature marvelously—it conforms to any vessel it occupies because it has no necessary form or meaning. The idea of flow is not limited to the convergence of parts that are inherently good or evil, or the necessity of taking the bad along with the good. It implies instead the interpenetration of good and evil, in that each contains the other in itself. Good and evil seem to be equal possibilities in the flow of experience, like ripples and waves that form momentary configurations in ever-moving bodies of water. In the context of the inhumanity of war, then, the opportunities for humaneness are always present. A sergeant states, "I look at that boy dying, I don't feel nothin'. I don't care about nothin' anymore," and Welsh responds, "Sounds like bliss." Welsh's cynicism suggests that the only kind of transcendence possible is simply numbness to pain. In action, however, he demonstrates an ability to change brutality into compassion. Welsh is the one who saves Witt from a court martial for being AWOL by reintegrating him into his unit. During the initial assault on the Japanese bunker, Welsh is the one who relieves a terrified soldier from duty. In the midst of that battle, Welsh is also the one who dodges a rain of fire to bring morphine to a dying soldier screaming in pain. Much as we saw in *Rashomon*, debates about good and evil are irresolvable, perhaps because words and concepts demand dichotomies that remain forever in opposition to each other. Only action and movement can pass beyond the "either/or" distinction that words create. Witt has concrete evidence when he tells Welsh: "I still see a spark in you."

To the Wonder is particularly evocative of movement—in the choreography of the actors, in the camerawork, and in the story itself. In terms of plot, the film is a story of romantic love between the American Neil and the single mother Marina whom he meets in Paris. Neil brings Marina and her ten-year-old daughter Tatiana to his native Oklahoma, where he takes a job as an environmental inspector. At first, life is happy, but their love unravels and Marina returns to Paris. Neil gets involved with an old childhood friend named Jane but this relationship too falls apart. Marina returns to Oklahoma, where she and Neil reunite and marry, only to flounder once more when Marina has a tryst with a local carpenter. As one might expect, there are no dialogues or character portrayals that explain why these relationships take these turns. Instead, Malick shows us an ongoing pattern of togetherness seguing into separation and merging back into union. Love is also the flow of opposites and this movement itself stands in for the story that is bigger than the particulars of any two individuals. In a voiceover, Marina asks, "What is this love that loves us? That comes from nowhere? From all around. The sky. You, cloud. You love me too." The images during this narration are of flowing water in a stream.

The focus on movement is accentuated by how much Marina dances her way through the landscape. This includes not only the plains of Oklahoma, which Malick favors in the glow of sunset gold, but the interior of Neil's large suburban house and even the supermarket where Marina whirls with sundry dry goods. The *New York Times* review refers rather derisively to Marina's "serious commitment to twirling" (Scott 2013), which is replicated to a lesser degree by Jane. As Olga Kurylenko (Marina) reports, "Every actor has to move in a Terrence Malick film— that's the requirement. If you stop, he'll tell you, 'No, no, keep moving.' You can't be static. It's a choreography." Jessica Chastain (Mrs. O'Brien) confirms that working with Malick is like being part of "a ballet dance company without a soloist. We're all moving together, and that includes the cinematographer, the focus puller, the camera operator, Terry and the actor. It's all five of us contributing to the shot, to seeing what the moment is" (Hynes 2013). Chastain's choreography in *Tree of Life* includes partnering with a butterfly and even floating in midair. *To the Wonder* is notably dynamic in its camerawork. Malick has persistently favored the mobility of the handheld camera, but the cinematography of *To the Wonder* is in constant motion, as if its point of view is that of flowing water itself. The camera—and the audience along with it—is the constantly moving stream that courses in and out of the lives of Marina, Neil, and Jane. We eavesdrop on a snatch of conversation and glimpse a moment before flowing on to another vista in the human landscape. The minimal role of dialogue in all of Malick films reaches its height in *To the Wonder*, which favors movement both in the viewer and what is viewed above all else.

As with Jack's dream of resurrection and reconciliation at the end of *Tree of Life*, *To the Wonder* also concludes with a dreamlike vision of hope. The final scene depicts Neil in a different house with two young children. The view then cuts to Marina lying in a dew-drenched field, through which she ambles until her face is caught in the orange-yellow glow of sunlight. She turns and the final shot is of Mont St. Michel. The voiceover in this final sequence has Marina saying: "Love that loves us. Thank you." The presence of the young children suggests that some years have passed since the previous scene in which Marina and Neil appear to have divorced and Marina boards a plane back to France. Prior to this departure, however, Neil makes peace with Marina's infidelity by kneeling before her and taking her hands in his, as if seeking forgiveness himself. The montage of images suggests a period of reflection as Neil accompanies Father Quintana during his ministry with the ill and the wretched, during which we can hear the voice of Father Quintana reciting the Prayer of St. Patrick. He ends with the lines: "Flood our souls with your spirit and life, so completely that our lives may only be a reflection of yours. Shine through us."

The origins of love and hate cannot be fathomed, and so the more fundamental question becomes what ultimately moves us to one or the other. The voice of Private Train asks, "How did we lose the good that was given us? Let it slip away. Scattered. Careless. What's keeping us from reaching out, touching the glory?" Innate to this question is the presumption that it is always possible to reach out and touch the glory. Darkness and light are features of the same face, and therefore both are possible at all times. With the right movement of vision and action, it is possible to render "all things shining."

Conclusion

Malick's invitation to create the story through open-ended filmmaking recapitulates the Buddhist visions offered by the films examined in this book. Like the Bodhisattva Guanyin who looks down and hears the cries of all beings in Kim Kiduk's *Spring, Summer, Fall, Winter . . . and Spring,* Malick's camera takes in the rhythms of human action, reflecting its sorrows but also suggesting another reality behind it. Similar to the way the Korean film collapses the distance between samsara and nirvana, Malick juxtaposes wretchedness and grace and wonders if they are really separate things. And like the varying discernments of the ghost-wife in Nonzee Nimibutr's *Nang Nak* and of the rape in Akira Kurosawa's *Rashomon,* Malick uses his characters to demonstrate that how and what an individual sees determines the qualities of their actions and the worlds they occupy. Finally, like the non-diegetic filmmaking of Hirokazu Kore'eda's *Maborosi,* which favors landscapes and incidental moments over narrative omniscience, Malick fills his frames with the breathtaking visions that are possible once dualistic ways of constructing meaning are transcended in favor of a synchronous and nondualistic insight. What results is filmmaking that showcases the distinct virtuosities of film as a visual medium.

By the time we reach the works of Terrence Malick, all signs of the Buddha's presence have been erased. But this is in accord with Mahāyāna conceptions of the dharmakāya, which is the ultimate body of the Buddha and the source of its many manifestations. The dharmakāya in itself is beyond form because it is fundamentally empty. By the same token, when a vision of the Buddha is obtained, it is incumbent upon the seer to deconstruct it:

> Having thought: "Did these Tathāgatas come from somewhere?
> Did I go anywhere?" he understands that those Tathāgatas
> did not come from anywhere. Having comprehended that
> his body did not go anywhere either, he thinks: "These Triple
> Worlds are nothing but thought." (PraS 3L)

In early Buddhist understandings of the Buddha, he is absent because he has attained nirvana and thus disappeared from the wheel of samsaric existence. With the rise of Mahāyāna traditions, the ultimate and empty dharmakāya is ever-present in the world but invisible because it cannot be reduced to any particular form. And because the dharmakāya is invisible, "To see the Buddha in his dharmakāya, one must know what a Buddha knows—one must *be* a Buddha" (Gifford 2011, 160). But as the layout of Borobudur demonstrates, to be a Buddha also means descending back into the world of forms as the place where one can see in the manner of the Buddha himself. It is this final portion of Borobudur with which we will conclude our consideration of the contemporary medium of film and its Buddhist possibilities.

CHAPTER 7

Descent into the World

Buddhist Visionary Practices

The practice of seeing the Buddha, as attested in classical Buddhist scriptures, is called *buddhānusmṛti* (Pāli: *anusatti*), which means a meditative contemplation that "recollects" the Buddha and "calls him to mind." In the Pāli texts, this practice entails a short recitation of the qualities of the Buddha, such as the description that he is "perfected in knowledge" and "the teacher of gods and humans."[1] Focusing on the spiritually wholesome qualities of the Buddha is thought to be beneficial by displacing afflicted thoughts, thereby producing an alteration in consciousness. In Mahāyāna Buddhism, the practice of buddhānusmṛti evolved to include explicit visualization of the Buddha's body. Hence, the physical qualities of the Buddha become objects of focus, and one is instructed to concentrate on how the Buddha is "with all the finest aspects, handsome, beautiful, lovely to behold, and endowed with bodily perfection" (PraS 8A). The recitation of iconic features, such as the thirty-two marks of the Great Man enumerated in both Pāli and Sanskrit sources, clearly point to the use of images as an aid in buddhānusmṛti practice (Zurcher 2013, 500).

Visionary experiences are central in Mahāyāna Buddhism, as attested in the Pure Land and Perfection of Wisdom texts,[2] and the *Gaṇḍavyūha*, which "self-consciously embraces imaginative and projective vision as an integral part of Buddhist practice" (McMahan 2002, 112). References to visualizing Buddhas and Buddha-lands are made across Mahāyāna sources, and although the names and even the techniques of the practices vary, "in essence [they are] the same developed form of buddhānusmṛti" (Harrison 1992, 224). The Chinese *nienfo* (Japanese: *nembutsu*) of Pure Land Buddhism is one version of buddhānusmṛti, in which chanting the name of the Buddha Amitābha accompanies the practice of visualization. So is the deity yoga of Tibetan tantra, in which Buddhas and bodhisattvas in the image of benevolent and wrathful deities serve as objects of meditative contemplation.[3]

An important and common feature of these visualization practices—which is emblematic of their shared heritage—are repeated reminders that the Buddhas both seen and visualized are ultimately empty. The early Mahāyāna visualization text called *Pratyutpanna-buddha-saṃmukhāvasthita-samadhi* ("the samadhi of direct encounter with the buddhas of the present") states that "when in this way one obtains the samādhi of emptiness by concentrating on the Tathāgatha without objectification, that is known as the calling to mind of the Buddha" (PraS 3F). To call the Buddha to mind without seizing upon that experience as the apprehension of an independent and objectively existing reality is to discern in the proper way. Hence, recollecting the Buddha is for the purpose of seeing properly, as the Buddha himself did, and what is actually recollected simply provides an opportune occasion:

> Attention is shifted away from the professed religious value or significance of the ritual acts themselves and directed instead toward a critique of the fundamental processes by which they (together with all other phenomena) are conceived. (Stevenson 1986, 65)

In the logic of this meditation, then, calling the Buddha to mind is only one way of attaining the discernment of emptiness. While the figure of the Buddha is an overt reminder of the qualities that he attained and the wisdom he achieved, "any type of activity or circumstance—religious as well as mundane—can serve as an equally effective ground for meditative discernment" (Stevenson 1986, 77).[4] In fact, if the point of meditation is the discernment of emptiness and emptiness is the mark of all things, this seems to mandate a movement away from the Buddha to the wider world itself as the field of practice.

The temple Borobudur appears to visually and ritually embody this sentiment. In her detailed study of the temple, Julie Gifford argues that the stairs that allow ascent and descent through the monument functioned as the locus of a significant ritual. This ritual would be the

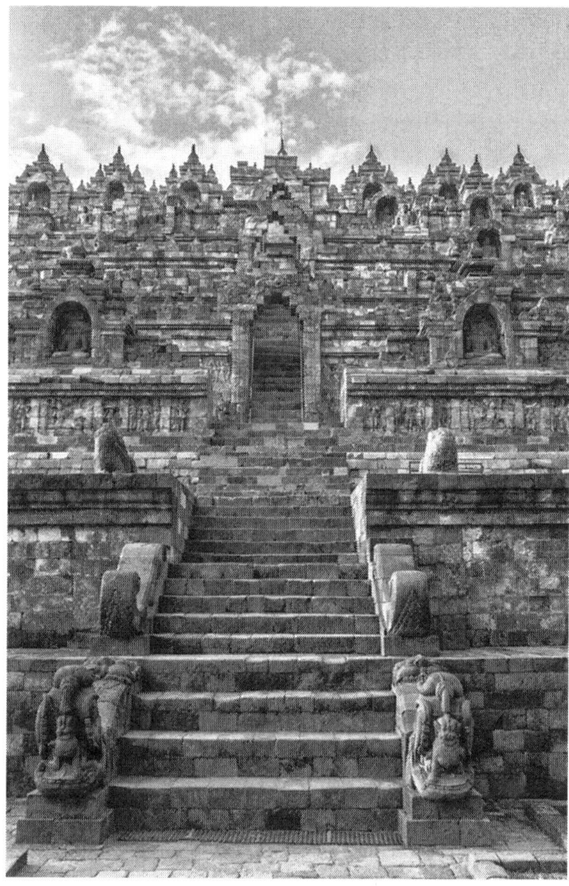

FIGURE 7.1. The perspective from the bottom of the stairs of Borobudur provides a clear view of the niche Buddhas, who appear to accompany beings descending the temple. (Photograph by Alexander Ipfelkofer)

final act in the experience of Borobudur, comprising the descent and exit from the temple after having climbed all the way to the empty stūpa at its center. The descent and departure is just as important as the experience of Borobudur itself:

Having performatively constituted himself as an advanced bodhisattva on the terraces, the celebrant returned from the purified fields to the world, bringing the soteriological power of the cosmic Buddhas with him. This is entirely in keeping with the Mahāyāna virtue of compassion, which the bodhisattva demonstrates by remaining in saṃsāra, returning to the world again and again for the sake of saving all sentient beings. (Gifford 2011, 165)

Gifford's argument for this reading of the descent from Borobudur is based on traditional legend, ritual, and images. After the Buddha taught the Dharma to his mother in the Trāyatrimśa heaven where she had been reborn (and where the first image of the Buddha was fashioned from sandalwood), Śākyamuni descended back to earth by way of a jeweled ladder formed by the god Śakra.[5] This famous episode from the Buddha's life is represented in Indian, Southeast Asian, and Tibetan Buddhist art and ritually reenacted in contemporary Theravādin societies when monks descend their hilltop monasteries after the rainy season retreat. Laypeople line the bottom of the hill to make offerings of food and supplies, and this auspicious opportunity to make merit is called *Devorohana*, or "coming down from the deva world" (Gifford 2011, 167). With this ritual enactment, monks function as stand-ins for the Buddha and embody the bodhisattva principle of being physically present in the world for the sake of devotees.

The logic of emptiness says that the historical Buddha was only one manifestation of an ultimately formless emptiness, which is why Buddhas proliferate in the course of Buddhist tradition—particularly as bodhisattvas whose raison d'être is to be present in the world. The ritual progression of Borobudur suggests that anyone who ascends and then descends from this microcosm of the dharmakāya world can also fulfill the role of a bodhisattva. The "visual rhetoric" of Borobudur strongly intimates this by displaying multiple images of the Buddha that are visible from the bottom of the stairs. Looking up the steps provides the best vantage point on the 432 niche Buddhas carved into the top of the gallery walls. These Buddhas are separate from the seventy-two stūpa Buddhas on the open-air terraces. The niche Buddhas adorn the galleries that form the lower part of the temple, and every level of these niche Buddhas is visible from the bottom of the stairs. This creates an interesting visual effect:

The niches draw the eye from one Buddha figure to another, and because the stairs introduce a vertical element, the eye is

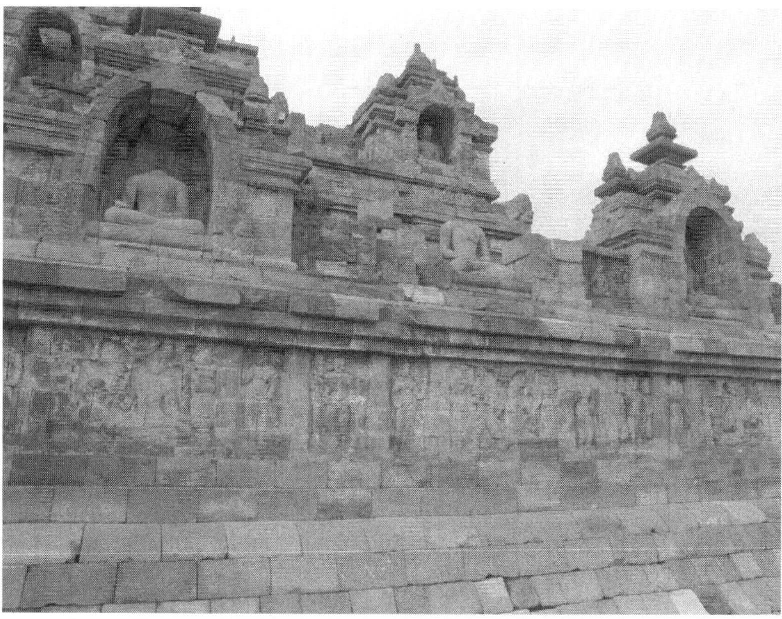

FIGURE 7.2. A close-up of some of the 432 niche Buddhas on top of the gallery walls. (Photograph by Robert DeCaroli)

> naturally drawn up and down. When one scans the monument is this way, it creates a visual illusion of movement. This illusion of movement helps the images in the niches function as a representation of the Buddha's descent. (Gifford 2011, 167)

The suggestion of this descent accompanies the view of the person coming down the stairs, as if he or she is in the company of the Buddha. More than this, the kinship and even equivalence between the Buddha and descending person are implied. It is in the nature of Buddhas to descend into the world and by that token, those in the world fulfill the function of being Buddhas. Buddhas and bodhisattvas, after all, never walk the earth in their cosmic forms but rather take on earthly manifestations such as Śākyamuni or the Dalai Lama. In the circulatory logic of the bodhisattva ideal, what goes up must come down and what is in the world is ultimately equivalent to what is supposedly above it in the formless realm of the dharmakāya.

This logic has been tapped in this book to argue that film instantiates a seamless continuity with the ritual, visual, and meditative practices of traditional Buddhism. This means considering film as more than a way to inform audiences by depicting the life of Buddhist figures or by "drafting" mainstream movies to showcase Buddhist teachings. The movement away from overt Buddhist signs draws our attention to film itself as a ritual practice, above and beyond its obvious capacities as an educational tool. One does not learn any discursive Buddhist content from the films of Terrence Malick but rather undergoes experiences, and what makes them Buddhist are the qualities of disciplined and attentive participation that they enable.

Film as Visionary Practice

This is perhaps more evident in non-feature films that are relatively free of the requirements of normal storytelling. I will consider two instances that form bookend examples, and demonstrate how they replicate and extend Buddhist forms of ritual practice. The first work is Anthony Cerniello's video *Danielle* (2013), whose eponymous subject ages from a young girl to an elderly woman in the space of less than five minutes. This work utilizes the capacity of film to collapse time to the extreme—or at least considerably more than Kim Kiduk's *Spring, Summer, Fall, Winter . . . and Spring*. The second example is Andy Warhol's art film *Empire* (1964), which deliberately slows down its image capture of the Empire State Building to produce a film that is more than eight hours long. This film considerably extends Kore'eda's and Malick's long takes on the nonnarrative moment. Both *Danielle* and *Empire* take advantage of the technological capabilities of their medium to create distinctive viewing experiences. Commentators therefore pay a lot of attention to the mechanics of their technical manipulations. My interest here, in contrast, is in the ritualized practices of seeing that they instantiate and elicit.

Anthony Cerniello's *Danielle* opens on a frontal headshot of a young Asian girl against a completely white background, accompanied by the low hum of a synthesizer. For the full duration of the video the girl looks directly at the viewer and does not move except for some occasional blinking and subtle eye movements. The primary thing she does is to age, marked only by the intermittent pulsing of the synthesizer from its otherwise steady hum. The remarkable thing about this act of aging is how imperceptibly the girl's face alters right in front of

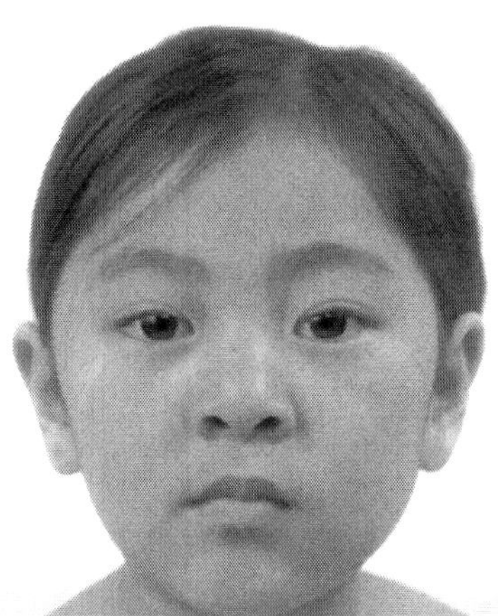

FIGURE 7.3. Danielle as she appears 8 seconds into the video.

the viewer's eyes—for the first full minute, the growth of the subject is virtually undetectable until one realizes that she has matured into an adolescent by about a minute and a half into the video. At two minutes she is a woman, and a minute after that the lines around her eyes and the loosening of the skin on her chin and neck has put her well into middle age. The video concludes at four minutes and twenty seconds,

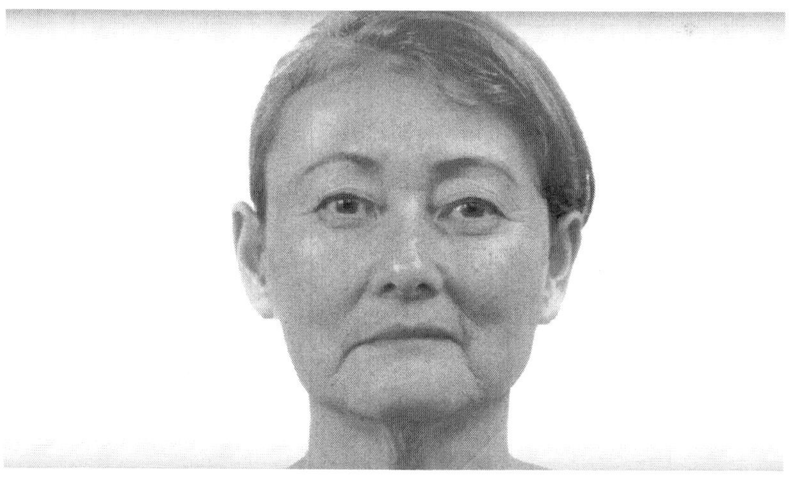

FIGURE 7.4. Danielle as she appears 4 minutes and 17 seconds into the video.

when Danielle appears to be in her sixties. Her hair is not yet completely white, and her lightly spotted skin is still unmarked by the full cascade of wrinkles that marks truly advanced age.

Cerniello's video is available on Vimeo with the following tag: "I attempted to create a person in order to emulate the aging process. The idea was that something is happening but you can't see it but you can feel it, like aging itself." Cerniello's artistic and technological feat was created through a combination of photography and animation, using footage of his friend Danielle and her youngest cousins to her oldest female relatives. Cerniello, who is a professional film editor, scanned and edited the montage of photos, and afterward his collaborators Nathan Meier, Edmund Earle, and George Cuddy brought the images to life through animation. The result replicates the experience of watching one's own children grow, particularly the potent combination of the daily contact that blunts awareness of change, on the one hand, and then the sudden shock and awakening to how much the person has altered, on the other. The process happens in front of one's eyes but it is imperceptible and can only be experienced as a startling aftereffect.

Time-lapse photography has been widely utilized to document long-term change and processes, of course. *Danielle* calls to mind the photographer Noah Kalina, who took a daily self-portrait for twelve and a half years, from January 11, 2000, to June 30, 2012, and posted them all to his website with the title *Everyday*. The resulting video of 4,514 photographs has a run time of 7:41 at ten frames per second. Unlike *Danielle, Everyday* is documentary art that evinces the actual life of one person, starting at the age of nineteen, who is caught in the vagaries of the everyday as his changing environment, dress, and hair length flash at lightning speed across the screen. Compared to the subject of *Danielle*, however, Kalina ages only twelve years in almost twice the amount of time, and the jumpiness of the rapid-fire succession of photos with its distracting variations do not create the focused mood of Cerniello's work. Raw footage of "real life," in other words, sometimes displays less than what artifice can, such as the digitally manipulated images of the multiple people comprising Danielle.

Buddhist visualization practices are also a form of artifice that creates visions for the sake of seeing more clearly. Discerning the truth of old age, illness, and death is a standard trope of Buddhist practice, and one that has required artistic technologies in order to underscore what is usually too invisible to be taken in. The well-known tale of Kisāgotamī tells of the young mother who sought out the Buddha to cure her dead child and who is told instead to collect a mustard seed from a household that has not known death. She fails, of course, and the fruitless task awakens her to the truth of life and she becomes a follower of the Buddha.[6] The conceit of Kisāgotamī's naivete—that she really needed to personally knock on doors to confirm that death comes to all families—is a literary contrivance that encourages one to inhabit a truth that is normally and perhaps purposefully forgotten. This narrative stratagem—and its brevity—is necessary to awaken a kind of vision that runs much deeper than simple intellectual knowledge of human mortality.

The fact of constant change and the simultaneous births and deaths that construct all events—most particularly the putative self or person—is one of Buddhism's most central visions. And it is one of the most difficult to discern (most of all within oneself) because we can only look at ourselves within the same time scale in which change actually occurs, and to exist within that process makes it difficult to see as an explicit object. The *Satipaṭṭhāna Sutta* (M 10), which is one of the foundational texts on mindfulness meditation, prescribes a practice that again reflects on the process only after the fact. This is the famous charnel ground meditations in which the practitioner is instructed to contemplate corpses in nine distinct stages of decay, from only a few days dead, when it is bloated, livid and oozing matter, to its last stages when it turns into a heap of bleached bones and then dust. The progression of decomposition is rather finely parsed, distinguishing between stage three, for example, when there is a skeleton with some flesh and blood held together by tendons, and stage four, when there is a blood-smeared skeleton with no flesh but still held together by tendons. If *Danielle* were to move past old age into death and beyond, the charnel ground meditations could function very well as a script for those successive states.

The *Satipaṭṭhāna Sutta*'s meditational instructions comprise one early artistic method of producing Buddhist visions, made necessary by the limits of ordinary experience. One can wonder to what degree actual charnel grounds cooperated in offering up neatly arranged corpses and skeletons arrayed according to the nine stages of decay. Clearly it is the *text* of the *Satipaṭṭhāna Sutta* itself and its clinically ordered distinctions that produce the desired effect of mentally enlivening Buddhist understandings of the nature of human existence. The text says, in fact, that the practitioner contemplates "*as though* he were to see a corpse thrown aside in a charnel ground" (M I.58; emphasis added) rather than instructing monks to actually go to the charnel grounds. To be sure, the premise of the meditations suggests that visual prompts—that is to say, actual bodies—were readily embraced as aids to mental visualization. In the *Visuddhimagga*, Buddhaghosa instructs monks to go and meditate upon actual corpses—but only after taking careful precautions. After warning against the possibility of encountering robbers on the road and wild beasts on the charnel grounds, Buddhaghosa also instructs the meditator to remain at some distance from the corpse—lest he gag at the smell or become frightened by the sight, and also to avoid corpses of the opposite sex in order to avoid "the wrong kind of excitement" (Vm VI, 12–42). Unstructured experience can have a way of derailing meditative practice and its aim of generating the appropriate internal vision—in this case, insight into the truth of impermanence and the inevitable decay of the body. The point of contemplative practice is to produce and maintain such insight at will, unencumbered by the distractions of normal life situations. The *Satipaṭṭhāna Sutta* is not only more readily available than actual corpses, it is less encumbered by potential hindrances. Hence, art is necessary.

The art of *Danielle* shares the *Satipaṭṭhāna Sutta*'s strategy of focusing our attention on the passage of time and is better at supplying the visual experience that texts can only evoke through description. The fact that Danielle is actually a montage of many people and the fact that the aging process is simulated is a fine actualization of the Buddhist view that the illusion of art is necessary to awaken to the illusory nature of life itself, resulting from its ephemerality. The power of art to focus the attention and sustain awareness is superior to the dulling effects of "real life," and Buddhist contemplative practices are themselves a kind of internal cinema of the mind that aims to vivify what the tradition takes to be ultimately real. The ability to do this takes disciplined effort, and works like *Danielle* are in lock-step with the practice of scaffolding the kind of vision that in time is supposed to become independently and internally sustained.

The technology of film works in more than one way and can go in the opposite direction of slowing down our experiences. If the fast-forwarding effect of *Danielle* works in tandem with Buddhist meditations on the ephemerality of life and its inescapable endings, a film such as *Empire* resonates with Buddhist ritual practices that cultivate the capacity to see things in the proper way by holding one's gaze. *Empire* was filmed from the forty-first floor of the Time-Life Building. Andy Warhol and

his crew shot six hours and thirty-eight minutes of footage but the film
is projected at a slower speed to create a movie of over eight hours in
length. The Museum of Modern Art in New York possesses the original
film and provides this description of the work:

> *Empire* consists of a single stationary shot of the Empire State
> Building filmed from 8:06 p.m. to 2:42 a.m., July 25–26,
> 1964. The eight-hour, five-minute film, which is typically
> shown in a theater, lacks a traditional narrative or characters.
> The passage from daylight to darkness becomes the film's nar-
> rative, while the protagonist is the iconic building that was
> (and is again) the tallest in New York City. Warhol lengthened
> *Empire*'s running time by projecting the film at a speed of
> sixteen frames per second, slower than its shooting speed of
> twenty-four frames per second, thus making the progression to
> darkness almost imperceptible. Non-events such as a blinking
> light at the top of a neighboring building mark the passage of
> time. According to Warhol, the point of this film—perhaps
> his most famous and influential cinematic work—is to "see
> time go by." (http://www.moma.org/collection/works/89507)

Warhol's aspiration to exhibit time going by is analogous to Cerniello's desire to see the aging process, and despite its opposing strategy
of slowing time down rather than speeding it up, the theme of imper-
ceptibility marks both. *Empire* visualizes time through changes in the
environment rather than in the edifice itself, which is relatively immobile.
What moves instead are the changes in natural light as well as the onset
of artificial lighting such as the floodlights that come on at night, and
the blinking light on the top of an adjacent tower. Some entities are
made to defy perishability, at least compared to human lives, and so its
own invisible timeline of change and eventual decay must be marked by
external events that move at a faster pace.

The fact that Warhol chose to slow down these visible markers of
time—such as the coming of night—is noteworthy. *Empire* was shot in
the middle of the summer when the sun traces its longest arc over the
sky and creates the lengthiest and most gradual of sunsets. By slowing
that process even further, the progression to darkness is extended and
made almost imperceptible. If the purpose of the film is to see time go
by then it handicaps the effort by slowing the pace to near stillness,

rendering the experience akin to staring at a painting. The actress Mary Woronov in fact stumbled upon this insight during a 2008 Warhol retrospective at the Gershwin Hotel in midtown Manhattan, where *Empire* was projected on the lobby wall:

> I realized that Andy never meant to do a film. He was doing a painting. Pop art put the image back in painting and Andy took it even further and put the image on film instead of canvas. He wasn't directing, he was painting. It's only taken me 40 years to realize that these films were never meant to screen in a theater, where I thought they were boring. They were meant to hang on a wall. They are Andy's greatest paintings. (http://www.warholstars.org/empire.html)

If we imagine *Empire* as a painting on a wall that one can come back to at different times to see the subject under different conditions, then we might be reminded of Claude Monet's depictions of Rouen Cathedral, which he captured at different times of day and in different seasons through over thirty paintings in the years 1892 and 1893. His purpose was to call attention to the effects of lighting, and this extensive exercise in aesthetic observation also has deep philosophical implications. If the appearance of the cathedral changes in different atmospheric conditions, is each instance of appearance that of the same cathedral or of different entities? Does the identity of the cathedral lie in some extrasensory plane beyond its changing appearances or is it constituted in the very act of observation—which can only take place under the varying conditions of light that make visual perception possible at all? The apparent solidity of monuments such as the Rouen Cathedral and the Empire State Building become questionable in the wake of art that poses the question of what exactly it is that one sees from one moment to the next. Monet's Cathedral series raises doubts about the inherent stability of the object it portrays, and so does *Empire*. The latter in a sense folds Monet's multiple depictions of the same building into one continuous work by slowing film almost to the point of stasis, on the one hand, while simultaneously encompassing the changes wrought by the movement of time, on the other.

What *Empire* features that paintings cannot, however, is the suggestion that the viewer should remain focused on it for its full eight-hour duration. A film is supposed to be watched from beginning to end even when it embodies only the barest whisper of a story, thereby commanding one's time to a degree that static portraits do not. The film's equivalence in length to the standard workday suggests the labor of the undertaking and pushes the viewing experience to the level of a contemplative discipline. If one were to seriously undertake a full screening of *Empire*, without drifting off into daydreams and other mental distractions, a primary way of concentrating on this barely-moving image might be to scrutinize its constituent elements until the whole entity is committed to memory. While the gradual evolutions in Warhol's portrait of the Empire State Building raises questions about its ultimate stability (in the manner of Monet's cathedrals), its long temporal duration invites an intense visual encounter with the form and provides the opportunity to instantiate and fix it within one's own mind.

Staring fixedly at an object for hours on end is common in Buddhist meditation practice, particularly in the kind of visualization rituals already discussed in this and previous chapters. Consider the depictions of Maitreya's abode in the third gallery of Borobudur, specifically panels III-20 to III-39, each of which features one aspect of the palace interior by turns—such as the bells, the banners, the lotus blossoms, and other objects that festoon the scene. Julie Gifford argues that this series of compositions both depicts what the pilgrim Sudhana sees and what the pilgrim to Borobudur is also encouraged to see, which is a meditative visualization of a purified Buddha-field: "Not only do they depict the visual elements found in a purified field, the . . . sequences also recapitulate the meditative procedure by which the practitioner builds up a complex mental picture of a purified field from a series of vividly imaged parts" (2011, 82). Panels III-20 to III-39 break down a single scene into multiple images in order to guide the observer in focusing on discrete features piece-by-piece so that one may finally assemble a mental picture of the whole.

Empire does not isolate the elements of its subject one at a time, of course, but rather invites a sustained scrutiny of an empirical object whose physical reality—in contrast to Maitreya's palace—appears to be indisputably real. But the questions raised above about its actual stability can be engaged further by considering the *Amitāyurdhyāna Sūtra* ("sūtra on the meditation on Amitāyus"),[7] which focuses on otherworldly visions and provides a different perspective on what it means to experience something as existing. As one of the three central Pure Land texts in Chinese and Japanese Buddhism, the *Amitāyurdhyāna Sūtra* gives instructions on how to obtain a vision of the Buddha Amitābha (Chinese: O-mi-to fo; Japanese: Amida) and his Western Pure Land by meditating on thirteen successive objects. The first six visualizations focus on the Pure Land and begin with contemplating the setting sun in the West until one is "able to visualize it clearly, whether your eyes are open or closed" (AdS 342a). Then one is told to visualize other elements such as the water, the ground, and the trees of the Pure Land, providing descriptions that guide the imagination. Because the Pure Land is by definition somewhere other than in the present world, the point of these exercises is to actively create the Pure Land in one's own mind—as if this is akin to actually going there. Seeing an entity in the world, on the one hand, and imagining it in the mind, on the other, elide together as equal acts of consciousness.[8]

As a result, the act of vividly bringing objects to life in the mind is repeatedly exhorted. For example, the text instructs one to: "Envision the western direction as entirely flooded by water. Then picture the water as clear and pure, and let this vision be distinctly perceived" (AdS 342a). Sometimes the guided visualizations are lengthy and detailed, such as in the contemplation of the trees of the Pure Land:

> Visualize each one and then form an image of seven rows of trees, each being eight thousand yojanas high and adorned with seven-jeweled blossoms and leaves. Each blossom and leaf has the colors of various jewels. From the beryl-colored blossoms and leaves issues forth a golden light. From the crystal-colored [blossoms and leaves] issues forth a crimson light. . . . Coral, amber, and all the other jewels serve as illuminating ornaments. Splendid nets of pearls cover the trees. Between these seven rows of nets covering each tree there are five hundred koṭis of palaces adorned with exquisite flowers, like the palace of the Brahmā king, where celestial children naturally dwell. (AdS 342b)

The description of the trees goes on for some time in this manner with the aim of helping the practitioner construct a detailed and precise image. One is repeatedly told to visualize the objects until they appear to be actually present. The text instructs, "See all of these as clearly and distinctly as if you were looking at your own image in a mirror" or "as if you were seeing an object in the palm of your hand" (AdS 343a). Generating a vivid internal image (*nimitta*) is the objective and object of such concentration practice. Having faith in Amitābha and his Pure Land means instantiating them through such visionary experiences rather than just making doctrinal proclamations of belief.

The actual existence of the Empire State Building is not the object of much debate, to be sure, but exercising contemplation of it can cultivate the same mental powers as visualizing the Pure Land. Despite the instant recognizability of this iconic building, even those in everyday proximity probably do not look at it closely or long enough to mentally reproduce it in detailed or lifelike form. Even if one were to make such an attempt, real-life situations do not readily provide a good vantage point on the subject—such as access to the higher floors of the Time-Life Building—nor the freedom to sit and stare at it in the midst of daily activities. This is not to suggest that there is some inherent virtue to contemplating and committing a view of the Empire State Building to memory. Rather, the objective is to cultivate the capacity to purposefully stay with a phenomenon in an undistracted manner and thereby develop the ability to actively determine what worlds and realities one occupies. This capacity can be cultivated by taking mundane objects as focal points, which offer easier points of departure for visualization practice.

For this reason, even Buddhist contemplation practices focus on simple and ordinary objects, such as the *kasiṇa* meditations described in the Pāli canon and systematized by Buddhaghosa in the *Visuddhimagga*. Perhaps the simplest kasiṇa is the earth kasiṇa, which is a clay disk that can be the size of a bushel or a saucer that is to be manually constructed if there is no access to a natural plot of earth such as a ploughed area or a threshing floor (Vm IV, 22–23). In the water kasiṇa and the fire kasiṇa meditations, one can again choose to concentrate on natural formations such as a lake or lamp flame, or manufacture an appropriate object expressly for the purpose of meditation, such as a bowl of water or a special fire. The use of ordinary objects and events is notable: the air kasiṇa meditation includes noting the tops of plants and trees moving to and fro in the wind and feeling the touch of the breeze upon one's body (Vm V, 9), and the light kasiṇa meditation can be practiced by concentrating on the circle of light cast on the floor by the sun or moonlight passing through a hole in the wall (Vm V, 21). But one can alternatively create such phenomena artificially, suggesting the interchangeability of nature and artifice when it comes to the single goal of cultivating the mental ability to concentrate.[9]

Medieval Chinese and Japanese Pure Land masters report having had intense visions as the result of their visualization practices, aided by other ritual tools such as sleep deprivation and countless mantra repetitions. This led them to render their experiences in painting and sculpture that in turn functioned as prompts for their followers' visualization practices, further extending the synergy between art and experience.[10] This co-dependency seems to be invoked by the *Amitāyurdhyāna Sūtra* in a brief passage that Julian Pas (1974, 112) reads as a later philosophical interpolation to the text. It appears in the section describing the eighth meditation practice, which is a visualization of the Buddha:

> [B]uddha tathāgatas have cosmic bodies [dharmadhātu-kāya], and so enter into the meditating mind of each sentient being. For this reason, when you contemplate a buddha, your mind itself takes the form of his thirty-two physical characteristics and eighty secondary marks. Your mind produces the Buddha's image and is itself the Buddha. (AdS 343a)

The meaning of this last sentence has been given somewhat varying interpretations by different masters, but they converge on the idea that the visions of the meditating mind are no different from the objective reality of the Buddha and Buddhahood.[11] The dharmakāya is invoked here and it again enables a transition from the Buddhas seen to a focus on the mind that does the seeing. The passage goes on to say, "The ocean of perfectly and universally enlightened buddhas thus arises in the meditating mind" (AdS 343a). It is the *act* of seeing the Buddha that makes him real, and therefore the Buddha is no different from, and exists within, the artistic imagination that actively chooses and constructs what to see. This is not to say that Buddhas are merely a figment of the imagination. This short philosophical interlude does not undermine the countless Pure Land devotees who have believed in the empirical existence of Amitābha's paradise in the West. But affirming the empirical reality of something does not entail ontological materialism either, particularly in a tradition such as Buddhism that is chiefly concerned with how human perceptions color what is seen in the world. For this reason, "Pure Land Buddhists would say that the Pure Land is immediately given through *phenomenal experience*, and in this sense is empirically verifiable" (Becker 1984, 147; emphasis added).

The ability to have such a phenomenological experience must be cultivated, however, and it is not simply given to the devotee. This is not a matter of constructing a wishful fantasy in order to mask the painful reality of the mundane world but rather of counteracting the weight of default human illusions with more felicitous ones. Filmic art such as Warhol's *Empire* can actively contribute to such an effort, and the perspective provided by Buddhist practice neutralizes the accusations of facetiousness or cynicism that are often directed to modernist art of this kind. Warhol's deceptively simple challenge to "watch time go by" underplays the phenomenological questions *Empire* provokes: Wherein does the reality of an object exist but within our evolving and unstable experiences? *Empire* provides a canvas on which to paint and possibly increase each viewer's ability to choose and sustain a vision of things, and given the history of Buddhist practice, such cultivation is difficult to separate from religious actions.

Conclusion

Erik Zurcher notes that the Mahāyāna emphasis on the universal unreality of emptiness automatically commits it to iconoclasm:

> Since the true Buddha-nature is beyond all imagination, no image can ever do justice to it. Icons are, in the last analysis, as useless as anything else as a means to reach the Absolute, for ultimate truth can only be approached by rejecting all images, both mental and material. (2013, 485)

Zurcher goes on to note, however, that this iconoclastic stance is balanced by "the equally important Mahāyāna concept of 'expedience' or 'adaptation.' . . . Since the ultimate Truth as such is inaccessible, we need concepts, words and images to approximate it" (2013, 502). This is certainly correct, but more needs to be said.

As so many observers of Buddhist tradition have noted, the Western conception of "religion" and its emphasis on doctrinal systems can skew our understanding of Buddhist practice. Specifically, we are too ready to apply the familiar concepts of credo and orthodoxy to Buddhist teachings, as if what Buddhists call the Dharma is above all a set of empirical and metaphysical propositions to which all followers must assent. But the Buddha's teachings are in fact "a set of practical and experiential techniques rather than a body of discursive knowledge" (Samuel 2008, 139). Thus, even the teaching of emptiness is an invitation to an experience that is enabled by words, analogies, parables—and ultimately, images. Words and images are not mere approximations of a reality beyond this one but rather what activates our imaginations, and their resulting experiences. Seeing the Buddha and the qualities he embodies—regardless of the medium or material—is thought to engage our minds in the wholly auspicious manner required to become a Buddha oneself. This meditation is its own end rather than the means to a destination beyond the present world. The way art allows one to perceive the world—in contrast to the distracted operations of the everyday mind—brings Buddhas to life everywhere. And this manner of seeing the Buddha is in fact to see what the Buddha himself saw.

Notes

Chapter 1. Seeing Like the Buddha

1. The thirty-two marks are not exclusive properties of the historical Buddha but thought to be characteristics of the Great Man, which can also include *cakravartins* ("wheel turning monarchs") who rule according to Buddhist teachings. The thirty-two marks are listed in the *Lakkhana Sutta* ("discourse on the marks") of the *Digha Nikāya* (D 30) and the *Brahmāyu Sutta* of the *Majjhima Nikāya* (M 91). Some of these attributes include golden skin, blue eyes, a long tongue, and a penis concealed in a sheath.

2. And to be clear, not all individuals who accepted the idea of Buddha-nature thought the concept extended to inanimate objects. The Buddha-nature of the insentient (*wuqing foxing* 無情佛性) was the subject of great controversy in early Chinese Buddhism, but it was supported by Huiyuan (334–416) of the Pure Land tradition, Jizang (549–623) of the Chinese Madhyamaka school, and Zhanran (711–782) of the Tiantai lineage. See Koseki (1980) for a discussion of Jizang, and Sharf (2002, 246–49) for a discussion of an eighth-century Chan text, the *Treasure Store Treatise*, which affirms the Buddha-nature of grass and trees.

3. Tathāgathagarbha doctrine is not the property of a single Mahāyāna school, but an idea that is found in various texts. Important early sources include the *Tathāgatagārbha Sūtra*, the *Śrīmālādevīsiṃhanāda Sūtra*, the *Anūnatvā-pūrṇatvanirdeśa Sūtra*, and the *Mahāparinirvāṇa Sūtra*, all of which were composed in India between 200 and 350 CE. This early tathāgathagarbha tradition is summarized in the *Ratnagotravibhāga* (also known in Tibetan as the *Uttaratantraśāstra*), an early-fifth-century Sanskrit text now preserved through Tibetan and Chinese translations.

4. The idea of "Buddhist aniconism" refers to the fact that images of the Buddha are notably absent until the first century CE. Scholars have debated why this is the case, and whether or not Buddhists deliberately avoided representing the Buddha in the early centuries (Huntington 1990). Explicit iconoclasm is voiced in East Asian Chan/Zen Buddhism, as a part of its antinomian attitude

toward all religious forms, including rituals and scriptures in addition to images. The Zen emphasis on emptiness doctrine leads to denunciations of all religious forms as unnecessary. See Sharf (2002, 44–46, 252–53) on the Ox Head lineage, and Adamek (2007, 218–26) on the Bao Tang, both southern schools of Chinese Zen.

5. See Pamela Winfield's (2013) comparison of Kūkai (774–835), the image-loving founder of Japanese esoteric Buddhism, and Dōgen, the iconoclastic founder of Japanese Sōtō Zen. Even Dōgen, however, tacks back and forth between rejecting and utilizing images.

6. Reverend Jump's essay was originally published for private distribution to his New Britian, Connecticut, congregation in 1910. It is reprinted in *Film History* 14, no.2 (2002).

7. See Freedberg (1989), ch. 8, "*Invisibilia per Visibilia*: Meditation and the Uses of Theory," for an account of medieval theological justifications of religious images as moving texts for the illiterate. The justifications are consistent with Reverend Jump's recommendations of motion pictures. See also Reinhartz (2004) for a consideration of the Jesus film genre, including Gibson's film, as a continuation of traditional Christian art.

8. Fredriksen's essay "History, Hollywood, and the Bible: Some Thoughts on Gibson's *Passion*" first appeared in the Society of Biblical Literature's SBL Forum (March 2004) and was reprinted in *The Journal of Religion and Film* (Feb. 2004, vol. 8:1). This volume of the journal is entirely dedicated to Gibson's film.

9. Vairocana Buddha is thought to have made his first literary appearance in the *Brahmajāla* (*Brahma Net*) *Sūtra*, a purportedly Mahāyāna Sanskrit text translated into Chinese by Kumārajīva in 406 but actually composed in China in the mid-fifth-century. Vairocana, which means "he who comes from the sun," is described as the Primordial Buddha from whom all other Buddhas emanate, and as the embodiment of emptiness. Vairocana is a significant figure in Chinese Huayan and Tiantai Buddhism, Japanese Shingon, and Tibetan tantric Buddhism.

10. Unsurprisingly, dharmakāya is another synonym for tathāgathagarbha. See the *Śrīmālādevīsiṃhanāda Sūtra*, which states, "This Dharmakāya of the Tathāgatha when not free from the store of defilement is referred to as the Tathāgathagarbha" (Wayman and Wayman 1976, 98). The dharmakāya and tathāgathagarbha are the same things distinguished by undefiled and defiled states.

11. This story appears in the *Ekottarāgama*, the Sanskrit version of the *Aṅguttara Nikāya* that was translated into Chinese in the late fourth century. See Zurcher (2013, 485–86) for an account of the tale. It is also recounted by the Chinese Buddhist pilgrim Xuanzang (602–664) in his famous account of his travels to India called *Xiyouji* ("journey to the West"). See Beal 1980 for the translation. The story appears in vol. 2, 254–56.

12. This is a slightly modified version of Beal's translation. The *Guanfo sanmei haijing* 觀佛三昧海經 ("the scripture of the sea of samādhi of visualizing the Buddha"), which was translated into Chinese by Buddhabhadra in Chang'an sometime between 408 and 429 CE, also contains a version of the sandalwood image story in which the image walks and talks to the Buddha.

13. Naturally, there are numerous Chinese legends about how the Udayana image was brought to that country. See Sharf (1996) for accounts of three of them.

14. See Cameron Warner (2011) on the controversy regarding the Jowo Buddha, whose appearance was altered when the founder of the Geluk school Tsongkhapa (1357–1419) added a crown. The controversy that ensued focused nominally on the Buddha's appearance—did Śākyamuni ever actually wear a crown?—but the underlying concern was that the crown, which covered the Buddha's cranial protuberance and its protective rays of light, could potentially diminish the image's ritual power.

15. See Schopen (1988–89), Schober (1997), and Swearer (2004) for discussions of the cult of images in India, Burma, and Thailand, respectively.

16. Mahāyāna Buddhists articulated a three-body (*trikāya*) theory that redefined the rūpakāya as the nirmāṇakāya, or "manifestation/emanation body" that can take many historical forms other than the Buddha. It also postulated the *saṃbhogakāya* ("enjoyment body") as a third body that contains the Buddha's immeasurable merit and the supernatural abilities associated with it. This body is the reward for incalculable periods of bodhisattva practice. See Griffiths (1994) for discussion of the trikāya theory as articulated in third- to ninth-century Indian Mahāyāna *śāstra* literature, which Griffiths defines as "doctrinal digests" that attempt to "give systematic and authoritative expression to Buddhist doctrine" (1994, 30). See also Xing (2005) for discussion of the Mahāyāna sūtra literature that gave rise to the trikāya theory.

17. We can see a similar kind of classification system in Theravāda Buddhism with its distinction between three different kinds of relics: corporeal relics, relics of use (the Bodhi tree), and relics of commemoration (images). These categories are not the same as the Tibetan classification of emanation bodies but they display a similar impulse to recognize the many and different ways in which the Buddha is present in the world. See Trainor (1997, 89) on the Theravāda classifications.

18. This idea of the dharmakāya as the qualities of the Buddha was first developed by the Sarvāstivāda school in the second century, which listed eighteen attributes of the Buddha culled from early sutras. They are the ten powers, the four kinds of intrepidity, the three foundations of mindfulness, and the great compassion. These qualities are sometimes structured into the three divisions of *śīla* (morality), *samādhi* (concentration), and *prajñā* (wisdom). In the third and fourth centuries, the Mahāyāna came up with its own entirely different list of

eighteen attributes that can be found in the Perfection of Wisdom literature. See Xing (2005) for discussions of Sarvāstivāda and Mahāyāna dharmakāya theories.

19. The *Mahāpadāna Sutta* of the *Digha Nikāya* (D 14) recounts how the Buddha revealed to his followers his knowledge of the lineage of cosmic Buddhas, of which he is the seventh. The Buddha has this knowledge by virtue of the divine eye that also gives him knowledge of his many previous lives. See Reynolds (1997) and Woodward (1997) for discussions of how this tradition of enumerating past and future Buddhas evolved into ever-longer lineages.

20. The *Daśabhūmika Sūtra* originated as an individual early Mahāyāna text but was incorporated as the twenty-sixth chapter of the *Avataṃsaka Sūtra* (which is an amalgamation of independent scriptures) in the late third to fourth centuries in Central Asia.

21. This metaphor appears in Vasubandhu's *Abhidharmakośa* I.16. The image of molten gold that can be shaped into many forms is used in the early Chan text *Treasure Store Treatise* to talk about images of the Buddha (Sharf 2002, 253).

22. Gomez (1977) describes how this idea developed within the mythico-magical framework of ancient India, where people believed ascetics developed magical powers (ṛddhi), including vikurvana—the ability to transform or multiply one's own body. This common folk belief was appropriated by Buddhists to thread a middle course between nihilism and ontological fundamentalism by rendering illusions into signs of emptiness that are powerful in awakening beings to their reality. Griffiths (1994) details the development of these Buddha bodies in their technical distinctions as "manifestation" (*nirmāṇa*) and "communal enjoyment" (*sambhoga*) bodies.

23. The cremation and veneration of bodily relics is a practice indigenous to the northeastern region of Magadha where Buddhism originated, which is geographically distinct from the brahmanical stronghold in the northwestern Indus River valley. Another explanation of the Buddha's cremation, along with the other rites performed during his funeral, may be that he was treated like a king according to Hellenistic and Near Eastern practice (Strong 2007). There is evidence that the remains of Alexander the Great and King Menander were preserved and worshipped as greatly auspicious. The ambivalent nature of relic worship is also an issue in contemporary Thailand, which has experienced brahmanical influence. The display and veneration of mummified corpses is extremely popular even though dead bodies are generally considered to be inauspicious. These corpses include not only that of Buddhist monks but infants and fetuses, the veneration of which seems to go back to native practices (McDaniel 2011, 173).

24. Campany (1991) examines Chinese Buddhist miracle tales about the *Lotus Sutra*, which was revered as a holy object and believed to have the ability to move and act, much like King Udayana's sandalwood image. This cultural

evidence confirms that Buddhist texts stood in for the person of the Buddha in the same manner as his physical relics and images.

25. *The Sutra on the Merit of Bathing the Buddha* is the Chinese monk Yijing's (635–713) translation of a Sanskrit text that is no longer extant. Daniel Boucher speculates that it is perhaps an amalgamation of two other texts available in eighth-century translations—one on stūpa worship and one on image worship (1995, 59). Regardless of the provenance of the text, it demonstrates how Buddhists harmonized competing practices by looking for their soteriological and philosophical underpinnings.

26. One can add living human beings other than the historical Buddha to this list. The tulku tradition of Tibetan Buddhism recognizes lineages of incarnate lamas who are understood to be living Buddhas. This practice is specifically sanctioned in terms of the idea of the manifestation bodies, or *nirmāṇakāyas.* See Bogin (2013) for a discussion of Buddha-body theory in relation to the tulku tradition.

27. Eckel (1992, 101) traces the various meanings of the Dharma as (1) the collection of teachings, (2) the path to enlightenment, (3) the goal of enlightenment, and (4) nondual awareness. The last concept of Dharma collapses the means-end linearity of the second and third definitions, in that nondual awareness is a mental state that comprises both path and goal. Eckel traces this idea to the Perfection of Wisdom literature, as well as the Yogācāra works of Vasubandhu and Dignāga.

28. This is an unpublished translation of Qiu Wei's poem by Paula Versano.

29. The recent publication, *Buddhism Goes to the Movies*, by Ronald Green (2013), uses American films such as *Fight Club, Waking Life*, and *I Heart Huckabees* to talk about Buddhist teachings such as the Four Noble Truths and Dependent Origination, for example. *Buddhism and American Cinema*, edited by John Whalen-Bridge and Gary Storhoff (2014), also utilizes the practice of looking at American films (such as *Lost in Translation* and *American Beauty*) through Buddhist concepts. The Hollywood Zombie genre has also been the focus of Buddhist readings (Moreman 2008, 2010; Walker 2012; Herman 2014).

30. The base of Borobudur with the *Karmavibhanga* images is actually hidden by an encasement that was added in the middle of the construction process, around 792. This has created scholarly debate as to whether the reason was structural or ideological. The argument for the latter is that given the overtly Mahāyāna worldview of Borobudur, the *Karmavibhanga's* images of tortures and punishments in hells for evil deeds were perhaps deemed incompatible with the Mahāyāna message of universal salvation. Thus, the images were covered up by a later architect/priest who took charge of construction. I follow Gifford in favoring the structural interpretation, thereby rendering the visual program of Borobudur into a deliberate and integrated process that moves from what are

considered lesser visions to more enlightened ones. In either case, however, the idea of multiple visions of Buddhahood remains.

31. There have been debates as to whether Borobudur is a stūpa, a storied palace (*prasada*) that represents the bodhisattva path to enlightenment, or a maṇḍala (Gifford 2011, 21–47). None of these suggestions are mutually exclusive. In any case, the nested circles-within-squares configuration echoes the "palace-architecture" maṇḍala common to Tibet and Nepal, which features a principal deity in the center ringed by multileveled square palaces with openings in the four cardinal directions.

32. Samuel (2008, 225) confirms this basic feature of the maṇḍala as comprising a center "with non-central components [that] are treated as emanations of that centre and reducible to it." He suggests that the maṇḍala reflects the political model of "a supreme king at the centre in relation to whom lesser kings are expected to be local projections rather than independent rulers" (226–27). This model was appealing to Chinese and Tibetan kings from the sixth century on, who favored maṇḍalas with the figure of Vairocana Buddha at the center adorned with imperial imagery.

Chapter 2. The Karmic Narrative of
Spring, Summer, Fall, Winter . . . and Spring

1. There are 547 jātakas in the *Jātakatthavannana* of the Pāli canon (found in the *Khuddaka Nikāya*). Aryaśura's *Jātakamālā* ("garland of birth stories") is a fourth-century collection of thirty-four tales in Sanskrit that has been particularly popular in India and Tibet. For an account of the jātakas and their variant collections, see Reynolds (1997).

2. The *Apadāna* is a collection of some six hundred verse-biographies of monks and nuns written during the last two centuries BCE. They elaborate upon earlier oral poems about Buddhist monks and nuns known as the *Theragāthā* and *Therīgāthā*, respectively. All three works form parts of the *Khuddaka Nikāya*, along with the *Jātakatthavannana*. Indian avadāna tales were written well into the thirteenth century CE, drawing from the apadānas, jātakas, and folklore. See Sarkar (1981) for a study of the history and nature of the jātaka and avadāna genres, as well as their relation to each other.

3. Early Western scholars of Buddhism have in fact considered the extensive biographical narratives that are also the subjects of art and popular piety as inferior and watered-down renditions of Buddhist philosophy, as Woodward recounts (1997, 41).

4. The *Vimānavatthu* ("stories of mansions") and *Petavatthu* ("stories of the departed"), also contained in the *Khuddaka Nikāya*, are perhaps the most explicit in accounting for the types of deeds that land people in Buddhist heavens

or the hellish realms of hungry ghosts, respectively. In contrast, the *Apadāna* accounts for those who have attained Buddhist liberation.

5. See my article, "Religion, Science, and the Truth about Karma" (Cho 2014) for a discussion of the moral function of karma doctrine in traditional Buddhist societies in Asia. I explicitly reject the idea that it has functioned as a form of Buddhist theodicy, and I also reject the relevance of empirical verifications of karma doctrine (such as rebirth in heavens and hells), seeing it instead as a way of actively shaping moral experience.

6. The practice of self-cremation is attested in China as early as the fourth century. It was part of an array of "abandoning the body" practices to honor the Buddha or enact bodhisattva compassion—such as sacrificing one's own body to feed hungry beasts. Self-cremation seems to be a Chinese innovation that had no precedents in Indian Buddhism, although the *Lotus Sutra*'s story of the Bodhisattva Medicine King who immolates himself serves as the blueprint for the Chinese practice. Although suicide is technically forbidden in Buddhism, self-cremation has been valorized in East Asian Buddhism as a sign of Buddha-hood. For an in-depth study of this history, see Benn (2007).

7. For the cult of images in India, see Kinnard (1999), especially chapter 3; for its development in China, see Kieschnick (2003), particularly chapter 1. Swearer (2004) provides an ethnographic account of image consecration rituals and practices in Thailand. Miracle tales regarding Buddha images can be found in the Korean *Samguk Yusa* ("legends of the three kingdoms"), which is partially translated in Grayson (2001).

8. Donald Lopez (1992, 147) reports that Har Dayal has calculated these three aeons to be equivalent to 384 X 10 [58] years. The source for this information is not cited.

9. The three poisons at the center of the Wheel of Life (*bhavacakra*) are represented by a bird, snake, and pig. The bird, which is frequently glossed as a cock in Western Buddhist literature, stands for lust or positive attachment because of its tendency to mate for life. The snake represents anger, hatred, or negative attachment generally. The pig is ignorance, which is thought to be the cause of both lust and aversion.

10. See Buswell and Gimello (1992) for an overview of evolutions in Buddhist conceptions of the path (*mārga*), which range from highly structured and enumerated charts of religious progress—such as the ten stages of the bodhisat-tva path—to anti-mārga traditions that draw on emptiness doctrine to radically revise the discourse on nirvana. According to Buswell and Gimello, even the most antinomian strains of Buddhism never reject the idea of path and prog-ress, but they reimagine nirvana as a "non-abiding" that never settles anywhere and allows one "to embark on a continuing transformation, to participate in unfettered change and in unbounded interrelation with all things and beings" (1992, 22). See Groner (1992) and Bielefeldt (1992) for discussions of East Asian

Buddhist notions of innate Buddhahood that radicalize notions of the Buddhist path, particularly in Japan.

11. For example, the *Sutra on the Merit of Bathing the Buddha* states that the consequence of bathing the Buddha image "is that you and the great multitude of men and gods will presently receive wealth, happiness, and long life without sickness; your every wish will be fulfilled. Your relatives, friends, and family will all be at ease. You will bid a long farewell to the eight conditions of trouble and forever escape the fount of suffering. You will never again receive the body of a woman, and will quickly achieve enlightenment" (Boucher 1995, 67).

12. See my study of the seventeenth-century Korean novel *Dream of the Nine Clouds*, and the broader consideration of the dream narrative genre with its Buddhist themes (Cho Bantly 1996).

13. The Chinese title of the film is also different from the translation: "three times" stands in for the original "zuihao de shiguang" (最好的時光), which is more accurately translated as "the best of times."

Chapter 3. The Meditative Discernment of *Nang Nak*

1. Chinese zhiguai first flourished during the Six Dynasties (220–589) and continued through the Tang (618–906). Zhiguai is not an exclusively Buddhist genre but rather folktales of anomalies that reflect Buddhist, Daoist, and shamanic influences. Some zhiguai collections, however, were compiled by Buddhists for didactic purposes, such as the *Mingxiangji* ("manifesting the dead"), *Huanyuanji* ("requiting grievances"), and *Yuminglu* ("the dead and the living"). See Campany (2012) for a translation of *Mingxiangji* and Campany (2015) for translations from numerous zhiguai sources. Japanese setsuwa collections were compiled during the Heian (794–1185) and Kamakura (1185–1333) periods, the first being the 116 tales of the *Nihon ryōiki* of the early eighth century. Japanese setsuwa tend to be more explicitly Buddhist because they were collected by monks as source material for sermons. See Nakamura (1997) for a critical discussion and translation of the *Nihon ryōiki*, and Reider (2001, 2002) for discussions of early modern Japanese setsuwa.

2. The Nō drama and otogizoshi both date to the Muromachi (1336–1573) period, but whereas Nō was an aristocratic art form, the picture performances of otogizoshi tales were directed toward a broader spectrum of audiences in commercial centers such as Kyoto and Nara. What is particularly interesting about the picture performances is the active role that Buddhist monks and nuns reputedly played in producing the picture books and forming the class of professional storytellers (Ruch 1977; Araki 1981). See also Mair (1989) for a discussion of the Buddhist origins of the Chinese tradition of picture perfor-

mances based on *bianwen,* or "transformations texts," which can be linked to later vernacular fiction.

3. This part of the film is based on the tale *"Jasei no in,"* or "A Serpent's Lust," in Ueda's *Ugetsu Monogatari.*

4. This part of the film is based on *"Asaji ga yado,"* or "The Reed-Choked House," in Ueda's *Ugetsu Monogatari.*

5. Tambiah (1968) and Veidlinger (2006) note the dominance of oral literature in Thailand even into the early modern era. This is true of the manner in which Buddhist teachings were transmitted even after the textualization of the Pāli canon into manuscripts in Sri Lanka in the first century BCE. In this context, it is not surprising that folk tales such as *Nang Nak* seem to lack textual origins.

6. The *Nang Tantrai* cannot be dated because the surviving manuscripts date back only to the nineteenth century. But it is clearly related to the south Indian reworking of the *Pancatantra* known as the *Tantropakhyana,* and both its Sanskrit and Tamil versions are attested before the year 1200. See Ginsberg (1967) for a full review of existing manuscripts. The *Nang Tantrai* was reprinted in 1869 under the direction of Prince Badintharaphaisansophon, during the reign of King Chulalongkorn, and Buddhist monks were involved as copyists.

7. The *Trai Phum Phra Ruang* (*Trai Phum*) was written around 1345 by Phya Lithai, heir to the Sukhothai throne in central Thailand. This act of Buddhist piety, which enhanced Phya Lithai's political charisma, was undertaken in close consultation with Buddhist advisors and Pāli Buddhist sources. Therefore, the content of *Trai Phum* faithfully echos orthodox Theravāda Buddhism but also communicates "the profundities of the doctrine to those who possessed only a minimum of religious sophistication and training" (Reynolds and Reynolds 1982, 7). The focus of the text is a description of the thirty-one realms of the three-world cosmology that is standard in Buddhism. This includes descriptions of the six realms of rebirth that are a part of the *kāmaloka,* or the world of desire. Given the authority of the author, its claim to orthodoxy, and its accessibility, the *Trai Phum* has been a significant influence on the Thai Buddhist imagination up to the modern period. See Reynolds and Reynolds (1982) for an introductory discussion and translation.

8. It is useful to keep in mind that the Buddhist doctrine of karma functions as an explicit challenge to brahmanical conceptions of personhood, which justified the social hierarchy by asserting absolute, species-type differences between castes (Bronkhorst 2011b, 50). In contrast, the Buddhist view is that "one's status in society is not a function of one's inherent nature, but of the quality and direction of one's values, intentions and actions—one's karma" (Hershock 2007, 181). Opposition to the brahmanical notion of an inherent nature leads to the Buddhist emphasis on mind and attributes of consciousness as the determining factors of existence.

9. Hayashi's (2003) ethnographic study of Thai village Buddhism describes how the figure of the wandering ascetic monk, in particular, simultaneously promotes meditation and Buddhist discipline as forces for taming native spirits: "The mechanism for driving out evil spirits . . . is to convert them to Buddhism, to bring them into the Buddhist world and thereby render the power of the world beyond impotent" (242).

10. As Pāli text scholars have noted, Buddhist cosmology is described in terms of both physical places and mental/meditative states (Hamilton 1999; Gethin 1997). The form and formless worlds of the three-world schema are explicitly correlated to levels of meditative states (*dhyānas*), for example. The physical and mental readings of cosmology are not treated as mutually exclusive options. Rather, they correspond to each other. The *Trai Phum* begins its discussion of hells by accounting for both the physical and mental factors that lead to rebirth there.

Chapter 4. *Rashomon* and the Indiscernible Emptiness of Being

1. Kobayashi (1979) and Kelsey (1982) draw on post–World War II Japanese *Konjaku* scholarship to refute the long-standing belief that the collection was put together by the aristocrat Minamoto Takakuni (1004–77). The current theory that the compiler was instead a Buddhist monk is ultimately speculative and the exact identity is unlikely to be determined, short of new evidence coming to light. Manuscript evidence, however, suggests the likelihood of one Kakuju (1084–1140), a monk of the Tōdaiji temple in Nara. An alternative theory poses the possibility of a Tendai monk in residence at Mt. Hiei, the Tendai headquarters. See Kelsey (1982, 13–16) for discussion of the evidence of these two possibilities.

2. While setsuwa often recount encounters with native spirits and ghosts, as examined in the last chapter, they also include tales of miracles performed by the Bodhisattva Guanyin and travels to Buddhist hells. Both Chinese zhiguai and Japanese setsuwa originate in popular oral narratives and should not be confused with religious scriptures. Nevertheless, they have indelibly colored the Buddhist religiosity of these societies: "The genre's liminal position—betwixt and between ideological persuasions and religious traditions, dealing with the spirit world but from the point of view of ordinary life and in texts deemed non-canonical—is one of the main reasons for its importance for understanding early medieval Chinese religious and cultural history" (Campany 1996, 27).

3. See Nakamura (1997) for a translation of the *Nihon ryōiki*, the earliest of these setsuwa collections that was compiled by the Buddhist monk Kyōkai

from 810–823. Appendix E of this book provides a list of all thirty Japanese setsuwa collections, including dates and authors, if known.

4. Kelsey (1981) focuses on the "Buddhification" of native Japanese snake myths in which the thunder deity takes the form of a snake in order to cause trouble for humans. In the *Nihon ryōiki* and *Konjaku monogatarishū*, these snakes convert to Buddhism and defend it against other native spirits. In the Buddhist reinterpretation of these menacing snakes, they are beings in an unfortunate form of rebirth due to attachment to worldly desires: "Now violence is no longer seen as something impersonal, arising from somewhere outside of the individual, but rather as something arising from within" (Kelsey 1981, 111). This is parallel to the Buddhist treatment of ghosts in *Nang Nak*.

5. The *Konjaku monotagarishū* comprises thirty-one books. The first five focus on Indian Buddhism, particularly the life of the Buddha, his teachings, his followers, and tales of karma in the jātaka style. The next five focus on the spread of Buddhism to China. These first ten volumes import many stories from collections of Chinese Buddhist tales, such as *Fayuan zhulin* ("forest of gems from the Dharma garden"), compiled in 668, *Mingbaoji* ("record of karmic retribution"), ca. 659, and *Jingliu yixiang* ("aspects of Buddhist doctrine"), ca. 516. Books 11–20 are Japanese Buddhist tales, and Books 21–31 contain the so-called secular tales, which begin with histories of the imperial, aristocratic, and warrior families. "Rashōmon" and "In a Grove" appear in Book 29, as the eighteenth and twenty-third stories, respectively. For English translations of these and other *Konjaku* setsuwa, see Dykstra (1998–2003).

6. The Korean text known as *Samguk yusa* ("legends of the three king-doms"), a thirteenth-century anthology compiled by Iryon, is another example of literature preserved by a Buddhist monk. It begins with founding legends of the three ancient kingdoms of Korea and moves on to tales about the transmission of Buddhism to Korea, as well as miraculous stories about Buddhist images and monks. This act of preservation has earned Iryon the title of Korea's first folklorist (Grayson 2001, 14). See Grayson (2001) for a partial translation of the work.

7. "Nose" and "Hellscreen" are adaptations of setsuwa from the thir-teenth-century collection *Uji shūi monogatari* ("collection of tales from Uji"). See Mills 1970 for a study and translation.

8. The Pāli texts of Theravāda Buddhism are not the dominant sources of East Asian Buddhism, which favor Mahāyāna texts. But the *Nikāyas* were translated into Chinese and I draw upon them to illuminate the imagery of a Japanese film. This does not entail the claim that the compiler of the *Kon-jaku*, or Akutagawa, or Kurosawa were schooled in Pāli texts and intended to invoke them.

9. This metaphor appears in the *Dhammasangaṇi* of the Theravada Abhidharma corpus. It is also elaborated by Buddhaghosa in his *Aṭṭhasālinī*

(252–53). See Gethin (1997) for a translation. See also Fuller (2005, 79–81) for a discussion.

10. Fuller (2005) provides a comprehensive survey of the "right-views" enumerated in the *Nikāyas* and concludes that they can be subsumed under two general categories: the view that actions have consequences, and the teaching of the insubstantiality of the self. Because Buddhism assumes the close relationship between thought and action, Buddhist right-view is something "practiced, not adopted or believed in" (2005, 126). Wrong views are those that deny that actions have consequences and make either eternalist or nihilist pronouncements about the self. Demonstrating the same thought-action nexus, Buddhist sources affirm repeatedly that the problem with such wrong-views is that they are forms of greed and attachment.

Chapter 5. The Depth of Shadows in *Maborosi*

1. The English transliteration of the movie's title, *Maborosi*, omits the "h" in "shi." When I use the phrase "maboroshi no hikari" I reinsert the "h" that the proper transliteration of the Japanese word requires.

2. The practice of *Fudaraku tokai*, or "passage to Fudaraku," is similar to the Pure Land practice of self-immolation by drowning for the purpose of reaching the Western Pure Land of Amida Buddha. Fudaraku tokai is attested in a variety of literary sources from the ninth to the nineteenth centuries. Eyewitness accounts by Jesuits in the sixteenth century describe how Buddhist devotees set sail from the Western coast in small boats and then jumped into the water after tying themselves down with rocks. Moerman (2007) provides an account of Fudaraku tokai based on literary and visual sources.

3. Kamo no Chōmei (d. 1216), author of *Hōjōki* ("record of the ten-foot-square hut"), writes in his *Hossinshū* ("tales of religious awakening"), "Because of a desire for reputation, or out of pride or envy, people may foolishly think that they can attain birth in the Pure Land by drowning or by making a lamp of their body. . . . This is absolute delusion" (quoted in Moerman 2007, 274). Chōmei's admonition attests to devotees who lacked the mental discipline to self-immolate in the required state of calm.

4. The *Daodejing* ("the classic on the way and virtue") is attributed to the ambiguous historical figure Laozi, who tradition has composing this text in the sixth century BCE. The oldest manuscripts date to the fourth century BCE, however, and the question of authorship is far from settled. The *Zhuangzi* has a firmer author in the philosopher Zhuang Zhou of the fourth century BCE, and along with the *Daodejing* form the two fundamental texts of philosophical Daoism that was influential throughout East Asia.

5. Yūgen is originally *yuxuan* in Chinese, and the term was used to describe the profundity of the *Daodejing* and *Zhuangzi*, particularly their concep-

tions of the Dao. Starting from the third century, *yuxuan* was used to explain the emptiness doctrine taught by the Prajñāpāramitā (Perfection of Wisdom) and Mādhyamika (Middle Way) schools. Further on, the term was applied to the Chan/Zen concept of *wu* 無 (Japanese: *mu*)—literally, "absence," which is often translated as "non-Being" and derives from the emptiness concept. See Konishi (1991, 186) for further discussion.

6. Fujiwara Shunzei was a poet and critic who is credited with invigorating the traditional Japanese short poem called *waka*. Although a low-ranking court official, Shunzei hailed from a distinguished literary family that includes his son Fujiwara Teika and granddaughter Fujiwara Toshinari no Musume. Shunzei took Buddhist vows at the age of sixty-three and composed his major critical work, *Korai fūteishō*, thereafter, in 1197.

7. Tendai Buddhism was originally Tiantai Buddhism in China, founded by Tiantai Zhiyi (538–597) and brought to Japan by Saichō (also known as Dengyō Daishi, 767–822), who established the Enryakuji temple on Mt. Hiei near Kyoto as a center for Tendai study and practice. Tendai Buddhism dominated Japan during the Heian and Kamakura periods, and exerted strong influence on the later school of Zen. Tendai's emphasis on the *Lotus Sutra* and the doctrine of original enlightenment (*hongaku*), which does not distinguish absolutely between nirvana and samsara, was utilized by Shunzei and others to justify the "worldly" realm of poetry and the arts as no different from Buddhist practice.

8. Kamo no Chōmei is best known for his literary essay, *Hōjōki* ("record of a ten-foot square hut"), which was written along with the *Mumyōshō* during his years as a Buddhist recluse after he retired from the imperial poetry office around 1204. The *Hōjōki* centers on the Buddhist theme of impermanence, with its descriptions of the natural disasters that befell the people of Kyotō. *Hōjōki's* account of the comparatively peaceful life in a simple hut outside of the capitol has rendered this work a classic in the genre of "recluse literature."

9. Konishi (1991, 520–26) notes that of the roughly two hundred plays in the current Nō repertoire, only one ("Sanshō") is humorous, and it is highly unpopular. The comic spirit of *sarugaku* has been corralled into the performance genre known as Kyōgen, which is now staged as an interlude between Nō performances. The impact of *shushi* on the development of Nō is visible not only in the latter's solemnity but also in plots that involve priests, dreams, and rebirth.

10. Shunzei utilizes the discussion of *shikan* (Chinese: *zhiguan*) offered by Zhiyi, the founder of Tiantai Buddhism. The *shi* (止) of shikan is the Sanskrit term *śamatha*, which is the meditative practice of calming the mind. The *kan* (観) is *vipaśyanā*, or insight meditation. See LaFleur (1983, 90) for a translation of Shunzei's discussion from the *Korai fūteishō*.

11. The Jetavana Monastery, located in Sāvatthi, was built for the Buddha by the wealthy layman Suddata Anāthapindika. The Buddha is said to have spent nineteen rainy seasons at Jetavana, and gave many of his teachings there. Zeami states in his treatise *Fūshikaden* ("teachings on style and the flower") that

during the dedication ceremony the Buddha's evil cousin Devadatta caused a disruption by having unbelievers cry and dance wildly. The Buddha thereupon had three of his chief disciples—Ānanda, Śāriputra, and Pūrna—perform sixty-six entertainments to calm the interlopers and allow the Buddha to continue with the dedication (Zeami 1984, 32).

12. Bo Zhuyi (772–846) was a Chinese official who passed the prestigious *jinshi* exam at the precocious age of twenty-nine, which entitled him to a series of high positions in the Tang dynasty court. Along with Du Fu (712–770) and Li Bai (701–762), Bo Zhuyi is considered one of the greatest poets during the golden age of Chinese poetry. Bo never entered the Buddhist order, but engaged in serious study and discussion of Buddhism, particularly beginning in the period of his political exile in 815. He spent considerable time in the Zen temples of Mount Lu, and built a small retreat on the mountain to which he returned between subsequent official appointments.

Chapter 6. The Visual Cinema of Terrence Malick

1. "Auteur theory" is a phrase associated with film criticism advanced in the 1950s by the so-called French New Wave filmmakers, particularly François Truffaut, and the periodical *Cahiers du Cinéma.* The basic idea of auteur ("author") theory is that the director is the author and creative force behind a film, which reflects his or her personal vision.

2. At the time of writing, however, Malick has had two films in post-production: *Voyage of Time,* a documentary, and *Knight of Cups,* a feature film. Both were slated to be released in 2014, but *The Hollywood Reporter* (February 25, 2014) reports that Malick's production company, Sycamore Pictures, was in the process of settling a lawsuit filed by investors in *Voyage of Time* for Malick's failure to have completed the film.

3. Malick is famously private, refusing most interviews and skipping the red carpet for his own film premiers. As a result, insights into his artistic process and ambitions come primarily from his actors and crew, such as his cinematographer Emmanuel Lubezki.

Chapter 7. Descent into the World

1. In the Pāli *Nikāyas,* the full recitation of the Buddha's qualities is: "The Blessed One is accomplished, fully enlightened, perfect in true knowledge and conduct, sublime, knower of worlds, incomparable leader of persons to be tamed, teachers of gods and humans, enlightened, blessed" (M I. 37). In the seventh chapter of Buddhaghoṣa's *Visuddhimagga,* the fifth-century text that systemati-

cally condenses Theravāda teachings, these epithets of the Buddha are grouped as one of six recollections that form the subject of concentration meditation.

2. The Pure Land sūtras are the *Longer Sukhāvatīvyūha Sūtra* and the *Shorter Sukhāvatīvyūha Sūtra*, which originated in India, and the *Amitāyurdhyāna Sūtra*, which was composed in Central Asia or China. The Perfection of Wisdom (*Prajñāpāramitā*) texts include most famously the *Heart Sūtra* and *Diamond Sūtra*, but also include *The Perfection of Wisdom in 8000 Lines* and *The Perfection of Wisdom in 25,000 Lines*.

3. This deity yoga is visualized in maṇḍala practice, which is one of the more conspicuous elements of Buddhist Tantra. One of the most elaborate maṇḍalas is the Kālacakra, with 722 deities, but the earliest maṇḍala form (dating to the early fifth century) features the four Buddhas of the four directions: Akṣobhya in the East, Ratnaketu in the South, Amitāyus in the West, and Dundubhiśvara in the North. Geoffrey Samuel notes that as meditation practices, "these can be seen as a logical extensions of the meditative procedure involving the summoning of the presence of the Buddha [buddhānusmṛti]" (2008, 226).

4. Stevenson is speaking here of the meditative practice described by the Tiantai master Zhiyi (538–597) as the samādhi of *suiziyi* (隨自意), which Stevenson translates as "cultivating samādhi wherever mind is directed." The literal meaning of suiziyi is "following one's mind." Suiziyi is one of four types of meditation techniques that Zhiyi describes in his *Mohezhiguan* ("treatise on calming and insight").

5. This legend is recounted in the *Dhammapada Commentary* and is part of a larger tale about the Buddha performing the Twin Miracle in which he causes jets of water and fire to simultaneously issue from every pore of his body. Burlingame (1921, 35–56) provides a translation.

6. The story of Kisāgotamī originates in the Pāli canon, particularly the *Therigatha*, or the verses about Buddhist nuns that are now part of the *Khuddaka Nikāya*. Kisāgotamī also appears briefly in the *Anguttara Nikāya* to ask the Buddha for instruction in the Dharma (A 8.53) and in the *Saṃyutta Nikāya* (S 5.3), where she faces down Māra.

7. The extant Chinese version of this text was supposedly translated from the Sanskrit by the Buddhist monk Kālayaśas in the first half of the fifth century. But scholars believe the text originated either in central Asia or China and was back translated into the Sanskrit title. The Chinese title is *Guanwuliangshoufojing*.

8. The Chinese term that is translated as "to visualize" is *xiang* (想), which is made up of the characters for "appearance" (相), and "mind" (心). Julian Pas glosses this as meaning that "when the outside object [appearance] is grasped by the mind, one has the subsequent action of either thinking or imagining" (1974, 100–101). Hence, to visualize means "the act or power of forming mentally visual images of objects not present to the eye" (1974, 101). This equalizes the act of memory, or the mental visualization of forms seen in

the past, and the act of imagining, which is the visualization of forms that exists only in the mind.

9. Buddhaghosa lists ten kasiṇa meditations in all: earth, water, fire, air, blue, yellow, red, white, light, and limited-space. These meditation practices are forms of concentration practice that leads to the four levels of *dhyāna* absorption.

10. Huiyuan (334–416), the founder of the Donglin Temple on Mount Lushan, encouraged both meditation on the Pure Land, and the painting of imagery conducive to such visualization; Shandao (613–681), the Chinese Pure Land master who exerted strong influence on Hōnen (1133–1212) and Shinran (1173–1263) of the Japanese Jōdo Shinshū sect, had trance experiences that he translated into sculpture; Genshin (945–1017), the Tendai monk and devotee of Amida Buddha, painted both hells and the Pure Land that inspired Amida worship in Japan (Becker 1984, 140–41).

11. In his translation of this passage from the *Amitāyurdhyāna Sūtra*, Inagaki footnotes a number of traditional interpretations, such as "there is no buddha apart from one's true nature," "the Buddha does not exist apart from one's mind," "no buddha exists apart from this meditating mind," and "since this mind is the *Bodhi*-mind and the cause of buddhahood, it becomes a bud-dha" (2003, 100 n.33).

References

Adamek, Wendi L. 2007. *The Mystique of Transmission: On an Early Chan History and its Context*. New York: Columbia University Press.

Akutagawa, Ryūnosuke. 2006. *Rashōmon and Seventeen Other Stories*. Selected and Translated by Jay Rubin; With an Introduction by Haruki Murakami. New York: Penguin Books.

Araki, James T. 1981. "*Otogi-*zōshi and *Nara-ehon:* A Field of Study in Flux." *Monumenta Nipponica* 36, no. 1: 1–20.

Barthes, Roland. 1982 [1970]. *The Empire of Signs*. Translated by Richard Howard. New York: Hill and Wang.

Bashō. 2000. *Narrow Road to the Interior and Other Writings*. Translated by Sam Hamill. Boston and London: Shambhala.

Beal, Samuel, trans. 1980. *Si-Yu-K. Buddhist Records of the Western World: Chinese Accounts of India*. Translated from the Chinese of Hiuen Tsuang. Four Volumes. Delhi, India: Bharatiya.

Becker, Carl B. 1984. "Religious Visions: Experiential Grounds for the Pure Land Tradition." *Eastern Buddhist* 17: 138–53.

Benn, James A. 2007. *Burning for the Buddha: Self-Immolation in Chinese Buddhism*. Honolulu: University of Hawaii Press.

Bentor, Yael. 1996. *Consecration of Images and Stūpas in Indo-Tibetan Tantric Buddhism*. Leiden, New York: Brill.

Bielefeldt, Carl. 1992. "No-Mind and Sudden Awakening: Thoughts on the Soteriology of a Kamakura Zen Text." In *Paths to Liberation: The Mārga and its Transformations in Buddhist Thought*, edited by Robert E. Buswell and Robert M. Gimello, 475–505. Honolulu: University of Hawaii Press.

Bogin, Benjamin. 2013. *The Illuminated Life of the Great Yolmowa*. Chicago: Serindia.

Bordwell, David, Kristin Thompson, and Janet Staiger. 1985. *The Classical Hollywood Cinema: Film Style and Mode of Production to 1960*. New York: Columbia University Press.

Boucher, Daniel, trans. 1995. "Sutra on the Merit of Bathing the Buddha." In *Buddhism in Practice*, edited by Donald Lopez, 59–68. Princeton: Princeton University Press.

Bo Zhuyi. 2000. Translated by Burton Watson as *Bo Juyi: Selected Poems*. New York: Columbia University Press.

Bronkhorst, Johannes. 2011a. *Buddhism in the Shadow of Brahmanism*. Leiden, Boston: Brill.

———. 2011b. *Karma*. Honolulu: University of Hawaii Press.

Burlingame, Eugene Watson. 1921. *Buddhist Legends. Translated from the Original Pāli Texts of the Dhammapada Commentary*. Volume Three. Cambridge: Harvard University Press.

Buswell, Robert E., and Robert M. Gimello. 1992. *Paths to Liberation: The Marga and Its Transformations in Buddhist Thought*. Honolulu: University of Hawaii Press.

Campany, Robert. 1991. "Notes on the Devotional Uses and Symbolic Functions of *Sūtra* Texts as Depicted in Early Chinese Buddhist Miracle Tales and Hagiographies." *The Journal of the International Association of Buddhist Studies* 14, no. 1: 28–72.

———. 1996. *Strange Writing: Anomaly Accounts in Early Medieval China*. Albany: State University of New York Press.

———. 2012. *Signs from the Unseen Realm: Buddhist Miracle Tales from Early Medieval China*. Honolulu: University of Hawaii Press.

———. 2015. *A Garden of Marvels: Tales of Wonder from Early Medieval China*. Honolulu: University of Hawaii Press.

Chang, Justin. 2011. "Review: 'The Tree of Life.'" *Variety*, May 16.

Childs, Margaret. 1987. "The Influence of the Buddhist Practice of *Sange* on Literary Form: Revelatory Tales." *Japanese Journal of Religious Studies* 14, no. 1: 53–66.

Cho, Francisca. 2009. "Buddhism." In *The Routledge Companion to Religion and Film*, edited by John Lyman, 162–77. London, New York: Routledge Press.

———. 2014. "Buddhism, Science, and the Truth about Karma." *Religion Compass* 8, no. 4: 117–27.

Cho Bantly, Francisca. 1996. *Embracing Illusion: Truth and Fiction in the Dream of the Nine Clouds*. Albany: State University of New York Press.

Chōmei, Kamo. 1968. *Mumyōshō*. Translated by Hilda Kato. *Monumenta Nipponica* 23, no. 3/4: 351–430.

Cleary, Thomas, trans. 1993. *The Flower Ornament Scripture: A Translation of the Avataṃsaka Sūtra*. Boston and London: Shambhala.

Cohen, Hubert. 2003. "The Genesis of *Days of Heaven*." *Cinema Journal* 42, no. 4: 46–62.

Conroy, Melissa. 2007. "Seeing with Buddha's Eyes: *Spring, Summer, Fall, Winter . . . and Spring. Journal of Religion and Film*. October 11 (2).

Cuevas, Bryan J. 2007. "The Death and Return of Lady Wangzin: Visions of the Afterlife in Tibetan Buddhist Popular Literature." In *The Buddhist Dead: Practices, Discourses, Representations*, edited by Bryan J. Cuevas and Jacqueline I. Stone, 297–325. Honolulu: University of Hawaii Press.

———, and Jacqueline I. Stone. 2007. "Introduction." In *The Buddhist Dead: Practices, Discourses, Representations*, edited by Bryan J. Cuevas and Jacqueline I. Stone, 1–31. Honolulu: University of Hawaii Press.

Deacy, Christopher. 2001. *Screen Christologies: Redemption and the Medium of Film*. Cardiff: University of Wales Press.

DeCaroli, Robert. 2004. *Haunting the Buddha: Indian Popular Religions and the Formation of Buddhism*. Oxford, New York: Oxford University Press.

Denby, David. 2013. "Commitments: 'To the Wonder' and 'The Company You Keep.'" *The New Yorker* April 15.

Doll, Susan, and Greg Faller. 1986. "Blade Runner and Genre: Film Noir and Science Fiction." *Literature Film Quarterly* 14, no. 2: 89–100.

Doniger, Wendy. 1998. *The Implied Spider: Politics and Theology in Myth*. New York: Columbia University Press.

Dykstra, Yoshiko, trans. 1998–2003. *The Konjaku Tales*. Three Volumes. Osaka: Intercultural Research Institute, Kansai Gaidai University.

Ebert, Roger. 1999. "The Thin Red Line." January 8. http://www.rogerebert.com/reviews/the-thin-red-line-1999.

———. 2013. "To the Wonder." April 6. http://www.rogerebert.com/reviews/to-the-wonder-2013.

Eckel, Malcolm David. 1992. *To See the Buddha: A Philosopher's Quest for the Meaning of Emptiness*. San Francisco: Harper San Francisco.

Feeney, F. X. 1999. "Human, All Too Human." *Los Angeles Weekly*, January 15–21.

Fredriksen, Paula. 2004. "History, Hollywood, and the Bible: Some Thoughts on Gibson's *Passion*." *The Journal of Religion and Film* 8, no. 1.

Freedberg, David. 1989. *The Power of Images: Studies in the History and Theory of Response*. Chicago: University of Chicago Press.

Fuhrmann, Arnika. 2009. "*Nang Nak*—Ghost Wife: Desire, Embodiment, and Buddhist Melancholia in a Contemporary Thai Ghost Film." *Discourse* 31, no. 3: 220–47.

Fuller, Paul. 2005. *The Concept of Ditthi in Theravada Buddhism: The Point of View*. London, New York: RoutledgeCurzon.

Gethin, Rupert. 1997. "Cosmology and Meditation: From the Aggañña Sutta to the Mahāyāna." *History of Religions* 36, no. 3: 183–217.

Gifford, Julie. 2011. *Buddhist Practice and Visual Culture: The Visual Rhetoric of Borobudur*. London: Routledge.

Ginsberg, Henry. 1967. "Thai Literary Tales Derived from the Sanskrit *Tantropākhyāna* with Special Reference to the *Piśācapakaraṇam*." Master's Thesis, University of Hawaii.

Gomez, Luis. 1977. "The Bodhisattva as Wonder-Worker." In *Prajñāpāramitā and Related Systems: Studies in Honor of Edward Conze*, edited by Louis Lancaster, 221–61. Berkeley: University of California Press.

Grayson, James Huntley. 2001. *Myths and Legends from Korea: An Annotated Compendium of Ancient and Modern Materials.* Surrey: Curzon.

Green, Ronald. 2013. *Buddhism Goes to the Movies: Introduction to Buddhist Thought and Practice.* London, New York: Routledge.

Griffiths, Paul. 1994. *On Being Buddha: The Classical Doctrine of Buddhahood.* Albany: State University of New York Press.

Groner, Paul. 1992. "Shortening the Path: Early Tendai Interpretations of the Realization of Buddhahood with This Very Body (*Shokushin Jōbutsu*)." In *Paths to Liberation: the Mārga and its Transformations in Buddhist Thought*, edited by Robert E. Buswell and Robert M. Gimello, 439–73. Honolulu: University of Hawaii Press.

Hallisey, Charles and Anne Hansen. 1996. "Narrative, Sub-Ethics, and the Moral Life: Some Evidence from Theravāda Buddhism." *Journal of Religious Ethics* 24, no. 2: 305–27.

Hamilton, Sue. 1999. "The 'External World': Its Status and Relevance in the Pali Nikaya." *Religion* 29, no 1: 73–90.

Harrison, Paul M. 1992. "Commemoration and Identification in *Buddhā-nusmṛti*." In *In the Mirror of Memory: Reflections on Mindfulness and Remembrance in Indian and Tibetan Buddhism*, edited by Janet Gyatso, 215–38. Albany: State University of New York Press.

Hayashi, Yukio. 2003. *Practical Buddhism among the Thai-Lao: Religion in the Making of a Region.* Kyoto: Kyoto University Press.

Hemphill, Jim. 2013. "Lyrical Images." *American Cinematographer* 94, no. 4. Online version.

Henderson, Gregory, and Leon Hurvitz. 1956. "The Buddha of Seiryōji: New Finds and New Theory." *Artibus Asiae* 19, no. 1: 4–55.

Herman, Peter. 2014. "We Are the Walking Dead: Robert Kirkman's Zombies and Buddhist Body Image." *Implicit Religion* 17, no. 4: 433–42.

Hershock, Peter. 2007. "Valuing Karma: A Critical Concept for Orienting Inter-dependence Toward Personal and Public Good." In *Revisioning Karma: The Ebook*, edited by Charles Prebish, Damien Keown, and Dale S. Wright. Journal of Buddhist Ethics Online Books.

Holt, John Clifford. 2007. "Gone But Not Departed: The Dead among the Living in Contemporary Sri Lanka." In *The Buddhist Dead: Practices, Discourses, Representations*, edited by Bryan J. Cuevas and Jacqueline I. Stone, 326–44. Honolulu: University of Hawaii Press.

Huntington, Susan L. 1990. "Early Buddhist Art and the Theory of Aniconism." *Art Journal* 49, no. 4: 401–408.

Hynes, Eric. 2013. "Muses in Motion, Captured on Camera." *New York Times*, April 10.

James, David. 2002. "Im Kwon-Taek: Korean National Cinema and Buddhism." In *Im Kwon-Taek: The Making of a Korean National Cinema*, edited by David James and Kyung Hyun Kim, 47–83. Detroit: Wayne State University Press.

Jump, Herbert. 2002. "The Religious Possibilities of the Motion Picture." *Film History* 14, no. 2: 216–28.

Kelsey, W. Michael. 1981. "Salvation of the Snake, the Snake of Salvation: Buddhist-Shinto Conflict and Resolution." *Japanese Journal of Religious Studies* 8, no. 1: 83–113.

———. 1982. *Konjaku Monogatari-shū.* Boston: Twayne.

Kieschnick, John. 2003. *The Impact of Buddhism on Chinese Material Culture.* Princeton: Princeton University Press.

King, Sallie B. 1991. *Buddha Nature.* Albany: State University of New York Press.

Kinnard, Jacob. 1999. *Imaging Wisdom: Seeing and Knowing in the Art of Indian Buddhism.* Surrey: Curzon.

Knee, Adam. 2005. "Thailand Haunted: The Power of the Past in the Contemporary Thai Horror Film." In *Horror International,* edited by Steven Jay Schneider and Tony Williams, 141–59. Detroit: Wayne State University Press.

Kobayashi, Hiroko. 1979. *The Human Comedy of Heian Japan: A Study of the Secular Stories in the Twelfth-Century Collection of Tales, Konjaku Monogatarishū.* Tokyo: Centre for East Asian Cultural Studies.

Konishi, Jin'ichi. 1991. *A History of Japanese Literature.* Volume Three. Translated by Aileen Gatten and Nicholas Teele. Edited by Earl Miner. Princeton: Princeton University Press.

Koseki, Aaron L. 1980. "Prajñāpāramitā and the Buddhahood of the Non-Sentient World: The San-Lun Assimilation of Buddha-Nature and Middle Path Doctrine." *JIABS* 3, no. 1: 16–33.

LaFleur, William. 1983. *The Karma of Words: Buddhism and the Literary Arts in Medieval Japan.* Berkeley: University of California Press.

———. 2002. "Suicide off the Edge of Explicability: Awe in Ozu and Kore'eda." *Film History* 14, no. 2: 158–65.

Laozi. 1963. *Daodejing.* Translated by D. C. Lau as *The Tao-te-Ching by Lau Tzu.* Penguin Classics.

Lopate, Phillip. 1999. "Above the Battle, Musing on the Profundities." *New York Times,* January 17.

Lopez, Donald S. Jr. 1992. "Paths Terminable and Interminable." In *Paths to Liberation: the Marga and its Transformations in Buddhist Thought,* edited by Robert E. Buswell Jr. and Robert M. Gimello, 147–58. Honolulu: University of Hawaii Press.

Mair, Victor. 1988. *T'ang Transformation Texts: A Study of the Buddhist Contribution to the Rise of Vernacular Fiction and Drama in China.* Cambridge: Harvard University Press.

Marran, Christine L. 2002. "Tracking the Transcendental: Kore'eda Hirokazu's 'Maboroshi.'" *Film History* 14, no. 2: 166–69.

May Adadol, Ingawanij. 2007. "*Nang Nak*: Thai Bourgeois Heritage Cinema." *Inter–Asia Cultural Studies* 8, no. 2: 180–93.

Maslin, Janet. 1998. "The Thin Red Line Film Review: Beauty and Destruction in Pacific Battle." *The New York Times*, December 23.

McDaniel, Justin. 2011. *The Lovelorn Ghost and Magical Monk: Practicing Buddhism in Modern Thailand*. New York: Columbia University Press.

McMahan, David. 2002. *Empty Vision: Metaphor and Visionary Imagery in Mahayana Buddhism*. London, New York: RoutledgeCurzon.

Meiland, Justin, trans. 2009. *Garland of the Buddha's Past Lives* by Aryasura. Two Volumes. New York: New York University Press.

Mills, D. E. 1970. *A Collection of Tales from Uji: A Study and Translation of Uji Shūi Monogatari*. Cambridge: Cambridge University Press.

Mills, Mary Beth. 1995. "Attack of the Widow Ghosts: Gender, Death, and Modernity in Northeast Thailand." In *Bewitching Women, Pious Men: Gender and Body Politics in Southeast Asia*, edited by Aihwa Ong and Michael G. Peletz, 244–73. Berkeley: University of California Press.

Moerman, D. Max. 2007. "Passage to Fudaraku: Suicide and Salvation in Premodern Japanese Buddhism." In *The Buddhist Dead: Practices, Discourses, Representations*, edited by Bryan J. Cuevas and Jacqueline I. Stone, 266–99. Honolulu: University of Hawaii Press.

Moreman, Christopher M. 2008. "A Modern Meditation on Death: Identifying Buddhist Teachings in George A. Romero's *Night of the Living Dead*." *Contemporary Buddhism* 9, no. 2: 151–65.

———. 2010. "Dharma of the Living Dead: A Meditation on the Meaning of the Hollywood Zombie." *Studies in Religion* 39, no. 2: 263–81.

Nakamura, Kyoko Motomochi. 1997. *Miraculous Stories from the Japanese Buddhist Tradition: The Nihon Ryōiki of the Monk Kyōkai*. Cambridge: Harvard University Press.

Newman, John. 2000. "Vajrayoga in Kālacakra Tantra." In *Tantra in Practice*, edited by David Gordon White, 587–94. Princeton: Princeton University Press.

Olivelle, Patrick, trans. 2008. *Life of the Buddha by Aśavaghoṣa*. New York: New York University Press.

Parker, Joseph. 1999. *Zen Buddhist Landscape Arts of Early Muromachi Japan (1336–1573)*. Albany: State University of New York Press.

Pas, Julian F. 1974. "Shan-Tao's Interpretations of the Meditative Vision of Amitāyus." *History of Religions* 14, no. 2: 96–116.

Reider, Noriko. 2001. "The Emergence of 'Kaidan-shu' The Collection of Tales of the Strange and Mysterious in the Edo Period." *Asian Folklore Studies* 60, no. 1: 79–99.

————. 2002. *Tales of the Supernatural in Early Modern Japan: Kaidan, Akinari, Ugetsu Monogatari.* Lewiston: The Edwin Mellon Press.

Reinhartz, Adele. 2004. "Passion-ate Moments in the Jesus Film Genre." *The Journal of Religion and Film* 8, no. 1.

Reynolds, Frank. 1997. "Rebirth Traditions and the Lineages of Gotama: A Study in Theravada Buddhology." In *Sacred Biography in the Buddhist Traditions of South and Southeast Asia*, edited by Juliane Schober, 19–39. Honolulu: University of Hawaii Press.

————, and Mani Reynolds. 1982. *Three Worlds According to King Ruang: A Thai Buddhist Cosmology.* Berkeley: Asian Humanities Press.

Richie, Donald. 1974. *Ozu.* Berkeley: University of California Press.

Rimer, J. Thomas, and Yamazaki Masakazu. 1984. *On the Art of the Nō Drama: The Major Treatises of Zeami.* Princeton: Princeton University Press.

Ruch, Barbara. 1977. "Medieval Jongleurs and the Making of a National Literature." In *Japan in the Muromachi Age*, edited by John W. Hall and Toyoda Takeshi, 279–309. Berkeley: University of California Press.

Russell, Catherine. 2011. *Classical Japanese Cinema Revisited.* New York: Continuum.

Ryōkan. 1996. Translated by Ryūichi Abe and Peter Haskel as *Great Fool Zen Master Ryōkan. Poems, Letters, and Other Writings.* Honolulu: University of Hawaii Press.

Sarkar, S. C. 1981. *A Study on the Jātaka and the Avadānas: Critical and Comparative.* Calcutta: Saraswat Library.

Samuel, Geoffrey. 2008. *The Origins of Yoga and Tantra: Indic Religions to the Thirteenth Century.* Cambridge and New York: Cambridge University Press.

Schober, Juliane. 1997. "In the Presence of the Buddha: Ritual Veneration of the Burmese Mahamuni Image." In *Sacred Biography in the Buddhist Traditions of South and Southeast Asia*, edited by Juliane Schober, 259–88. Honolulu: University of Hawaii Press.

Schopen, Gregory. 1975. "The Phrase 'sa pṛthivīpradeśaā caityabhūto bhavet' in the *Vajracchedikā*: Notes on the Cult of the Book in the Mahāyāna." *Indo-Iranian Journal* 17: 147–81.

————. 1988–89. "On Monks, Nuns, and 'Vulgar' Practices: The Introduction of the Image Cult into Indian Buddhism." *Artibus Asiae* 49, no. 1–2: 153–68.

Schrader, Paul. 1996. "Notes on Film Noir." In *Film Noir Reader*, edited by Alain Silver and James Ursini, 52–63. New York: Limelight Editions.

Scott, A. O. 2013. "Twirling in Oklahoma, Dervish for Love." *The New York Times,* April 11.

Sharf, Robert H. 1996. "The Scripture on the Production of Buddha Images." In *Religions of China in Practice*, edited by Donald S. Lopez Jr., 261–67. Princeton: Princeton University Press.

———. 2002. *Coming to Terms with Chinese Buddhism: A Reading of the Treasure Store Treatise*. Kuroda Institute Studies in East Asian Buddhism 14. Honolulu: University of Hawaii Press.

Shimizu, Yishiaki. 1992. "Multiple Commemorations: *The Vegetable Nehan* of Itō Jakuchū." In *Flowing Traces: Buddhism in the Literary and Visual Arts of Japan*, edited by James H. Sanford, William R. LaFleur, and Masatoshi Nagatomi, 201–33. Princeton: Princeton University Press.

Shulman, David. 2012. *More Than Real: A History of the Imagination in South India*. Cambridge and London: Harvard University Press.

Stevenson, Daniel B. 1986. "The Four Kinds of Samādhi in Early T'ian-t'ai Buddhism." In *Traditions of Meditation in Chinese Buddhism*, edited by Peter N. Gregory, 45–98. Honolulu: University of Hawaii Press.

Strong, John S. 2007. "The Buddha's Funeral." In *The Buddhist Dead: Practices, Discourses, Representations*, edited by Bryan J. Cuevas and Jacqueline I. Stone, 32–59. Honolulu: University of Hawaii Press.

Swearer, Donald. 2004. *Becoming the Buddha: The Ritual of Image Consecration in Thailand*. Princeton: Princeton University Press.

Tambiah, Stanley J. 1968. "Literacy in North-East Thailand." In *Literacy in Traditional Societies*, edited by Jack Goody, 86–131. Cambridge: Cambridge University Press.

Tanizaki, Jun'ichirō. 1977 [1933]. *In Praise of Shadows*. Translated by Thomas J. Harper and Edward G. Seidensticker. Stony Creek, CT: Leete's Island Books.

Teiser, Stephen. 1988. *The Ghost Festival in Medieval China*. Princeton: Princeton University Press.

Trainor, Kevin. 1997. *Relics, Ritual, and Representation in Buddhism: Rematerializing the Sri Lankan Theravāda Tradition*. Cambridge and New York: Cambridge University Press.

Ueda, Akinari. 2007. *Tales of Moonlight and Rain*. A Study and Translation by Anthony H. Chambers. New York: Columbia University Press.

Vale, Eugene. 1972. *The Technique of Screenplay Writing*. New York: Grosset and Dunlap.

Veidlinger, Daniel. 2006. *Spreading the Dhamma: Writing, Orality, and Textual Transmission in Buddhist Northern Thailand*. Honolulu: University of Hawaii Press.

Walker, Beverly. 1975. "Malick on *Badlands*." *Sight and Sound* 44, no. 2: 82–83.

Walker, Seth M. 2012. "'Whatever It Is, We All Carry It': Tanha and AMC's The Walking Dead." *Nomos Journal* October 9.

Warner, Cameron David. 2011. "Re/Crowning the Jowo Śākyamuni: Texts, Photographs, and Memories." *History of Religions* 51, no. 1: 1–30.

Wayman, Alex, and Hideko Wayman, trans. 1974. *The Lion's Roar of Queen Śrīmālā: A Buddhist Scripture on the Tathāgathagarbha Theory*. New York and London: Columbia University Press.

Whalen-Bridge, John. 2014. "What Is a Buddhist Film?" *Contemporary Buddhism* 15, no. 1: 44–80.

———, and Gary Storhoff. 2014. *Buddhism and American Cinema.* Albany: State University of New York Press.

White, David Gordon. 2000. "Tantra in Practice: Mapping a Tradition." In *Tantra in Practice*, edited by David Gordon White, 3–38. Princeton: Princeton University Press.

Winfield, Pamela D. 2013. *Icons and Iconoclasm in Japanese Buddhism: Kūkai and Dōgen on the Art of Enlightenment.* Oxford and New York: Oxford University Press.

Woodward, Mark R. 1997. "The Biographical Imperative in Theravada Buddhism." In *Sacred Biography in the Buddhist Traditions of South and Southeast Asia*, edited by Juliane Schober, 40–63. Honolulu: University of Hawaii Press.

Wright, Dale. 2007. "Critical Questions Towards a Naturalized Concept of Karma in Buddhism." In *Revisioning Karma: The Ebook*, edited by Charles Prebish, Damien Keown, and Dale S. Wright. Journal of Buddhist Ethics Online Books.

Xing, Guang. 2005. *The Concept of the Buddha: Its Evolution from Early Buddhism to the Trikāya Theory.* Routledge Critical Studies in Buddhism. Abingdon and New York: RoutledgeCurzon.

Zeami, Motokiyō. 1984. Translated by J. Thomas Rimer and Yamazaki Masakazu as *On the Art of the Nō Drama: The Major Treatises of Zeami.* Princeton: Princeton University Press.

Zeitchik, Steven. 2011. " 'Tree of Life' Cinematographer: 'It was like no set I ever worked on.' " *24 Frames: Los Angeles Times Blog*, January 14.

———. 2012. "Not All See the 'Wonder' of Terrence Malick, But His Actors Do." *Los Angeles Times,* September 12.

Ziporyn, Brook. 2012. *Ironies of Oneness and Difference: Coherence in Early Chinese Thought: A Prolegomena to the Study of Li.* Albany: State University of New York Press.

Zurcher, Erik. 2013. "Buddhist Art in Medieval China: The Ecclesiastical View." In *Buddhism in China: The Collected Papers of Erik Zurcher*, 477–512. Leiden: Brill.

Index